Ancient Rome
Documentary Perspectives

Second Edition

Edited and Translated by
Bradley P. Nystrom
California State University, Sacramento

Stylianos V. Spyridakis
University of California, Davis

KENDALL/HUNT PUBLISHING COMPANY
4050 Westmark Drive   Dubuque, Iowa 52002

Contents

II. THE ROMANS AT WAR

III. LITERATURE

IV. RELIGION

V. PHILOSOPHY

VI. ANCIENT LIVES

Preface

This second edition of *Ancient Rome: Documentary Perspectives* retains the basic scope and structure of the original version, though with the revision of much of what was previously included and the addition of new material we hope to have added to its depth and comprehensiveness. Our goal has been to produce a work which offers a good selection of readable translations which, taken together, present an accurate and balanced picture of the history and culture of ancient Rome. With this in mind, we have assembled an initial chapter consisting of what we believe is a solid collection of texts on political and social life and supplemented it with additional chapters on the military, literature, religion, philosophy and the lives and life styles of individuals and groups, both Roman and non-Roman. It is our hope that the book will be found useful not only by instructors teaching courses on the history of Rome, but also by those whose focus is on Roman culture.

B. P. N.
S. V. S.

I
Political and
Social Life

The Roman Constitution: Polybius, *Universal History* 6.11–17

The Greek historian Polybius of Megalopolis was a prominent politician and soldier of the Greek Achaean League. After being deported to Italy by the Romans in 167 B.C. he became a friend of Scipio Aemilianus and wrote a *Universal History* in forty books which is our main source for the middle period of the Roman Republic. In the sixth book of this work Polybius described the Roman constitution of the late third century B.C., which he considered an excellent example of the ideal "mixed constitution" of Aristotle and the Peripatetics because it contained monarchic, oligarchic and democratic elements in a harmonious blend. In Polybius' view this superior constitution with its carefully constructed system of checks and balances was the basis of Rome's greatness.

The Roman constitution was comprised of three forms of government, each of which had a part in the regulation of the Roman state. Indeed, their respective shares of power had been so fairly and properly assigned that it was difficult even for a native Roman to say with certainty whether the whole system was an aristocracy, a democracy or a monarchy. And this is easy to understand, for if we concentrate on the power of the consuls, the constitution appears to be entirely monarchic and royal; if we look at the power of the Senate, the constitution seems to be aristocratic; and when we consider the power of the people it appears to be entirely democratic. The specific parts of the state governed by each of these three elements, not only in the past but even now, may be summarized, more or less, as follows.

The consuls, before leading out their armies, are the real masters of the government in Rome since all other magistrates, with the exception of the tribunes, are under their authority and obey their commands. They are the ones who introduce foreign delegations to the Senate. Moreover, the consuls bring urgent matters requiring deliberation to the Senate and attend to the details of the execution of its decisions. In matters of state requiring the people's approval it is their responsibility to become involved in them, to summon the assemblies of the people, to submit proposals before them and to enforce the decrees expressing the wishes of the majority. In the case of preparations for war and the conduct of campaigns in general the consuls enjoy the greatest power, for

2

they have the authority to demand from the allies any levies they consider necessary, to appoint military tribunes, to draft soldiers and to select those men who are best suited for military service. Moreover, when they are on active duty in the field the consuls have the power to punish anyone who serves under them. They have the right to spend as much of the public monies as they see fit and they are accompanied by a quaestor who readily complies with their orders. Thus, if we consider only the powers of the consuls we might quickly conclude that the Roman constitution is simply monarchic or royal.

Now let us move on the Senate. This body has, in the first place, control of the treasury and the authority to regulate all revenue and expenditures. For the quaestors have no power to disburse any public funds for the various functions of the government without the approval of the Senate, with the notable exception of payments made to the consuls. Similarly, the Senate controls what is by far the most important and largest of all public expenditures, namely the money which is spent by the censors every five years for the maintenance and construction of public buildings and public works in general, for it is the Senate that appropriates this money. Moreover, all crimes committed in Italy which are subject to public scrutiny, such as treason, conspiracy and assassination, are investigated by the Senate. Likewise, if an individual or a community desires the settlement of a dispute through arbitration, or claims the right to be compensated for damages, or needs help or protection the Senate has the authority to deal with these problems. The Senate also has authority in the area of foreign relations. It sends embassies abroad to settle disputes, offers advice, requests, demands and sometimes accepts submissions of the enemy, and declares war. In addition, the Senate determines what kind of reception should be given to foreign ambassadors who come to Rome and what answers they should receive from the Roman government. All of these matters are under the authority of the Senate. The people have no say in them. As a result, when the consuls are absent a resident of Rome would assume that the constitution is entirely aristocratic. In fact, this is the conclusion reached by many Greek states and foreign kings, for all of their dealings in Rome are with the Senate.

At this point one might reasonably ask whether the people have any constitutional powers, since the Senate performs so many functions, and especially the management of all revenues and expenditures, and the consuls have supreme authority in matters pertaining to preparations for war and the conduct of military operations in general. There is indeed a role for the people to play, and it is an important role. For the people alone have the power to grant honors and impose punishments, and it is these things that hold together kingdoms and constitutions and human society generally. For where a definite distinction between these two is not made, or is made but not enforced, there nothing can be properly managed since it is impossible to achieve this goal when good and evil men enjoy the same honors. Thus, the people alone decide

3

in matters of life and death, and the people's court tries some of the cases in which crimes are punished with a fine, especially cases involving ex-magistrates who have held the highest offices of state. There is a practice connected with these matters which is commendable and worthy of mention. This is that those individuals on trial for their lives at Rome have the legal right to depart freely and openly and condemn themselves to a life of voluntary exile if even one of the tribes whose votes are required to pronounce the sentence has not yet voted. These persons find safety in the regions of Naples, Praeneste, Tibur and other towns with which legal arrangements have been made. To continue, it is the people who bestow on those who deserve it the noblest reward of virtue in the state: election to high office. The people also possess the power to pass or reject laws and enjoy the most important right of all, that of deliberating on questions of war and peace. Moreover, when alliances, peace proposals and treaties are made, it is the people who ratify or reject them. These functions might well lead one to the conclusion that the people enjoy the greatest power in the state and that the Roman constitution is democratic.

Now that I have explained the ways in which political power is distributed among the various elements in the state, I will show how each of these different elements has the power, when it so chooses, to oppose or work in harmony with the others. The consul, when he begins a campaign and is invested with all the powers which I have previously described, gives the impression of having absolute power in the execution of his responsibilities; yet he needs the support of the people and the Senate, for he cannot possibly bring his work to a successful conclusion without them. For it is obvious that the legions he commands need constant provisioning, but nothing can be supplied to them, neither grain nor clothes nor pay, without the approval of the Senate, and so all the activities of the consuls can be brought to a halt if the Senate decides to be deliberately negligent or obstructive. Also, the Senate has the power to decide whether a consul shall bring any projects to completion, since it has the power either to replace him with another consul at the expiration of his one year term of office or retain him in command. Moreover, the Senate has the authority either to publicly praise and augment the successes of the consuls or, if it wishes, to downplay and minimize their importance. This is because the so-called triumphs in which the consuls bring the concrete evidence of their achievements before the eyes of the citizens cannot be organized or celebrated unless the Senate allocates the necessary funds. It is absolutely essential for the consuls to be on good terms with the people no matter how far from home they carry their operations for, as I have said before, it is the people who ratify or reject the terms of treaties. It is also important that, when laying down their office, the consuls are obligated to give an account of their conduct to the people. Thus, the consuls have good reason for seeking to stay in favor with both the Senate and the people.

The Senate, which enjoys great authority, as I have already pointed out, has the legal obligation to consider the views of the masses in conducting public affairs and to comply with the wishes of the people. In fact, the Senate cannot enforce the death penalty as a punishment for offenses against the Republic unless the people first approve of its decision. Even in the case of drafting laws which directly involve the Senate, the people alone have the authority to endorse or reject them. This applies, for example, to laws that take away certain honors and offices from the senators and even reduce their properties. However, the thing which should be emphasized most is that when the tribunes of the people decide to exercise their veto power the senators not only cannot pass a law but are even barred from holding meetings, both formal and informal. The tribunes of the people, of course, are legally required to enforce the decrees of the people in all cases and, most of all, to respect their wishes. As a consequence, the Senate is always aware of the power of the people and cannot possibly ignore their wishes.

The people of Rome are not independent of the authority of the Senate and cannot ignore its wishes as a body or as individuals. For the censors are the officials authorized to give out the countless contracts for the repair of existing public buildings and the construction of new ones throughout Italy as well as the contracts involving the collection of revenues from various rivers, harbors, farms, mines and lands, and all the properties that fall under the jurisdiction of the Roman state. All of these activities involve the people at large, and there are few individuals in Rome who do not seek to benefit from them. Some of them buy contracts from the censors for themselves, others enter into partnerships with the contractors and still others serve as security for these contractors or even mortgage their properties to the Roman treasury for them. It should be noted that the Senate exercises absolute control over all these contracts and activities for it alone has the authority to offer time extensions and to reduce, in part, the monetary obligations of the contractors, or even to release them entirely from any obligation to the Senate if they are unable to meet it as a result of circumstances beyond their control.

Much can be said of the means by which the Senate can cause great problems or, conversely, make life easy for the contractors, for this body has final authority in these matters. Most important of all, however, is the fact that in most trials involving serious charges, both public and private, the justices are drawn from the membership of the Senate, and so all Roman citizens are in awe of it. Since they can never be certain when they may be in need of its good will the people are careful not to ignore or actively resist its wishes. Likewise, people do not thoughtlessly oppose the will of the consuls, for they know that one day they may have to serve under them in a campaign when the consular authority is absolute.

Secessio: Livy, *History* 2.31–33

The efforts of the Roman *plebs* to acquire greater social and political rights during the so-called Struggle of the Orders were often well-organized actions which demonstrated an acute awareness of the needs and vulnerabilities of the senatorial party. One of the means by which the plebeians sought to implement their demands was *secessio*, a general strike in which they withdrew from the city, thereby depriving it of their labor and military service. Five instances of *secessio* are recorded between 494 and 287 B.C., although only the historicity of the last is beyond doubt.

The first instance of *secessio* is described by Livy, who tells us that it was precipitated by plebeian resentment of the debt-bondage into which many of the common people had fallen as a result of their failure to repay loans made to them by patrician lenders. His account also offers one of the many possible explanations of the origin of the tribunate, a magistracy established for the purpose of protecting the *plebs*.

Even though the Romans had won three victories, both the senatorial party and the plebeians remained anxious about Rome's domestic problems, for the money-lenders had used all of their skill and influence to confound not only the common people but the Dictator himself. After the consul Vetusius returned to Rome, Valerius' first official act was to propose to the Senate that it should declare its policy concerning the men who had fought so bravely despite the fact that they had earlier been bound over for debt. His proposal was rejected, whereupon Valerius responded with these words: "I see that I do not please you by advocating social harmony. Well, by God, it won't be long before you will wish that men as reasonable as I am spoke on behalf of the plebs. I will not disappoint the people any longer, nor will I continue serving in this office without accomplishing anything. I was made Dictator because of the exigencies of war and internal discord. We have won peace with our neighbors, but here at home the cause of peace is being thwarted. We are on the road to anarchy, and I would rather face it as a private citizen than as Dictator." So saying, he resigned his office and left the Senate. The people understood that he had resigned because of his indignation over the way in which they had been mistreated. He had not kept his promise to liberate them, but his failure had not been his fault, and so they escorted him to his house shouting assurances of their approval and their appreciation.

The senatorial party now began to fear that if the army was disbanded the discharged soldiers would lead the people in a return to their secret meetings and conspiracies. And so, although the troops had been raised by order of the Dictator, the Senate maintained that they were still under the authority of the consuls to whom they had sworn their oaths. Furthermore, by claiming that the Aequi had renewed their hostilities, the Senate was able to justify ordering their commanders to lead the legions out of the city. This order immediately brought the crisis to a head. At first, it is said, there was talk among the soldiers of assassinating the consuls, for they thought that one cannot be bound by an oath to a dead man. But then, when they had learned that a sacred obligation can never be dissolved by a criminal act, they decided instead to follow the advice of a certain Sicinius, who argued that they should simply ignore the consuls and go off to the Sacred Mountain which lies across the Anio about three miles from the city. The historian Piso says that they withdrew to the Aventine, but the version of the story which I have given is more generally accepted. There, on the Sacred Mount, and without any leader, they built a camp defended by a rampart and trench. They remained there for some days, keeping quiet and eating only what was necessary for subsistence. They did not seek to challenge their enemy, nor did the enemy challenge them.

In Rome there was a great panic, and the fear which had spread everywhere brought the city to a standstill. The plebeians who had been left behind by their friends in the army feared violence at the hands of the senators. The senators were afraid of the plebeians who remained in the city and wondered if they were safer with them there or out with those who had seceded. And there were other questions: How long would the deserters remain peaceful? What would happen if a war with some foreign power broke out in the midst of this crisis? It was clear that Rome's only hope lay in the establishment of harmony among its social classes and that their reconciliation would have to be accomplished at any cost.

The senators decided to send as their representative to the plebs Menenius Agrippa, an eloquent man who was well-liked by the common people because he was by birth a plebeian. They say that when he had been admitted into the camp on the Sacred Mountain he told them the following story in the simple style of the olden days:

"Long ago, before the parts of the human body were in agreement, as they are now, each part had its own ideas and expressed them in its own way. The parts were indignant because they had to put up with the worry and the bother of providing everything the belly needed, while the belly itself had nothing to do but lie there and enjoy all of the good things they gave it. For this reason they plotted against the belly; the hand would not bring food to the mouth, the mouth would not open for food, the teeth would not chew. By 'going on strike' in this way they hoped to starve the belly into submission, but instead these parts and all of the others grew weak to the point of death. And so they realized that the belly, too, has an important job to do, and that it does not keep the nourishment they give it for itself, but shares it in proper proportion with each of the parts by depositing it in the blood which it makes in the process of digestion."

Menenius was so successful in pointing out to the plebeians the similarity of the revolt of the body parts to their action against the senatorial party that their anger was cooled. The two parties now began to make progress toward a reconciliation, and in the end an agreement was reached according to which the plebeians were to be given magistrates of their own. These officials were to be sacrosanct and responsible for protecting the plebeians against the consuls. No member of the senatorial class was to be eligible to hold this office. And so the people chose the first "tribunes of the people," Gaius Licinius and Lucius Albinus. These two appointed three others to be their colleagues, one of whom was Sicinius, the same man who had called for the revolt and withdrawal to the Sacred Mountain. The identity of the other two tribunes is uncertain. According to some, only two tribunes were chosen on the Sacred Mountain, and the principle of their sacrosanctity was established there.

Debt-Bondage: Livy, *History* 2.23

During the early years of the Republic the plebians often suffered at the hands of merciless lenders who, because they had few competitors, were able to set their own terms. Interest rates were generally high and penalties imposed on defaulters could be extreme. According to the terms of one kind of loan contract, a creditor who had not been repaid had the right to seize the property and even the person of the borrower in order to satisfy the latter's obligation. Persons who had been bound over for debt were expected to work off their debt. It is certain that many did, though it is also true that because of this practice many ended their lives in slavery. The following account from Livy describes the extent of the problem of debt-bondage in the early years of the fifth century B.C.

Two dangers threatened Rome. First, war with the Volscians was imminent. Second, there was discord among the citizens, for the plebeians were filled with a burning hatred of the patricians. The main reason for their anger was the miserable condition of those who had been forced into virtual slavery because they had been unable to pay their creditors. These men complained that while they had been off fighting for their country's freedom and to increase its power, their fellow-citizens had taken advantage of their absence to enslave and oppress them. They claimed that the plebeians were better off in war than in peace and that the Roman ruling class posed a greater threat to their freedom than any foreign foe. Their growing bitterness erupted into rage when they learned of the victimization of one man in particular.

He was quite old, and he rushed into the Forum looking like someone who had suffered great evils. His clothes were filthy and the condition of his body was even more shocking, for he was extremely pale and emaciated. His long, scraggly hair and beard made him even more frightful. Despite his dreadful appearance he was recognized by a number of onlookers and word spread that he had once commanded units of the army. Some of the sympathetic observers said that he had received other military honors, and the man himself showed them scars on his chest which testified to his honorable conduct as a soldier of Rome.

A great crowd gathered around him, filling the Forum as though there was about to be a meeting of the assembly, and he was asked how he had fallen into such a terrible condition. He answered that while he had been away from his farm fighting in the Sabine War his crops had been devastated by the enemy, his cottage had burned down, his cattle had been driven off and all of his other belongings had been taken. It was just at that inopportune time, he said, that the government had levied taxes and he had been forced to go into debt to pay them. The interest on the money he owed had made his situation even worse, and then his creditors had taken his farm, which had belonged to his father and grandfather before him. In the end, like some disease that destroys every part of its victim, they attacked his very body. They seized him and took him away, not into slavery, but to the debtors' prison where he was to be executed. At this point the old man showed the crowd his back, which was horribly disfigured by the weals from his last whipping.

The sight of these, together with the man's story, caused a tremendous uproar which was not confined to the Forum, but spread throughout the entire city. Those who had fallen into debt-bondage ran into the streets from all directions, some of them even in chains, shouting and pleading for the support of their fellow-citizens. The response was dramatic, for the streets were soon filled with men who had flocked to join the uprising. Any senator who had been caught up among the mob was in great danger.

Cato on Women: Livy, *History* 34.2

In 215 B.C., during the Second Punic War, the Romans passed the Oppian Law which was intended to help orient the Roman economy to the demands of war by limiting the luxury items available to women. In 195 B.C. the tribunes Marcus Fundanius and Lucius Valerius proposed in the Concilium Plebis that the law should be repealed. Their proposal was enthusiastically supported by the women of Rome, many of whom, according to Livy, left their homes in order to persuade the men of the city to vote in favor of it. Ultimately, the Oppian law was repealed, but not without protest from those who considered the demands of the Roman women and their attempt to gain political influence dangerous and offensive. One of them was the famous conservative Marcus Cato. A passage from his speech against the tribunes' proposal appears below.

"My fellow citizens, if each of us had taken the trouble to keep his rights and authority as a husband safe from the women in his family we would have less trouble with women in society at large. But as things stand now our liberty has been destroyed at home by unmanageable women and trampled on by them even here in the Forum. Because we have not controlled them individually we now dread them collectively. I had always thought that the old fable about the women of the island of Lemnos who revolted and killed all the men was mere fiction, but now I see that any group can be dangerous if its members are allowed to have meetings and assemblies and secret consultations. . . .

Indeed, I was rather ashamed just a moment ago when I had to make my way through a crowd of women in order to get to the Forum. If my respect for their dignity and decency as individuals had not prevented me from subjecting them to the humiliation of being scolded in public by a consul, I would have said: 'What do you think you are doing, running around out of doors, blocking the streets and talking to other women's husbands? Couldn't you have made your requests to your husbands in your own homes? Or do you think you are more persuasive in public and with men married to someone else? Of course, if you were governed by a sense of modesty you would not think it right to concern yourselves with the business of passing and repealing laws—not even in your own homes.' That is what I would have said.

Our ancestors would not allow women to conduct business, not even their private business, unless they were supervised by a guardian. They wanted to keep women under the control of their fathers, brothers and husbands. But we (may the gods help us!) allow women to interfere in politics and mingle with us in our meetings in the Forum. Don't you realize that that is what they are up to right now out in the streets and on the corners? They are calling for the passage of the tribunes' bill and the repeal of the [Oppian] law. If you give loose rein to their wild nature you will be leaving it up to these untamed creatures to set the limits of their own license. Unless you act, the Oppian Law will prove to be the least of the things enjoined on women by custom and law which they will want to abolish because they think they are unjust. The truth of the matter is this: what they want is complete liberty or, rather, complete license."

Cato and Carthage: Plutarch, *Cato* 25.1–26.1

By the middle of the second century B.C. control of Roman foreign policy had fallen into the hands of the conservative forces led by Cato. Many factors contributed to the harsh means of dealing with foreign powers which they advocated, including the desire for spoils of war, the need for an abudant supply of slave labor, the desire of business interests for new fields of exploitation and a general distrust of foreign states. Rome's ruthless destruction of its rivals was particularly notable in 146 B.C. when, in the space of only a few months, Roman armies destroyed Carthage and Corinth, the two major commercial cities of the Mediterranean. The following excerpt from Plutarch's life of Cato describes the statesman's concern that Carthage would once again threaten Rome and his insistence that it be destroyed.

There are some who say that the destruction of Carthage was the last of Cato's accomplishments as a statesman. Indeed, it was Scipio the Younger who actually razed the city, but the war was undertaken by the Romans primarily on the counsel of Cato, who advised it for the following reason. He was sent to the Carthaginians and to Masinissa, the king of Numidia, in order to discover the reasons why they were waging war against each other. Masinissa had always been a friend to the Romans and the Carthaginians had been on good terms with the Romans ever since their defeat by Scipio Africanus had resulted in the loss of their empire and the imposition of a heavy tribute.

The Romans of his day generally supposed that Carthage was in very poor condition, but Cato found that this was not the case. The city was full of men of military age and rich in money and all kinds of military equipment. Morever, the people were proud. Thus, Cato concluded that rather than making any changes in its relations with Masinissa Rome should seek to put an end to the incredible growth of this city which was its ancient and irreconcilable enemy. Returning immediately to Rome, he informed the Senate that the defeats which Rome had previously inflicted upon the Carthaginians had done far more to diminish their imprudence than their strength and that, rather than weakening them, they had given them that kind of strength which derives from experience. He advised the senators that the Carthaginians were skirmishing with the

Numidians in order to prepare themselves for war with Rome and that they were taking advantage of the peace established by their treaty with the Romans to wait for the right time to attack.

They say that as he spoke he shook his toga and purposely let some African figs drop to the ground. Then, after admiring their size and beauty, he added that they came from a country just three days' sail from Rome. After this, whenever he offered his opinion on any issue he would always add these words: "And I also believe that Carthage must be destroyed."

Buying a Farm: Cato the Elder, *On Agriculture* 1–4

The Roman statesman Marcus Portius Cato, also known as Cato the Elder and Cato the Censor, was born in 234 B.C. at Tusculum. After serving as a soldier in the Second Punic War he held a number of public offices before becoming consul in 195 B.C. He won his greatest fame as censor, an office whose authority he used to attempt to reestablish the "old Roman" values which he feared had been abandoned by the Roman nobility. His *De Agri Cultura (On Agriculture)* glorified country life and offered instruction in the raising of livestock and the cultivation of vines, olives and fruits, all of which were important features of Roman agriculture in his day. The following excerpt contains Cato's suggestions to those interested in buying a farm.

Commerce can be a very profitable occupation, though it is sometimes dangerous. Similarly, one can become wealthy through money-lending, though this profession is not particularly honorable. Our ancestors held to this view and embodied it in their laws, according to which the penalty for usury was twice as severe as that imposed for thievery. From this we may infer that they considered usurers to be only half as desirable as thieves. When they wanted to praise some worthy man they would call him a "good husbandman" or a "good farmer," and the one who received such praise was thought to have been given the greatest of honors.

Now, I consider businessmen to be energetic fellows who are determined to make money; yet, as I said before, business is a dangerous career which involves certain risks. Farmers, on the other hand, make up that class from which come the strongest men and the bravest soldiers. Of all occupations theirs is the most honorable and their livelihood the most secure and viewed with the greatest respect. Moreover, there are no workers more committed to their occupations than farmers.

But now I must return to my subject. Let what I have written above serve as introduction to this essay on agriculture. When you are in the market for a farm you should take care not to make your purchase on impulse. Make every effort to inspect all the available properties and don't suppose that a single visit to any one of them is enough for such an important transaction; a good farm will look more attractive each time you inspect it.

15

Be sure to note how the neighbors keep up their places; well kept farms are a sign of a good district. The climate should be mild, not stormy, and the soil should be fertile. Ideally, a farm should be located in a healthy spot, such as at the foot of a mountain, and face south. There should be plenty of laborers and an adequate supply of water.

A good farm will be located near a prosperous town and close to the sea, a navigable river or a good and heavily traveled road. It will be in a region where farms are rarely sold and where people who do sell their land later regret having done so. Make sure that the farm has all the necessary buildings. You will want to make your purchase from someone who is a good farmer and a good builder, so don't be too quick to criticize a seller whose farming and building techniques are different from yours—he may have greater expertise than you do.

When you inspect a farm be sure to count the oil presses and wine vats; if there are only a few you can be sure that the place doesn't make much of a profit. On the other hand, there should not be a lot of unnecessary equipment, for a farm should be equipped and operated as economically as possible. Always remember that a farm is like a man: no matter how great its income there will be little left over if it incurs a lot of unnecessary expenses.

In my opinion, the ideal farm consists of about sixty-six well-situated acres with a variety of soils. Its vineyard is its most important part if it produces plenty of good wine. The garden is second in importance, then groves of willows and olive trees, a meadow, grainfields, a wood lot, an orchard of trees to support climbing grape vines and, finally, a grove of trees whose nuts can be used for feed.

When a farmer returns home after an extended absence he must first pay his respects to the household gods. He should then inspect his farm as soon as possible—preferably on the same day, but no later than the following day. After he has determined how work on the farm has been progressing he should call for his foreman and question him. Which tasks have been completed and which have not? Were the former completed in a timely manner? Will the latter be completed at all? How much wine was made? How much grain was harvested? Was anything else produced? When he has learned how much work has been done the farmer should consider how many laborers it took to accomplish it and the amount of time they took. If he decides that their performance is unsatisfactory the foreman will explain that he did his best but the slaves were sick, it rained, some slaves ran away or he was forced to do work on some public project. When he has finished giving his excuses the foreman should be brought back to an accounting of the various farm tasks and the work that has actually been done. Remind him that there are many jobs which can be done even on rainy days; storage jars can be scrubbed and patched with tar, buildings can be cleaned, grain can be shifted, manure can be hauled out to the manure pile, seed can be cleaned, old harnesses can be repaired and new ones made, and slaves can mend their tunics and hoods. Tell him, too, that even on festival days irrigation ditches can be repaired, road work can be done, brambles can be cut and cleared, the garden can be hoed, the meadow can be cleared, firewood can be bundled, thornbushes can be pulled, spelt can be ground and the farmstead can be made neater and more tidy in general. Finally, you might mention that, since the slaves (as he claims) were sick, it was not necessary to issue them such large rations. When you have explained these things to your foreman, tell him to finish the work which was not completed.

There are other things which must be done. You must go over cash and grain accounts and purchase fodder. Arrangements must be made for the storage of wine and oil, and it is important to consider their inventories and accounts. How much has been sold? Were payments made in full? Are there balances due? How much of the inventories is still marketable? Should security be taken on outstanding accounts? Are the inventories sufficient? You must purchase items needed for the year's operations, sell off surpluses and give orders for the work you want done on the farm. If there is work which must be let out under contract, make sure that you put your instructions in writing. Inspect your livestock and hold a sale. Sell your oil, if the price is right, and sell your surplus wine and grain. You should also sell your old and worn-out oxen, blemished cattle, blemished sheep, wool, hides, old wagons, old tools, old and sick slaves, and anything else that you don't need. A landower should be a seller, not a buyer.

When a landowner is young he should focus his attention on planting. He ought to *think* about building, but planting is not something to think about but to do. It is when you reach the age of thirty-six that you should begin building, but only if you have already finished your planting. In building, you should make sure that the number, type and capacity of your buildings are suited to the needs of your farm. A landowner needs a sturdy barn, a storage room and plenty of vats for oil and wine so that he will be able keep his products until such time as he can sell them for a good price. Such facilities will enhance his wealth, self-respect and reputation. He should have good presses so that the work can be done well. Olives should be pressed immediately after they are gathered in order to keep the oil from spoiling. Remember that we have a windy season each year when the olives are beaten off the trees; if you gather them right away and the presses are ready there will be no loss due to the storms and, besides, the oil will be greener and better. If, on the other hand, you allow the olives to lie on the ground or the floor they will spoil and the oil will be rancid. Any variety of olive will produce a good and greener oil if it is pressed promptly. An olive orchard of about eighty acres requires two presses if the trees are strong, thickly planted and well tended. You should have good mills of different sizes, so that when the stones are worn you may change. Each mill should have its own leather cords, six sets of handbars, six double sets of pins and leather belts. Greek pulleys run on double ropes made of Spanish broom. You can work more quickly with eight pulleys above and six below. If you use wheels the work will go more slowly but will not require as much effort.

You will need good stalls, sturdy pens and feed racks with spaced bars. If you make the latter with the bars about a foot apart the cattle will not scatter their feed.

Build your house according to your means. If you build a nice home on a good farm and place it in an attractive setting, so that you will be able to live decently in the country, you will like to go there and will do so more often. The result will be a better farm: the farmhands will behave better and profits will rise. . . . Remember the old saying: "The face is better than the back of the head" [*i.e.,* It is better to pay attention to matters than to turn away and ignore them]. Be a good neighbor, and don't allow your people to misbehave. If your neighbors like you it will be easier for you to sell your produce, find contractors to do work for you, and to hire extra farmhands. When you build the neighbors will help you with their labor, teams and materials. If hard times come, heaven forbid, they will gladly take your side.

The Rise of the Latifundia: Appian, *Civil Wars* 1.1.7

The great *latifundia,* or agricultural estates, were an outgrowth of Rome's conquest of its neighbors, much of whose land ended up in the hands of Roman patricians. Cheap slave labor, another product of Rome's expansionist policies, made the operation of the *latifundia* particularly profitable. In the following excerpt from his account of the civil wars of the late Republic, the historian Appian describes how, by taking advantage of inexpensive land and labor, the rich became richer.

As the Romans defeated one after another of the peoples of Italy they built towns on the lands they seized or, when a town already existed, they would enlist citizens to go and live in it. The idea was that these settlements would serve as outposts. Farmland was either given to the colonists, leased or sold. But since they were not yet in a position to allot those lands which had been devastated by war, and these made up the bulk of what they had won, they declared that for the time being anyone who was willing to work them could do so in return for part of the annual harvest, namely a tenth of the grain and a fifth of the fruit. Those who kept livestock were also required to make payment, either in cattle or sheep. The Romans established these policies in order to promote the growth of the Italians, whom the Romans considered the most hard-working of peoples, so that they would have plenty of allies close by. But the very opposite happened, for the rich claimed most of these lands and with the passing of time grew bold enough to suppose that they would never be taken from them. Moreover, they added to them any unclaimed adjacent strips and used both force and persuasion to take away the allotments of their poor neighbors. In the end they found themselves farming huge estates instead of small ones and relying on slave labor for farming and herding since free laborers could at any time be conscripted into the army. The ownership of slaves proved to be extremely profitable since they produced so many children and because these, being exempt from military service, did not have to face life-threatening dangers. As a consequence of all this, certain powerful men became exceptionally rich and the number of slaves soared. At the same time, the strength and number of the Italians declined, oppressed as they were by poverty, taxes and military service. And even when they were fortunate enough to enjoy a brief respite from these evils they could do nothing but pass the time in idleness, for the wealthy used slaves rather than free laborers to work their farms.

A Slave Revolt in Sicily: Diodorus Siculus, *Historical Library* 34.2

The expansion of Roman territory and influence during the late Republic and early Empire brought thousands of slaves to Rome. These unfortunate victims of Roman imperialism had little to protect them against the cruelty of their masters, and though some were treated with reasonable civility, many lived lives of unending torment. It is not surprising, then, that Roman slaves occasionally rebelled against their masters. The most famous slave rebellion was led by the Thracian gladiator Spartacus (73-72 B.C.). An earlier rebellion occurred in Sicily in 135-132 B.C. and was described by Diodorus Siculus in his *Library of History.*

. . . The slave revolt in Sicily broke out for the following reasons. The Sicilians, who had become very wealthy, began buying great numbers of slaves. They used to bring great bunches of them from their homelands to Sicily, where they would immediately mark their bodies with brands. They used the young men as shepherds and the rest for all the other jobs that needed to be done. The Sicilians were very hard on their slaves. They made little effort to provide for them the necessities of life, such as food and clothing. As a result, most of the slaves turned to robbery for their needs, and since they were organized into scattered groups, as if they were soldiers, there was bloodshed all over the island. The praetors tried to stop them but did not punish them. They were afraid of the power and influence of the landed gentry who owned the robber-slaves, and so they felt they had no choice but to turn a blind eye to the plundering of the land. The praetors feared the landowners because most of them were Roman equites, and it was the equites who served as judges when provincial magistrates were accused of misconduct.

The slaves, crushed by their hardships and frequently subjected to unreasonably brutal beatings, could not endure their treatment. Meeting whenever they got the chance, they discussed the possibility of a revolt until, in the end, they put their plan into action. Now, there was a certain Syrian slave who belonged to Antigenes of Enna—a man from Apamea [in Syria] who was a magician and wonder-worker. This slave claimed that he could foretell the future (the gods, he said, had commanded him to read it in dreams) and he had cleverly used this skill to take advantage of many people. In addition

20

to giving oracles based on his dreams he also pretended to have visions of the gods while he was awake, and during these he would act as if he was getting his information about the future directly from the gods themselves. Some of his predictions came true and others did not, but since people only paid attention to his successes he quickly earned a reputation as a prophet. He used a certain trick to breathe fire and flame from his mouth, all the while pretending to be possessed by some god and raving about the future. He would put fire and a bit of fuel in a nut, or something like a nut, that had a small hole on both sides. Then he would put this device in his mouth and breathe on it to produce sparks and, finally, a flame. Before the revolt he used to say that the Syrian goddess (Atargatis) appeared to him and told him that he would become king. He told this story to everyone, even to his own master. Everyone treated his claims as a joke, and so Antigenes, who had gotten into the spirit of the wonder-worker's quackery, would introduce Eunus, for that was his name, at his dinner parties and ask him questions about his reign and how he would treat each of his guests. Eunus would answer frankly that he would be moderate in his treatment of masters, and since he was such a marvelously colorful character Antigenes' guests would always break out in laughter. Some of them would give him tasty morsels from the table and ask him as they did so to remember their kindness when he became king. It just so happened that this charlatan did become king, and in return for the tidbits that were given to him in jest at dinner parties he demonstrated his sincere gratitude.

The revolt began in the following way. There was a man named Damophilus from the city of Enna who was at the same time very wealthy and very arrogant. He was extremely cruel to his slaves, and so was his wife, Megallis, who was just as eager as he was to punish them and treat them inhumanely in a hundred ways. Suffering from their abuse, the slaves became like wild animals and conspired to rise up against their master and mistress and murder them. Going to Eunus, they asked him if the gods approved of what they were about to do. Babbling his usual hocus-pocus, he assured them that the gods were on their side and convinced them to put their plan into action without delay. And so they immediately assembled an army of four hundred of their fellow slaves and, after having armed themselves with whatever weapons they could find, they attacked Enna under the leadership of Eunus, who breathed fire in order to inspire them. Whenever they entered a house they spilled blood. They did not even spare tiny babies; instead, they tore them from their mothers' breasts and threw them to the ground. And as for the women, I cannot bring myself to describe the brutal and indecent things they did to them before the very eyes of their husbands. By this time the attacking slaves had been joined by slaves from the city who demonstrated their savagery by first murdering their own masters and then looking for others to slaughter. When Eunus and his men learned that Damophilus and his wife were in a park near the city they sent some men who tied their hands behind them and abused them with insults as they brought them back. The only one who received mercy from the slaves was their daughter, for she was very kind and had always sympathized with the slaves and done what she could to help them. This shows that the slaves were not acting out of some kind of "natural savagery" of slaves but out of a desire to repay their former masters for their cruelty to them.

Now, the men who had been sent to find Damophilus and Megallis brought them back to the city and into the theater, where all of the rebels had gathered. Damophilus tried to save their skins by making a well-crafted appeal for mercy to the crowd. But then, when he began winning some of them over, Hermeias and Zeuxis, two men who hated him, denounced him as a liar and, without waiting for the other rebels to pronounce a judgment, one ran a sword through his chest while the other cut off his head with an axe. Eunus was then chosen king, not because he had courage or skill as a military commander, but because he was a wonder-worker and had prompted the revolt, and also because his name [which means "friendly" or "benevolent"] struck them as a good omen suggesting that he would be a kind ruler.

As soon as the rebels had made him their king, he called an assembly and executed all of the citizens of Enna except those who knew how to make weapons. These were bound in chains and put to work. He gave Megallis to the young slave girls, who tortured her and then threw her over a cliff. He himself murdered his own masters, Antigenes and Pytho. Then, after placing a crown on his head and dressing himself like a king, he announced that his wife, who was also from Apamea in Syria, would be queen. Next, he chose a royal council consisting of men who seemed to have the necessary intelligence. One of these was a certain Achaeus (who also happened to be an Achaean by birth), a man who was good both at making plans and carrying them out. Within three days Eunus had armed as best he could a force of more than six thousand men. In addition to these he had others who would fight with axes and hatchets, slings, sickles, stakes and even kitchen skewers. With these men he roamed about, ravaging the entire countryside. And then, when he had recruited many other slaves, he even dared to attack the Roman generals. He defeated them many times because of the size of his army. He had more than ten thousand soldiers. . . .

Soon after, the rebels fought a battle with Lucius Hypsaeus, a general who had arrived from Rome. He commanded eight thousand Sicilian troops, but the slaves numbered twenty thousand and so they were victorious. Before long there were two hundred thousand of them and in their numerous battles with the Romans they had many successes and few defeats. When word of the revolt spread there were other revolts in other places. An uprising of one hundred and fifty slaves occurred in Rome, another thousand revolted in Athens, and there were rebellions in Delos and many other places. But the local magistrates called in the troops so quickly and punished the rebels so severely that the rebellion was put down and those who were considering joining it were deterred. But in Sicily things only got worse. The slaves captured cities, enslaved their inhabitants and cut whole armies to pieces. Finally, however, the Roman commander Rupilius recaptured Tauromenium after subjecting it to a siege so effective that the city was completely sealed off. The rebels inside were trapped under indescribably horrible conditions of suffering and hunger. At first they ate the children, then the women, and finally one another. . . .

In the end a Syrian slave named Sarapion betrayed the citadel. Rupilius seized all of the runaway slaves in the city and, after torturing them, he threw them over a cliff. He then marched against Enna, which he besieged just as he had Tauromenium, causing the rebels extreme suffering and dashing all their hopes. Cleon, one of the rebel commanders, came out of the city with a few men, but after a heroic struggle in which he was covered with wounds his dead body was put on display. Rupilius captured Enna by betrayal, for it was too strongly defended to be taken by force of arms alone. Eunus took his thousand bodyguards and fled in a cowardly way. . . .

. . . . He died in a manner befitting such a scoundrel at Morgantina [in central Sicily]. After this Rupilius scoured Sicily with a few picked troops and more quickly than anyone had hoped rid the island of every single robber-slave.

Tiberius Gracchus' Land Reforms:
Plutarch, *Tiberius Gracchus* 8–9

Historians generally recognize that Tiberius Gracchus was a man of high probity and sincere patriotism whose reforms might have preserved the Republic. However, he made serious tactical errors in the implementation of his land reform program, thus raising political passions and exposing himself to merciless persecution. But although Tiberius failed in his concrete designs, his political vision profoundly influenced Roman politics. In fact, he is widely regarded as the instigator of the revolution that led to the eventual destruction of the Republic.

Of the land gained by the Romans as a consequence of the conquest of their neighbors, part was sold by the government and part was made public. This public land was assigned by the authorities to those citizens of the Republic who were poor and landless, with the requirement that they pay a small rent to the public treasury. However, when the wealthy began to offer more substantial rents for the use of these public lands and to force the poorer people out, a law was enacted which made it illegal for any individual to hold more than three hundred acres of public land. This measure controlled for awhile the greed of the rich and protected the poor, who retained the land they had formerly rented. But then the wealthy were able to get possession of these lands by using false names until at last they claimed most of them as their own. The poor people who had lost their farms as a result of these tactics were now no longer ready to serve in war or interested in the education of their children. Thus, in a short time comparatively few free laborers remained in Italy, which was inundated with gangs of foreign-born slaves who were now employed by the rich Romans in cultivating the soil from which the free citizens had been driven. A close friend of Scipio, Gaius Laelius, made an effort to correct this injustice but was opposed by influential men. In order to avoid a civil disturbance, he soon gave up his effort and was consequently nicknamed "the Wise" and "the Prudent," for both of these are suggested by the Latin word *Sapiens*.

When Tiberius was elected tribune of the people he immediately proceeded to address this problem at the urging of Diophanes the rhetorician and Blossius the philosopher, as most writers say. Diophanes was a Greek refugee from Mytilene and Blossius was an Italian from Cumae who had received his education in his native city under the guidance of Antipater of Tarsus, who subsequently honored him by dedicating some of his philosophic lectures to him. Others argue that it was Cornelia, Tiberius' mother, who had the most profound influence on him, for it is known that she frequently chided her sons for the fact that the Romans referred to her as the daughter of Scipio instead of the mother of the Gracchi. And there are some who say that it was actually Spurius Postumius who was most responsible for his career. This man was the same age as Tiberius and his rival as a public speaker. When Tiberius returned home from the army he found that Postumius had surpassed him by far in reputation and influence and was highly respected. Tiberius, they say, then thought to outclass him by undertaking a daring political venture which he hoped would have an enormous impact on the people. His brother Gaius, however, informs us in one of his written works that when Tiberius went to Numantia through Tuscany and observed that the country was nearly depopulated (for he encountered only a few free farmers and shepherds there but found large numbers of imported barbarian slaves) he conceived the idea of pursuing the political course whose consequences were to prove so fatal to his family. Moreover, it is also quite certain that the people themselves were responsible for augmenting his zeal and determination by writing messages on the porches, walls and monuments of the city calling upon him to restore to them their lost farms.

Tiberius, however, did not draft his law without seeking the opinions and assistance of those citizens of Rome who were then most distinguished for their virtue and reputation. Among these were Crassus, the *pontifex maximus*, Mucius Scaevola, the jurist who was serving as consul at that time, and Appius Claudius, his father-in-law. In fact, one cannot find a more moderate and gentle law ever drawn up to combat such great injustice and greed. Those individuals who should have been punished for violating the law or, at least, should have lost their title to the lands which they had illegally occupied were now to receive compensation for surrendering their unlawful claims and giving up the public lands to needy citizens. Yet, despite the fact that Tiberius' reform legislation was very moderate, the avaricious rich were against both it and its author, who had by now aroused their anger and partisan spirit. As for the people, they were pleased by the land reform law and willing to forget the injustices of the past as long as similar abuses would be avoided in the future. The wealthy, therefore, attempted to mislead the people by telling them that what Tiberius really had in mind was a general redistribution of land as a means of overthrowing the government and creating a climate of general confusion.

But this scheme of the wealthy failed, for Tiberius, who championed an honorable and just cause and spoke with an eloquence that would have made a far less worthy plan seem attractive, was not an easy opponent to overcome.

Every time the people gathered around the rostra he would take the opportunity to speak on behalf of the poor: "The wild beasts of Italy," he used to say, "have their own dens and places of rest and refuge, but the men who fight and risk their lives for their country enjoy only the air and light of their homeland, for since they have no houses or settlements of their own they are forced to wander from place to place with their wives and children. The military commanders are guilty of a ludicrous deception when they exhort the common soldiers to fight for their sepulchers and altars, since there is not one among them who possesses a tomb or an altar. Indeed, they fight and die to preserve the luxury and wealth of others. They are known as the masters of the world but have not even one foot of ground to call their own."

The Legislation of Gaius Gracchus:
Plutarch, *Gaius Gracchus* 1, 4–7

Gaius Sempronius Gracchus became a champion of the Roman people after the assassination of his brother Tiberius who, as tribune in 133 B.C., proposed legislation aimed at recovering vast tracts of land from their wealthy *possessores* and making them available to poor, landless citizens. As tribune for the years 123 and 122 B.C., Gaius proceeded with his brother's reforms and, like him, earned the enmity of the senatorial class. He was murdered while serving his second term. The character and legislation of this remarkable Roman reformer are described by Plutarch in the following passage.

After his brother's death Gaius at first withdrew from public affairs and lived a quiet life at home, giving the impression of being a man without political ambitions who wanted to spend his life in inaction. Perhaps he was afraid of his brother's enemies or, on the other hand, he may have wanted to make them even more contemptible in the eyes of the people. In any case, he stayed at home, and there were some who went so far as to attack him personally by saying that he had repudiated his brother's reforms and turned his back on them. But he was still a very young man, in fact nine years younger than his brother Tiberius who had been killed before he turned thirty. As time went on, however, Gaius' true nature emerged and it became clear that he was completely averse to a life of indolence, decadent pleasures, drinking and making money. Further, the great effort he made to master the art of public speaking, an art which would support his aspirations to public office, showed clearly that he had no intention of spending the rest of his life in obscurity. When a friend of his named Vettius was brought to trial Gaius defended him so powerfully that the people were entranced and left almost ecstatic by his eloquence, which made other orators look like children by comparison.

It so happened that at about this time the lot fell on Gaius to go to Sardinia as quaestor for the consul Orestes. His enemies were delighted, and Gaius himself was pleased to go. He enjoyed serving in the army and was as well trained in war as he was in law. Moreover, even though he was not yet ready to get involved in politics and appear on the rostra, many of his friends and other citizens were calling insistently upon him to do just that, and so he welcomed the opportunity to leave the city. Such are the facts, and yet, in spite of them, there are those who claim that Gaius was a demagogue pure and simple who was far more eager to win the support of the people than his brother Tiberius. They are wrong. Gaius seems to have been drawn into public life by necessity rather than by choice, and this view is supported by Cicero, who says that Gaius had turned down offices and chosen to live a quiet life until his brother appeared to him in a dream and said, "Why are you hesitating, Gaius? There is no escape, for we were both destined to live and die as champions of the people."

Plutarch describes Gaius' successes as quaestor, various accusations made against him by his enemies, and the speech in which he defended himself

Once he had stirred the people with these words—he had a very powerful voice and spoke with absolute conviction—Gaius proceeded to introduce two laws. The first provided that no magistrate should be allowed to hold a second office if the people had dismissed him from his first. The second gave the people the power to prosecute any magistrate who banished a citizen without a trial. The first law was clearly intended to remove from office Marcus Octavius, who had been dismissed from the tribunate by Tiberius, while the second was aimed at Popilius, who as praetor had banished Tiberius' supporters. Popilius did not wait to stand trial but fled Italy immediately. Gaius himself rescinded the first law, saying that he spared Octavius at the request of his mother Cornelia. This pleased the people and they consented to the repeal of the measure, for they honored Cornelia as much for her sons as they did for her father. In fact, in later years they erected a bronze statue of her which bore the inscription: "Cornelia, Mother of the Gracchi." We also have some of the things Gaius said about her on an occasion when he was attacking one of his enemies in the rough language he used in the Forum: "What," he said, "are you insulting Cornelia, who gave birth to Tiberius?" And then, since the man had been accused of being a homosexual, he asked, "How dare you compare yourself with Cornelia? Have you borne children like hers? One thing is certain, all Rome knows you've slept with a man more recently than she has!" Such was the bitterness of his words, and there are many other examples which can be found in his writings.

Gaius now introduced a number of laws which he hoped would both please the people and undermine the power of the Senate. One of these was an agrarian law which divided public land among the poor citizens. Another, which pertained to the army, required that soldiers should be clothed at public expense rather than their own and also prohibited the conscription of anyone under the age of seventeen. A third law gave the Italians the right to vote and a fourth made provision for a grain supply and lowered prices for the poor. A fifth law dealt with the appointment of juries and had the effect of sharply curtailing the power of the Senate, for up until that time only senators had served as jurors in criminal cases, and so they had been greatly feared by the plebeians and equestrians. This same law also provided for the addition to the three hundred members of the Senate another three hundred selected from the equestrian class and gave the authority to appoint jurors to the whole six hundred. They say that Gaius worked harder for the passage of this law than for that of any other. Perhaps the most interesting in his campaign for its passage was that, whereas leaders of the people had customarily turned their faces towards the senate-house and the part of the Forum called the *comitium* when they spoke, Gaius now for the first time faced the people, and continued this practice from that time on. This small change in posture and deviation from tradition signified no small revolution in Roman public life, for it raised the question of whether the government of Rome was aristocratic or democratic. By facing the people Gaius was suggesting that politicians should address themselves to the people and not to the Senate.

When the people not only ratified this law but also gave him authority to appoint equestrians as judges, Gaius acquired nearly regal powers, and even the Senate could no longer ignore his opinions and advice. But these were always given in support of measures which brought honor and dignity to that body, such as the very equitable and honorable resolution concerning the grain which had been sent from Spain by the praetor Quintus Fabius. Gaius persuaded the Senate to sell it and give the money back to the cities which had supplied it and, not satisfied with this, to censure Fabius for making Roman rule intolerably harsh on a subject people. This decree won him great respect and good will in the provinces.

Gaius also proposed legislation for the founding of new colonies, the building of roads and the construction of public granaries. He took personal responsibility for the management and supervision of these diverse and elaborate projects and never showed the slightest fatigue in guiding them to their completion. In fact, he finished them with such astonishing speed that even those who hated and feared him were amazed to see what extraordinary talent he had for getting things done. As for the people themselves, they were astonished by the very sight of this man who, while pressed by crowds of contractors, artisans, public officials, military officers and men of letters, was able to make himself accessible and familiar to all of them, treating them with kindness and giving each of them the attention he deserved. In this way he discredited as envious slanderers all those who had represented him as a tyrannical, arrogant and violent man. He was, in fact, even more effective as a popular leader in his private dealings with individuals than he was in the speeches he gave from the rostra.

Gaius was especially enthusiastic about the building of new roads, and he took great care to make sure that these would be both useful and beautiful. His roads were laid out in straight lines across the country and were paved with dressed stone set on substructures of packed sand. Depressions were filled up, intersecting rivers and ravines were bridged and both sides of the roads were leveled or built up to the same height, so that the work had an even and pleasing appearance. In addition to this, Gaius had every road measured in miles —the Roman mile being a little less than eight *stadia* [about 95 yards less than the English mile]—and set up milestones to mark the distances. Other stones were placed at shorter intervals on both sides of the road so that riders would be able to mount their horses without assistance.

Hired Hands: Varro, *On Agriculture* I.17.2–3

Despite the land reform legislation of Tiberius Gracchus, which was intended to bring about a more equitable distribution of farmland, most of Rome's rural poor remained landless and dependent upon the wealthy landowners who offered them work on their great estates. The Roman writer Varro (116-27 B.C.) described the types of farm workers who labored there.

The tilling of a field is a task performed by men, whether slaves, free men or both. Some free men work the land themselves, as is the case with the landed poor, who do so with the help of their families. Others are hired hands who find work when the more difficult tasks, such as gathering in the vintage and haying, can be completed only with the help of additional free laborers. And then there are the ones we call *obaerarii*, [*i.e.*, laborers trying to work off their debts], many of whom can still be found in Asia, Egypt and Illyricum. With regard to all of these, my advice is this: it is more profitable to work difficult lands with the help of free men instead of slaves, and even on better land it is a good idea to use them for the heavier farm work, such as storing the vintage and the harvest. Cassius [*i.e.*, Cassius Dionysius, who translated the treatise of the Carthaginian Mago on agriculture] wrote that farmhands should be able to work hard, at least twenty-two years old, and take easily to work in the fields. You can tell whether they meet these requirements by observing the way they follow instructions and, in the case of new ones, by asking them what kinds of tasks they performed for their former bosses.

Optimates: Cicero, *In Defense of Sestius* 45–46; 48

The Senate's violent suppression of the Gracchan movement in the late second century B.C. encouraged the growth of opposition forces which would prove to be its undoing in the following century. One of the most visible responses to the Senate's policies was the crystallization of an anti-senatorial movement of *Populares,* citizens whose interests coincided more with those of the people of Rome in general rather than with those of the ruling aristocracy. The *Populares* should not be considered a democratic party, however, as has sometimes been the case, for there were as yet no political parties in Rome. Moreover, its members, mostly newly enriched businessmen, generally appear to have supported popular causes more for the purpose of winning popular support than out of sincere devotion to a liberal ideology. Nevertheless, they posed a serious threat to the wealthy members of the senatorial oligarchy, or *Optimates,* whose views were represented by Cicero in his oration in defense of Sestius.

There have always been two classes of men in Rome who have been eager to participate in politics and take charge of affairs of state. One of these aimed at becoming *Populares,* both in reality and in popular opinion, while the other aspired to be *Optimates.* The *Populares* were those who wanted their words and deeds to find favor with the people, while the *Optimates* sought the approval of the best citizens. And who are these "best citizens"? Their number is beyond counting, and if it were not for them the state would not exist. They are those who set public policy, and those who support them. They are the members of those classes to whom the Senate is open. They are citizens of Rome who live in towns and in the countryside, businessmen, and even freedmen.

As I said, the membership of this class is large and diverse, and so a brief summation of what they are all about will help to prevent misunderstanding. All those who are neither criminals, morally bankrupt, mad nor encumbered by embarrassing domestic scandals are *Optimates.* In other words, this "breed," as you call it, is comprised of honest men of sound mind who come from good families. Those government officials who seek to satisfy the desires of these men and to safeguard their interests and principles, since they are the defenders of the *Optimates,* are recognized as the most important of the *Optimates,* the most distinguished citizens and leaders of the state. And what is the goal of these men who steer the ship of state? What is the mark on which their gaze should be fixed? What is the destination for which they should set their course? Why, that which all sensible, good and prosperous men consider most desirable thing of all: peace with honor. All those who want peace with honor are *Optimates,* and those public officials who work to achieve it earn for themselves reputations as the very best of citizens and saviors of the state. Indeed, men should neither be so carried away by the honor of holding public office that they fail to work for peace, nor accept any peace that does not bring honor.

Now, an honorable peace must guarantee the integrity of the basic features of Roman life, features which our leaders must protect and defend even at the cost of their own lives: the rites of our religion, the auspices, the powers of our magistrates, the authority of the Senate, our laws and ancestral customs, the courts and their administration of justice, good faith in business dealings, our provinces and relations with our allies, the glory of our empire, the army and the treasury. He who would be the defender and champion of so many great interests must be a man of great spirit, great mind and great resolve, for in a state as large as ours there are always plenty of men who want to encourage unrest and revolution in the hope of escaping in these the punishment they deserve for the crimes they have committed, others who are afflicted by an innate madness that thrives on civil strife and sedition, and still others who, when faced with financial ruin, prefer to bring all of society down with them rather than suffer alone. When men like these find leaders to represent them and their corrupt desires, disturbances are aroused in the state. It is then that those who have sought the authority that comes with public office must be on their guard and, making full use of their knowledge and exercising the greatest care, hold their course until they reach the safe harbor of peace and honor without injury to any of the basic features of Roman life of which I have just spoken. I would be guilty of lying, gentlemen, if I were to say that the way to peace with honor is not rough, hard and full of danger and deceit, for I have always known that it is difficult and have greater experience of its demands than others do.

I do not deny that the task is a hard one. I admit that there are dangers, and that it is true that, as the poet said, "Many are the traps set for the virtuous." . . . .In earlier times the *Optimates* had even more to fear than they do now, for the desires of the people and what worked to their advantage did not always coincide with the public interest. When Lucius Cassius proposed a law to provide for voting by ballot the people thought their freedom depended on its passage. But the leaders of the state disagreed, for they feared that the impetuous masses might abuse the secret ballot and endanger the interests of the *Optimates*. Tiberius Gracchus proposed an agrarian law which delighted the people, for it provided plenty of food without work. But good men opposed it, for they saw in it a call to the people to exchange industriousness for laziness and a drain on the treasury.

Corruption in the Provinces:
Cicero, *Verrine Orations* 2.3.20–24

Gaius Verres was a notoriously corrupt politician who managed to secure a number of lucrative public offices, most notably the governorship of Sicily where he served for three years (73-70 B.C.). With no apparent regard for the rights of the Sicilians, Verres used his position to systematically strip them of their wealth, thus amassing for himself a vast fortune. On the expiration of his term of office the people of Sicily brought suit against Verres. They were represented by Marcus Tullius Cicero, whose spectacular prosecution of the case marked the beginning of his brilliant career as a lawyer and statesman. Cicero's *actio prima*, the first phase of his prosecution, was so effective that Verres abandoned his defense and went into exile at Massilia; thus, he had no occasion to deliver a second speech, the *actio secunda,* an excerpt from which appears below. Nevertheless, it provides us with a sample of Cicero's oratory as well as a description of the widespread phenomenon of corruption in the provinces.

I cannot describe for you, senators, the whole range and number of his crimes. It would be impossible to enumerate, one by one, all the ways in which he has brought suffering to his countless victims. With your permission, then, I will merely cite some representative examples.

There is a man from Centuripa named Nympho, a hard-working and industrious man who is a prudent and experienced farmer. He had a large farm which he he held as leasehold, a practice which is common throughout Sicily even among wealthy men such as he is, and he had invested a great deal of money in agricultural equipment. But Nympho was treated so unjustly by Verres that he was forced not only to abandon his farm but to flee Sicily and come to Rome to live in exile, as many of Verres' victims have done.

Verres had induced a tax collector to certify that Nympho had not made any return from the acreage he cultivated, a violation of that famous edict of his which had the sole purpose of winning him gains of just this kind. When Nympho declared that he was prepared to defend himself before an impartial court, Verres proceeded to appoint as arbitrators some truly "fine" men, namely that same physician of his, Cornelius, who is also known as Artemidorus, who in previous years had been the leader of Verres' faction in his hometown of Perga and led the raid which despoiled the local temple of Diana, his diviner Voluusius, and his crier Valerius. They convicted Nympho without giving him a chance to defend himself. And what penalty did they impose on him? Verres' edict made no mention of a specific penalty, and so the arbitrators sentenced Nympho to pay all of the grain he had harvested. Thus, the tax collector Apronius, instead of collecting the correct tax or carrying away only a portion of the grain which had been stored in a hiding place, took a full seven thousand bushels as a penalty for violating the edict, and this despite the fact that he had no contractual right to do so.

The wife of Xeno, a distinguished citizen of Menae, owned an estate which was leased to a tenant farmer. The tenant, however, had deserted his land because he could not endure the mistreatment he suffered at the hands of the tax collectors. Verres authorized the prosecution of Xeno on his favorite charge: not making the proper return on his acreage. Xeno denied any responsibility, pointing out that the farm had been leased to someone else. Verres instructed the court to find him guilty if, in the words of the edict, *"it shall appear that the size of the farm in question is greater than the area stated by the tenant."* Xeno argued that he had not been farming the land, a defense which should have been sufficient to relieve him of any liability, and that he was neither the owner nor lessor of the farm, which belonged to his wife who, being in charge of her own business affairs, had leased the land on her own initiative. He was defended by Marcus Cossutius, a man who was both distinguished and highly respected. Nevertheless, Verres managed to bring Xeno to trial, asking for a penalty of one thousand sesterces. And Xeno, though he knew the court would be composed of disreputable people, nevertheless agreed to accept its decision. Then Verres, in a voice loud enough for Xeno to hear, commanded his temple slaves to keep him in custody while the case was being tried and to deliver Xeno to him as soon as the proceedings were concluded. He added that, if found guilty, Xeno might be wealthy enough to consider a money penalty a mere slap on the wrists, but that he would find it hard to ignore a flogging. Intimidated by this threat of violence, Xeno agreed to pay the tax collectors as much as Verres asked.

Polemarchus, a decent, respectable citizen of Murgentia, was ordered to pay a tax of seven hundred bushels on a farm of only fifty acres. Because he refused he was taken off to Verres' home to be judged by him there. Verres was still in bed, however, and so Polemarchus was dragged into his bedroom, a privilege normally reserved for tax collectors and women. There he was roughed up and kicked so badly that he agreed to pay a thousand bushels although he had earlier refused to pay seven hundred.

Eubulidas Grospus is a man of good character, high birth and wealth, all of which make him the leading citizen of his home town of Centuripa. You should know, however, that this most distinguished citizen of a distinguished town ended up not only entirely without grain but with no more life and blood in his body than Apronius was pleased to leave him. Violence, torment and beatings induced him to pay not the amount of grain he should have paid, but what he was forced to pay.

In the same city there were three brothers named Sostratus, Numenius and Nymphodorus who abandoned their land because they were ordered to pay in taxes an amount greater than their entire harvest. Apronius, Verres' agent, then came to their farm with his band of thugs, seized all their equipment, carried away their slaves and drove off their livestock. Nymphodorus later went to see Apronius at Aetna and begged him to restore his property but Apronius had him arrested and suspended from a wild olive tree that grows in the forum there. Thus, this friend and ally of Rome, this farmer and landowner, hung from a tree in one of our empire's towns for as long as it pleased Apronius.

Senators, I have been describing for you the various injustices which have been done by giving you only a single example of each and thus leaving a great many unmentioned. I ask you to see with your own eyes, to imagine in your own minds, how from one end of Sicily to the other there were assaults by tax collectors, plunderings of farmers, savageries committed by Verres and the tyrannical acts of Apronius. Verres had nothing but contempt for the Sicilians; he didn't even consider them human. He believed that they would never take strong action against him and that you yourselves would not be much disturbed by word of his crimes.

Well, he was wrong about them, and his low opinion of you, too, was false. You might think that, as cruelly as he treated the provincials in Sicily, he would have courted the favor of the Roman *citizens* there, that he would have done his best to indulge them and keep them satisfied and on his side. Did he? Hardly! He hated and persecuted them more than any other group! I will say nothing here of the chains and the prisons, the beatings and the executions. I will pass over the crucifixions by which he sought to express to Roman citizens his humane and benevolent feelings toward them. I will speak of these things later. For the present I am discussing the tax on grain and how Roman citizens were treated on their own farms. And how they were treated, senators, you have already heard from the victims themselves. They have told you how they were robbed.

Perhaps you think that in a cause as noble as Verres' self-enrichment it is necessary for such things to happen and for justice and custom to be set aside. You might argue, senators, that as far as material losses are concerned there are none so damaging that they cannot be endured by a strong man with real spirit. But what if, while the defendant was governor, Roman equestrians had been violated without hesitation by Apronius? I do not mean men who are obscure and unknown, but famous and distinguished Roman equestrians like yourselves? Is that enough for you? Is there anything else you would like me to say, or should we settle Verres' case right now and proceed to the prosecution of Apronius? I promised him before I left Sicily that I would do so.

Moral Decline During the Republic:
Sallust, *Conspiracy of Catiline* 9–10

**Writing in the difficult years following the assassination
of Julius Caesar (44 B.C.), the Roman historian Sallust
considered the roots of the evils which plagued his country. In
his *Conspiracy of Catiline*, which describes a failed coup d'etat
in 63 B.C., Sallust argued that the decline of Rome was due in
large part to the abandonment of the civic values and high moral
standards which had made Rome great in the past.**

[The Romans of the early Republic] considered good morals to be of the
utmost importance both in peace and war. Social harmony was the rule and
greed was very rare. Justice and goodness were enforced not so much by laws
as by nature. These early Romans reserved their quarreling, discord and hostility
for the enemies of the state. Citizens vied with each other only for honor. When
they made offerings to the gods they spared no expense, while at home they
practiced frugality. They were loyal to their friends. By combining courage in
war and justice in peacetime they protected themselves and their country. For
example, in wartime soldiers were punished more often for attacking the enemy
against orders or for being too slow to obey the order to leave the field of
battle than for abandoning their standards or giving ground when hard pressed
by the enemy. A second example is the fact that the early Romans governed
their subjects with generosity rather than fear, and when wronged they sought
to forgive the offenders rather than seek vengeance.

But when Rome had grown great through hard work and justice, when
mighty kings had been vanquished in war and savage tribes and powerful
nations had been brought down, when Carthage, Rome's rival, had been toppled
and every land and sea had been opened to us, then Fortune turned against us
and brought confusion to all that we did. Those who had found it easy to bear
hard work and danger, anxiety and hardship, now discovered that the leisure
and wealth which most men find so desirable were a burden and a curse to
them. Lust for money grew among them, then the hunger for power, and these
two gave rise to every other kind of evil. Greed destroyed honor, honesty and
every other virtue, and taught men to be arrogant and cruel, to neglect the gods,
and to believe that nothing is too sacred to sell. Ambition made many men
false, leading them to say what they knew was not true, to choose friends and
make enemies with only personal advancement in mind and to pretend they

had good qualities which they did not have. At first these vices grew slowly, and sometimes they were punished. But in the end, when the disease had spread like a plague, Rome changed: a government which had once surpassed all others in justice and excellence now became cruel and unbearable.

Slave Labor in Spanish Mines:
Diodorus Siculus, *Historical Library* 5.36–38

Among the unluckiest of Roman slaves were those who were forced to work in the mines. In the following passage the Greek historian Diodorus Siculus describes the plight of the slaves who labored in the gold and silver mines of Iberia (modern Spain).

Ever since the Romans seized Iberia the greed of the Italians has brought them in droves to the province's mines, from which they have carried away untold wealth. They buy whole lots of slaves and turn them over to those who supervise the miners. The slaves then dig deep shafts in various places in hopes of finding the veins of silver and gold that run through the earth. The shafts they dig are not only very deep, but they also run many stades [a stade is about 607 feet] in length, and tunnels reach out from them at every angle, twisting back and forth under the earth, so that the miners can bring up from the depths the ore which gives their owners the profit they are after. . . .

The slaves who work in the mines produce unbelievable wealth for their masters but they themselves are destroyed by the digging they do day and night in the subterranean shafts. Many of them die because of the extreme suffering that fills their lives. They are given no chance to rest. Instead, under the overseer's lash, they have no choice but to live lives of terrible hardship and misery. Some of them manage to stay alive for quite some time, for they have strong bodies and hardy souls, but their suffering is so great that in their eyes death is more desirable than life.

Women and the Conspiracy of Catiline: Sallust, *Conspiracy of Catiline*, 23–25

In 63 B.C. Catiline, a young Roman aristocrat, attempted to overthrow the government of Rome. The unsuccessful *coup d'etat* was observed by the historian Sallust who recorded it in his *Conspiracy of Catiline.* The brief excerpt below describes the involvement of two women: Fulvia, who was one of the first to tip off authorities concerning Catiline's treasonous activities, and Sempronia, an aristocratic supporter of Catiline who was also the mother of Decimus Brutus, one of the assassins of Julius Caesar. Sallust considered Sempronia's behavior to be scandalous not only because of her involvement in the Catilinarian conspiracy but also because in all of her activities she exercised a degree of independence thought to be inappropriate for women in the Rome of her day. Interestingly, while Sallust clearly disapproves of Sempronia's actions, he also appreciates her for her ability.

One of the conspirators was a certain Quintus Curius, a man who came from a good family but who was knee-deep in infamy and crime. In fact, the censors had expelled him from the Senate because of his immoral behavior. He was an unreliable and foolish man who did not have the sense to keep his mouth shut even about his own misdeeds. Quintus had for a long time a mistress named Fulvia, who was also from a good family. When she began to frown on the mediocre gifts he gave her because of his declining fortunes he suddenly began to talk big; one moment he would promise her the moon, the next he would threaten to stab her unless she did what he asked. This was so unlike his normal manner that Fulvia demanded an explanation, and when she heard the reason for his arrogance she decided that she could not be a party to the concealment of such a serious danger to the state. Without revealing the name of her source, she told a number of people what she had heard about Catiline's plot. It was this information, more than anything else, that caused people to give their support to Marcus Tullius Cicero in his bid for the consulship. Up until this time the aristocrats were so jealous of this office that they would have thought it polluted if some outsider, no matter how distinguished, was elected to it. But now danger threatened, and jealousy and aristocratic pride had to be put aside.

Thus, Cicero and Gaius Antonius won the election and were returned as consuls—a serious setback for the conspirators. But Catiline was not discouraged. He went on devising ever more grandiose plans, establishing stores of weapons at strategic spots throughout Italy and raising money on his own or his friends' credit and sending it to a man named Manlius in Fiesole who later on was the one who opened hostilities.

It was at about this time that Catiline was attracting supporters of all kinds. These included a number of women who, in their younger days, had lived extravagantly on the money they earned by selling themselves. But now, their tastes unchanged but their incomes reduced because of their age, they had run into debt. Catiline believed that these women would be useful in stirring up the slaves and as arsonists. Their husbands, he thought, could either be persuaded to join his cause or murdered.

One of these women was Sempronia, who had often acted with masculine daring. Fortune had been very good to her in giving her high birth, beauty, a good husband and children. She had been well educated in both Greek and Latin literature, could play the lyre and dance better than any honest woman should and had many other qualities and accomplishments which tend to lead to decadence. She had almost no regard for honor and modesty, and it would be hard to say which she squandered more—her money or her honor. Her lust was so great that she approached men more often than they approached her. Even before she became involved with Catiline she had often gone back on her word, failed to pay her debts, been an accessory to murder and had become impoverished because of her expensive tastes. And yet her abilities were considerable. She could write poetry, make jokes and, as the occasion required, use modest, soft or rough language. She was, in fact, a woman of great wit and charm.

The First Triumvirate: Plutarch, *Crassus* 14–15

By 60 B.C. three of Rome's most prominent political figures found themelves in opposition to the Senate. Conservative senators had sought to prevent Caesar's bid for the consulship for the year 59 B.C., the Senate had refused Crassus' request for a reduction in the high price his equestrian friends had unwisely bid for the privilege of collecting taxes in Asia, and Pompey's promise in 62 B.C. to grant tracts of land to the veterans of his eastern campaigns had still not won senatorial approval. In order to overcome senatorial opposition, the three entered into an informal association known as the First Triumvirate (60 B.C.). While this arrangement proved useful for all of the triumvirs, it was Caesar who profited most. With the support of his fellow triumvirs Caesar was elected as consul for the year 59 B.C. and then went on to posts as governor of Cisalpine Gaul, Illyricum and Transalpine Gaul. Eventually he was able to make a dramatic return to Rome (49 B.C.) which resulted in his seizure of power.

Hoping to win election as consul, Caesar now returned from his command in Further Spain and found that Crassus and Pompey were once again at odds with each other. Unwilling to make an enemy of either of them by supporting the other, and well aware that his campaign would be hopeless if he lost the support of both, he did his best to reconcile them by arguing that by weakening each other they would also increase the power of men like Cicero, Catulus and Cato whose power would be minimal if only Crassus and Pompey would join their interests and supporters and run the government with a common goal and purpose. They were persuaded by his argument and so Caesar was able to forge from three individuals a single force of irresistible power which he would use to destroy the government of the Senate and the people of Rome. Each of his colleagues received a share of power equal to that of the other, but Caesar himself emerged as the most powerful of the three, for with their support he soon won election to the consulship, and while he held that office they voted him the command of armies and turned over to him the province of Gaul. Pompey and Crassus established Caesar in this position of strength believing that once he had been made secure in his share of the spoils they would be able to divide what was left at their leisure. Pompey's motive in all this was his insatiable appetite for power. As for Crassus, he had always been been greedy, but now he longed for the trophies and triumphs won in military exploits, the one area in which he believed he had not shown his superiority to Caesar. This longing gave him no rest until it ended in his inglorious death and a national disaster.

When Caesar came down from Gaul to the city of Luca many Romans went to meet him there, among them Pompey and Crassus. In private meetings these three decided to tighten their grip on the government and, in fact, to bring it completely under their control. Caesar, they determined, would keep his army, and Pompey and Crassus would be given provinces and armies of their own. The only way in which these things could be accomplished was through control of the consulship, and so they decided that Pompey and Crassus would stand for election as consuls the following year and that Caesar would do his part by writing to his friends and sending his soldiers to support them at the election.

Having reached this agreement Pompey and Crassus returned to Rome. But it wasn't long before people caught on to their plans and word spread that nothing good had come out of their meeting with Caesar . . . . "Why should these men want a second consulship?" many asked. "Why must they serve together a second time? Why not with other colleagues? Surely there are many men in Rome who are qualified to hold the consulship with Crassus and Pompey." Disturbed by such talk, the supporters of Crassus and Pompey now gave in to the temptation to use violence against those who spoke out against them. The worst moment came during an ambush they set for Domitius as he was coming down to the forum before daybreak with his followers. His torchbearer was killed and many were wounded, including Cato. Once their opponents had been routed and shut up at home by such means, Pompey and Crassus had themselves proclaimed consuls. Not long thereafter, they once more surrounded the rostra with armed men, removed Cato from the forum, killed some who put up resistance, and then passed decrees which added five years to Caesar's command in Gaul and gave the provinces of Syria and the two Spains to themselves. They cast lots for them; Crassus won Syria and Pompey received the Spanish provinces.

Caesar the Tyrant: Cicero, *On Duties* 3.21

In the following excerpt from his treatise *On Duties*, Cicero defends the murder of Caesar by arguing that the dictator's ambition and overthrow of the legitimate government of Rome had made him a dangerous enemy of the Roman people.

The tyrant deserved to die, for he thought he was justified in committing the worst of all crimes. Why do we bother to worry about petty offenses—inheritances illegally claimed and fraud in the marketplace? Here we have a man who aspired to make himself king over the people of Rome and master of the entire world, and he succeeded! Who but a madman would think that such ambition is morally correct? Who but an anarchist who yearns to see the destruction of law and liberty and thinks that an abominable thing, their suppression, is really something glorious? And what about those who say, on the one hand, that there is no place for a king in a state that was once free and should be free now, and yet argue, on the other, that kingship nevertheless offers great advantages to anyone who can claim it? How can I get such people to see the light? By the immortal gods, how can the filthiest and most grievous of crimes, the murder of one's own country, be advantageous to anyone? How can it benefit the murderer himself, even if his oppressed fellow-citizens give him the title "Father of His Country"?

The Assassination of Caesar:
Plutarch, *Julius Caesar* 57–58; 64–66

On the 15th of March in the year 44 B.C. a group of about sixty conspirators ranging from ex-Pompeians to his own followers carried out their plot to assassinate Julius Caesar. In their view the mockery which he had made of the Republic justified a crime vividly recounted by the Greek biographer Plutarch in the following excerpts from his account of the life of Caesar.

Caesar refused to listen to his friends when they urged him to protect himself and volunteered to serve as his personal bodyguard. In his view it was better to die than to live in perpetual fear of dying. Caesar considered the affection of the people his best and most effective protection and sought to keep the support of the masses by means of feasts and entertainments, free distribution of grain and the foundation of colonies for the benefit of his veterans. The most famous of these are Carthage and Corinth. It is interesting to note that these two cities, which had been occupied and destroyed by the Romans in the same year [46 B.C.], were now restored and repopulated by Caesar in the same year [44 B.C.].

Caesar managed to win the good will of the aristocrats through promises to bestow the offices of consul and practor on some of them and various other positions and distinctions on others. Because he relied upon the support of the people he gave each of them reason to hope that he might receive some special favor in the future. Thus, when the consul Fabius Maximus died just one day before the end of his term, Caesar made Caninius Rebilius consul for that day. As was customary, many people went to pay their respects to the new consul and escort him to the Senate, an event which prompted Cicero to comment: "Hurry up, fellows, or his term may expire before we get there" . . . .

[Caesar's offenses turned] the attention of the masses to Marcus Brutus who, besides being the nephew and son-in-law of Cato, was thought to be descended from the ancient Brutus on his father's side and from the noble family of the Servilii on his mother's. But the many honors and favors which he received from Caesar had cooled whatever desire he may have had to overthrow the new monarchy. After Pompey's defeat at Pharsalus Caesar had not only spared his life and granted his request to spare the lives of his men, but had continued to appoint him to important offices. As a matter of fact, that same year Caesar had given him the most important of the practorships and had chosen him, rather than his rival Cassius, to serve as consul four years later. It is said that Caesar had remarked on the latter occasion: "Cassius is more qualified, but I cannot say no to Brutus." Even after the assassination plot had been conceived and Brutus had been accused by some of being one of the conspirators, Caesar expressed his faith in him by making the gesture of placing his hand on his own body and saying to the accusers: "Brutus will wait for my skin," meaning that, in spite of Brutus' unquestionable ability to rule, he was not the kind of man who would show ingratitude by taking power in some base way. Those people who wanted to bring about political change in the state placed all their hopes in Brutus; however, since they did not dare to speak to him openly they resorted to leaving messages every night on the platform and state chair that Brutus used in his capacity as practor. Most of them contained lines such as "You are sleeping, Brutus" and "You are not Brutus anymore." When Cassius noticed that these messages were beginning to affect Brutus' sense of pride he intensified his efforts to influence him, for Cassius had his own reasons for hating Caesar (which I described in my account of Cassius' life). Likewise, Caesar was also suspicious of Cassius, and had once told his friends: "What do you think Cassius is after? He looks pale, and that bothers me." And again, on another occasion, when he was told that Antony and Dolabella were involved in a plot against him, Caesar said that he wasn't worried about such fat and sleek men, but that he feared the lean and pale type, meaning Cassius and Brutus. . . .

At this time Decimus Brutus, surnamed Albinus, entered the scene, a man in whom Caesar had so much confidence that he had made him his second heir, but who was, nevertheless, involved in the conspiracy with the other Brutus and Cassius. Fearing that the plot might be revealed if Caesar adjourned the Senate to another day, he derided and ridiculed the diviners [who had warned Caesar that his life was in danger] and told Caesar that if the senators felt slighted by this it would be his own fault, for they were meeting at his request and were prepared to vote unanimously that he be declared king of all the provinces with the right to wear a diadem in all areas but Italy, both on land and sea. If someone were sent to tell them to adjourn until some later date when Calpurnia's dreams were more favorable, what would his enemies say? Who, if he did not appear at the meeting of the Senate, would be willing to listen patiently instead to Caesar's friends defend his government as not at all arbitrary or tyrannical? But if he was certain that this was an unlucky day, it would be much better for him to go to the Senate himself and personally adjourn the session. As he offered this advice, Brutus took Caesar by the hand and led him forward. They had not gone far from his door when someone's servant tried to get close to him but failed, since a crowd had already surrounded Caesar. The servant made his way into the house, though, and placed himself under

Calpurnia's protection, asking her to keep him safe until Caesar returned home because he had some important information for him.

At this point Artemidorus of Onidus, a teacher of Greek philosophy who was acquainted with Brutus and his associates and had become aware of the plot, brought a note to Caesar in which he revealed what he knew. Observing that Caesar passed all of the notes that were handed to him to his servants, Artemidorus came as near to Caesar as possible and said: "Caesar, read this note alone and quickly, for it contains vital information which concerns you personally." Caesar took the note and tried several times to read it, but the crowds that were pushing toward Caesar in order to speak with him made this impossible. Nevertheless, he kept the note in his hand until he came to the Senate. Some say that the note was given to Caesar by someone else, since Artemidorus was prevented by the crowd from getting close to him.

It is possible these things might have happened by chance; however, the fact that the place where the Senate met that day and which was destined to be the stage for the impending drama was the same building that Pompey had built as an annex to his theater and contained his statue plainly shows that some supernatural power directed the action and arranged for the murder to occur in that particular place. They say that just before the assassination took place even Cassius, who was a follower of Epicurus, looked at the statue of Pompey and silently invoked his assistance, for this critical moment of grave danger seems to have made him forget all rationalism and filled him with emotion.

In the meantime, Caesar's loyal friend Antony, who was a strong man, was kept outside the Theater of Pompey by Brutus Albinus, who sought to delay his entrance by engaging him in a prolonged conversation. When Caesar himself entered the building the senators rose to show their respect for him and some of Brutus' accomplices came and stood behind his chair while others approached him on the pretense of wanting to add their support to Tillius Cimber's petition for the release of his brother from exile. These conspirators continued their appeals to Caesar until he came to his seat. When he sat down he refused their request, but they persisted in urging him to grant it until he began to be annoyed. At this point Tillius got hold of his toga with both hands and pulled it down from his neck, which was the signal for the assault. Casca delivered the first dagger blow to Caesar's neck but the resulting wound was not mortal or even dangerous since Casca, in initiating such a daring undertaking, was extremely nervous. Thus, Caesar was able to turn around and grab the dagger. At that moment both the victim and the assailant cried out, Caesar in Latin, "You villain, Casca, what is the meaning of this?" and Casca to his brother in Greek, "Brother, help!"

When the attack began those individuals in the building who had no knowledge of the plot were so amazed and horrified that they froze in their places and were not only unable to help Caesar or run away, but even to utter a single word. But those who were involved in the conspiracy now drew their daggers and completely surrounded Caesar. He saw their blades leveled at his face and eyes, and like a wild animal trapped in the hunt he met with blows in whatever direction he turned, for it had been agreed that all of the conspirators would participate in the actual assassination and stain themselves with his blood. This explains why even Brutus gave him a dagger blow in the groin. It is reported by some witnesses that Caesar tried to resist all the other attackers by shifting his body to avoid their blows and calling out for help, but that when he saw Brutus' drawn dagger he simply covered his face with his toga and gave up his struggle, falling, either by chance or because he was pushed in that direction by his assassins, at the foot of the statue of Pompey, which was drenched with his blood. Thus, one might have thought that Pompey himself presided over an act of revenge against his enemy, who now lay at his feet dying an agonizing death, for they say he received twenty-three stab wounds.

Antony and Cleopatra: Plutarch, *Antony 25–27*

The last of the Ptolemaic monarchs of Egypt, Cleopatra VII was one of the most remarkable women of antiquity. Her image was blackened by Roman propagandists who saw her as a serious obstacle to the expansion of their empire in the East and the seductress of two of Rome's best generals, but the portrait of a scheming, irresistibly beautiful Cleopatra was challenged by other writers who offered a more balanced portrait of the Egyptian queen. One of these was the Greek biographer Plutarch who, while acknowledging her effective use of her personal charm, also regarded the Queen as a brilliant woman whose talents were many and diverse. The following excerpt from his biography of Antony describes her first meeting with the Roman triumvir in 41 B.C.

Such being Antony's nature, the love for Cleopatra which he now began to feel was the very worst of all the evils that could have befallen him. It awakened and roused to a frenzy many of the passions that had been hidden and dormant in him and stifled and ultimately destroyed the good and redeeming qualities which still resisted corruption. Here is the story of how she made him her captive.

While he was preparing for the campaign against the Parthians, Antony sent a message to Cleopatra ordering her to meet him in Cilicia to respond to the accusation that she had raised a great deal of money for Cassius and supported him in his war against the triumvirs. But when his messenger, Dellius, saw her face and discovered what a subtle and clever conversationalist she was, he realized that Antony would never consider harming such a woman and that she would more likely gain influence over him. So he decided to flatter the Egyptian queen and advised her to go to Cilicia, in Homer's words, "dressed in fine array," and not to be afraid of Antony whom he described as the gentlest and most humane of generals. Dellius' words were persuasive, and since she had already seen the effect of her beauty on Julius Caesar and Gnaeus, the son of Pompey, she expected that she would have an even easier time bringing Antony under her control. For Caesar and Gnaeus Pompey had known her when she was still a girl with little knowledge of the world, but she was going to meet Antony at just that age when a woman's beauty is most splendid and she is at the height of her intellectual power. So Cleopatra set about making preparations for her journey, taking with her as many gifts and ornaments and as much money as her royal rank and the prosperity of her country allowed her to take, but she went putting her greatest confidence in her own powers of enchantment and seduction.

Although she received many letters from Antony and his associates summoning her to visit him she did not answer them, and when she finally did come she seemed to be mocking him. For she sailed up the river Cydnus in a barge with a gilded stern and spreading sails of purple, its rowers dipping their silver oars in time with the music of flutes, pipes and lutes. Cleopatra herself reclined under a canopy of golden cloth, adorned as Venus is in paintings, while boys dressed as Cupids stood on either side of her cooling her with their fans. Her maids, dressed like sea nymphs and Graces, "manned" the rudders and reefing-ropes, and exquisite fragrances from countless censers wafted from the ship and diffused along the banks of the river. Some of the locals ran alongside the barge from the mouth of the river to Tarsus while others hurried down from the city to behold the sight. Indeed, even the crowds in the market streamed away until Antony himself, seated on his tribunal, was left virtually alone as the word spread that Venus had come to revel with Bacchus for the sake of Asia.

Antony then sent a message to Cleopatra inviting her to dine with him, but she answered that she would prefer that he come to her. And so, wanting to give evidence of his courtesty and friendliness, he agreed to her proposal and went. When he arrived he found the preparations to be beyond description, but what impressed him most was the incredible number of lights. They say that so many of these were suddenly let down and displayed on all sides, and that they were so ingeniously arranged in groups forming rectangles and circles, that few spectacles were as beautiful or worthy of being seen.

The following day Antony invited the Queen to have supper with him. He had hoped to surpass her in splendor and elegance but failed so miserably that he was the first to make fun of his own poor wit and lack of sophistication. For her part, Cleopatra realized that Antony's humor was that of a soldier and commoner and adopted his own manner in her dealings with him without the slightest reluctance or reserve.

They say that her actual beauty was by no means unparalleled or of the kind that was likely to astonish those who saw her, but that her presence was irresistible to those who knew her and that the attractiveness of her person, her seductive conversation and the natural grace that was evident in everything she said and did were magical. When she spoke it was a pleasure to hear the sound of her voice, which she used like an instrument of many strings, switching effortlessly to whatever language she wished to speak. There were very few foreign languages for which she needed an interpreter, for she was able to converse without assistance with Ethiopians, Troglodytes, Hebrews, Arabians, Syrians, Medes and Parthians. It is said that she also learned several other languages, whereas the Ptolemaic kings who preceded her had scarcely bothered to learn the Egyptian language, and some of them had even lost the ability to speak Macedonian.

Augustan Autocracy: Tacitus, *Annals* 1.2–4

Despite his claims about his accomplishments in the *Res Gestae* and popular support throughout the Empire for his regime, not all Romans approved of Augustus. One of his critics was the historian Tacitus. Writing in the early years of the second century, Tacitus viewed Augustus' assumption of power from the perspective of one who had seen the unhappy consequences of what he regarded as monarchical rule.

When after the deaths of Brutus and Cassius the Republic no longer had an army, when [Sextus] Pompey had been crushed in Sicily, when, after Lepidus had been eliminated and Antony was dead, when even the Julian party had only Caesar left to lead it—it was then that Augustus, giving up the title of triumvir and saying that he was really nothing more than a consul who was content to protect the people with the authority of a tribune, began working to win over the army with gifts, the people with cheap grain and the whole Empire with the blessings of peace. As a result, his power grew steadily and he gradually took into his own hands the functions of the Senate, the magistrates and even the law. No one opposed him. The most spirited men had either fallen in battle or been eliminated during the proscriptions. The rest of the nobles found that accepting slavery without resistance was the quickest route to wealth and political power. They had profited from the revolution, and so now they preferred the security of the new order to the dangerous uncertainties of the past. The new regime was also popular in the provinces where the rule of the Senate and the people had been discredited by the feuding and greed of the government officials. The legal system had offered the provincials very little protection since it had been totally crippled by violence, favoritism and, most of all, bribery.

In order to make his position more secure Augustus made Claudius Marcellus, his sister's son and a mere youth, a priest and an aedile. He honored Marcus Agrippa, a commoner but a fine soldier who had fought with him to many victories, with two successive consulships. When Marcellus died, Augustus chose Agrippa as his son-in-law. He gave imperial titles to his stepsons, Tiberius Nero and Claudius Drusus, even though his own family was still intact, for he had already admitted Agrippa's children, Gaius and Lucius, into the imperial household and, while they were still youths, he had been extremely anxious (though he said he wasn't) to see them become consuls-elect and Princes of the Youth. After Agrippa died either untimely fate or the treachery of their stepmother Livia cut off both of them, Lucius Caesar as he was on his way to our armies in Spain and Gaius Caesar as he was returning from Armenia, suffering from a wound. By that time Drusus had long been dead and so the only remaining stepson was [Tiberius] Nero. Everything centered on him. Augustus adopted him as his son, made him his colleague in ruling the empire, appointed him his partner in exercising his tribunician power and paraded him before the troops—not, as before, because of his mother's schemes and conniving, but at her open suggestion. In fact, she had now gained such control over the aging Augustus that he had sent his only grandson, Agrippa Postumus, into exile on the island of Planasia. It is true that the boy had no good qualities aside from the courage which accompanies brute strength, but he had not been guilty of any serious offense. Curiously, Augustus gave Drusus' son Germanicus the command of eight legions on the Rhine and made Tiberius adopt him, even though Tiberius already had an adult son in his house. He did this to further strengthen and safeguard his position. There was no war at this time apart from a campaign against the Germans which was being fought to make up for the defeat of Quintilius Varus and his army rather than to increase the size of the empire or to gain any other worthwhile benefit. In Rome itself everything was calm and the magistrates continued to use their traditional titles. A new generation had grown up since Actium; most of the older people had been born during the civil wars—how few were left who could remember the Republic!

It was a different world. Not a trace was left of the old Roman morality. The ideal of political equality had been abandoned and everyone watched and waited for the commands of the emperor without the slightest fear for the present so long as Augustus, while he was still vigorous, was able to maintain his own position, that of his house, and the peace.

The Achievements of Augustus:
Augustus, *Res Gestae* (Monumentum Ancyranum)

The original of Augustus' *Res Gestae,* a record of his achievements engraved on two bronze tablets and placed near his Mausoleum in Rome, has been lost. Fortunately, fragmentary copies of this important document have survived in various provincial capitals of the Empire. Of these, the most complete is the one found in 1555 at Ancyra (modern Ankara), which preserves the greater part of the text in the original Latin and includes a Greek translation. It is known as the *Monumentum Ancyranum.*

By my own effort and at my own expense I raised an army when I was nineteen and used it to restore to the Republic the freedom of which it had been deprived by an oppressive faction. To reward me, the Senate, during the consulship of Gaius Pansa and Aulus Hirtius, and by means of various honorific decrees, added me to the ranks of its members and granted me both consular rank in voting and the *imperium.* Further, it commanded me, in my capacity as propraetor, to cooperate with the consuls in preserving the integrity of the republic. In the same year, after both consuls had been killed, the people elected me consul and triumvir and made me responsible for reforming the government.

I brought my father's murderers to trial for their crime, forced them into exile, and then, when they led an armed revolt against the Republic, defeated them twice in battle.

I was required to fight civil and foreign wars all over the world, both on land and at sea. When victorious I spared the lives of those citizens who begged my forgiveness, and I sought to preserve rather than annihilate those foreign nations which could be pardoned without posing a threat to our security.

Five hundred thousand Roman citizens served me under military oath. I settled just over three hundred thousand of these in colonies or restored them to their original homes when they had completed their terms of service, and to all of them I gave land or monetary rewards.

I captured six hundred ships above the class of trireme, smaller vessels not being counted.

I celebrated ovations on two occasions, curule triumphs on three and was acclaimed *imperator* twenty-one times. The Senate voted me additional triumphs, but I declined them. I also deposited laurels in the Capitol after fulfilling the the vows I took during each war. On fifty-five occasions the Senate decreed the offering of thanksgiving to the immortal gods for successful land and sea ventures carried out by me or by legates acting under my authority. The number of days on which such thanksgiving was offered in compliance with the Senate's decree was eight hundred and ninety. Nine kings or sons of kings were led before my chariot in my triumphal processions.

At the time I wrote this document I had served as consul thirteen times and had held tribunician power for thirty-seven years.

I declined to accept the dictatorship which was offered to me in person and in absentia by the people and the Senate during the consulship of Lucius Arruntius.

At the time of a critical grain shortage I consented to serve as commissioner of the grain supply and in a matter of days freed the people from the fear and danger of starvation. On that occasion I was offered a perpetual consulship, but I refused.

During the consulships of Marcus Vinicius and Quintus Lucretius, then of Publius Lentulus and Anaeus Lentulus and again of Paullus Fabius Maximus and Quintus Tubero, when the people and the Senate proposed that I should be made sole overseer of laws and morals with supreme powers, I declined to accept any authority without precedent among the customs of our forefathers. However, I was able to carry out the wishes of the Senate by exercising my tribunician power, and on five occasions the Senate granted my request for a fellow tribune to serve with me.

For ten consecutive years I have served as a member of the triumvirate for the revision of the constitution. For forty years, up to this very moment, I have served as *princeps senatus* [ranking senator]. I have also served as *pontifex maximus, augur,* member of the college of the fifteen commissioners in charge of religious affairs, member of the seven in charge of religious feasts, member of the Arval Brotherhood, member of the *Titii sodales,* and as a fetial.

By order of the people and the Senate I augmented the number of the paricians and revised the membership of the Senate on three occasions. During my sixth term as consul, when Marcus Agrippa was my colleague, I conducted a census of the people. After an interval of forty-two years I performed the *lustrum,* in which 4,063,000 Roman citizens were recorded. In the consulship of Gaius Censorius and Gaius Asinius I ordered a second census on the authority of my consular power; in this census 4,223,000 Roman citizens were recorded. By virtue of my consular power I conducted a third census during the consulship of Sextus Pompeius and Sextus Appuleius when my son Tiberius was serving as my colleague; at that time the number of Roman citzens counted was

4,937,000. By means of legislation I restored many of the customs of our ancestors and by personal example I set precedents for future generations to follow.

The Senate decreed that vows for my health should be made by the consuls and priests every five years. Thus, during my lifetime the consuls and the priests of the four main priestly colleges frequently sponsored games and the people of the Empire, both individually and collectively, constantly offered sacrifices for the sake of my health.

The Senate decreed that my name should be included in the ritual of the Salii, passed a law which proclaimed my person sacred and gave me tribunician power for life. I was offered appointment as Pontifex Maximus but declined, for I did not wish to succeed my colleague Lepidus in that office while he was still alive. When Lepidus, who had taken advantage of civil unrest to win the sacred office, died in the consulship of P. Sulpicius and C. Valgius, I took the office after an unprecedented number of people came to Rome for my election.

On my return to Rome from Syria the Senate consecrated an altar to Fortuna Redux near the temple of Honor and Virtue in the district of the Porta Capena and ordered the Vestal Virgins to offer annual sacrifices on it in commemoration of the day of my homecoming, which occurred during the consulship of Q. Lucretius and M. Vinucius and is called the Augustalia. On the same occasion the Senate bestowed on me an unprecedented honor by sending to meet me in Campania representatives of the praetors, tribunes of the people, the consul Q. Lucretius and other distinguished citizens. When I returned to Rome after successful campaigns in Spain and Gaul during the consulship of Tiberius Nero and Publius Quintilius, the Senate decreed the consecration of another altar, this one to Pax Augusta on the Campus Martius, and ordered the officials and priests and the Vestal Virgins to perform annual sacrifices on it.

The temple of Ianus Quirinus, whose gates our ancestors wanted closed when peace was won by victory on land or sea in the empire of the Roman people and which, from the foundation of Rome until my own time are said to have been shut only twice, were closed by order of the Senate three times during my principate.

As an honor to me my sons Gaius and Lucius Caesar, whom fortune took from me in their youth, were designated consuls by the Senate and people of Rome in their fifteenth year with permission to occupy the office again after an interval of five years. Moreover, the Senate decreed that they should take part in public affairs from the day they were introduced in the forum. Furthermore, the whole class of Roman equestrians bestowed on each of them the title of *Princeps Iuventulis* and presented them with silver shields and spears . . . .

I eliminated piracy from the seas. In my war against the pirates thirty thousand slaves who had run away from their masters and fought against the Republic were captured and returned to their masters for punishment. All Italy spontaneously swore allegiance to me and proclaimed me leader in the war that led to my victory at Actium. The same kind of allegiance was given to me by the provinces of Gaul, Africa, Sicily and Sardinia. More than seven hundred senators, eighty-three of whom had served or were to serve as consuls, and one hundred and seventy members of the priestly colleges fought under my command.

I expanded the borders of all those provinces of the Roman people located next to tribes which had not submitted to our power. I pacified the provinces of Gaul, Spain and Germany, regions bounded by the ocean from Gades to the mouth of the Elbe. I managed to keep the peace in the Alps, an area extending from the Adriatic to the Tuscan sea, and I did so without having to make unprovoked attacks on any of that region's tribes. My fleet penetrated an area never before seen by Romans, either by land or by sea, by sailing from the mouth of the Rhine eastward to the territories of the Cimbri. The Cimbri, Charydes, Senones and other peoples of that region dispatched envoys requesting my friendship and the friendship of the Roman people.

Under my guidance and authority two Roman armies marched almost simultaneously into Ethiopia and the region of Arabia known as Felix, where they defeated great forces of both nations and captured a large number of towns. In Ethiopia our troops marched as far south as the city of Nabata in the vicinity of Meroe and in Araia they marched as far as Mariba in the region of the Sabaei.

I annexed the land of Egypt to the Roman Empire. After the assassination of its king Ataxes I had the opportunity to make Greater Armenia a Roman province, but in accordance with the practices of our forefathers I chose to deliver that kingdom to Tigranes, the son of King Artavasdes and grandson of King Tigranes, relying on my stepson Tiberius Nero to handle the matter. When that same Armenian nation later became restless and rebelled against us, my son Gaius conquered it and delivered it to the Median king Ariobarzanes, the son of Artabazus, and, after the death of this king, to his son Artavasdes. When the latter was assassinated I sent Tigranes, a member of the Armenian royal family, into that kingdom. On the far side of the Adriatic, in the direction of the East and Cyrene, I restored all the provinces which were by then under the rule of various kings and, before that, I restored Sicily and Sardinia, which had been taken over by an army of rebellious slaves.

I established colonies of soldiers in Africa, Sicily, Macedonia, the regions of Spain, Achaea, Asia, Syria, Narbonese Gaul and Pisidia. In addition to these I established twenty-eight colonies in Italy which have already become very populous and famous.

As a result of my victories in battle I was able to recover in Spain, Gaul and Dalmatia many military standards which had been lost by other leaders. I forced the Parthians to return to Rome the spoils and standards of three Roman armies and to humbly seek the friendship of the Roman people. I deposited recovered standards in the inner shrine of Mars Ultor.

I annexed to the Empire of the Roman people, once they had been defeated by Tiberius Nero who was at that time my stepson and legate, the tribe of the Pannonii, who had never encountered a Roman army before my principate. I pushed the borders of Illyricum to the banks of the Danube. When a Dacian army crossed over to the southern side of that river it was routed under my guidance, and after that victory my army crossed the Danube and compelled the Dacian tribes to obey the orders of the Roman people.

Indian kings who had never before had contact with any Roman general often sent embassies to me. Likewise, embassies seeking our friendship were sent by the Bastarnae, the Scythians and the kings of the Sarmatians who occupy both banks of the Don. The kings of the Albani, the Hiberi and the Medians also sent embassies.

Two Parthian kings, Tridates and Phrates, the son of King Phrates, sought refuge in my court, as did Artavasdes of Media, Artaxerxes of the Adiabeni . . . .

The king of the Parthians, Phrates, son of Orodes, sent all of his sons and grandsons to me in Italy, not as the consequence of defeat in battle but as a means of ensuring our friendship by entrusting them to me as pledges of his loyalty. During my principate many other nations which had no previous diplomatic or friendly relations with us also came to know the good will of the Roman people.

The peoples of Parthia and the leaders of Media requested through their ambassadors and accepted my appointment of kings for them: Vorones, son of King Phrates and grandson of King Orodes for the Parthians, and Ariobarzanes, son of King Artavasdes and grandson of King Ariobarzanes, for the Medians.

During my sixth and seventh consulships, after I had put an end to civil war and had acquired supreme power in the Republic by universal consent of the Roman people, I returned my state power to the Senate and the Roman people. In response to this gesture the Senate decreed for me the title of Augustus and declared that the door-posts of my house sould be publicly adorned with laurels. A civic crown was placed over my door and a golden shield was set up in the Curia Julia which, as its inscription proclaims, was given to me by the Senate and the people as a reward for my valor, clemency, justice and piety. As a consequence of these honors, I enjoyed supreme authority in the state, although my power did not exceed that of my colleagues in the several magistracies.

During my thirteenth consulship the Senate, the equestrians and the Roman people unanimously determined to bestow on me the title of *pater patriae* and decreed that it should be inscribed in the vestibule of my house, in the Julian senate house, in the Forum Augustulum and on the pedestal of the chariot which was placed there by order of the Senate as an honor to me.

I wrote this document in my seventy-sixth year.

The Deification of Augustus: Dio Cassius, *Roman History* 56

Within a matter of days after his death in 14 A.D. the Roman Senate met to formally declare the immortality and divinity of the emperor Augustus. The following excerpt from Dio Cassius' *Roman History* describes the eagerness with which the senators sought to pay him these extraordinary honors and the beginning of an era in which the political values of the Republic would give way before the increasing importance of the imperial personalities.

The Senate proclaimed that Augustus was one of the immortals, established a college of priests and holy rituals for him and made Livia, who had already been designated Julia and Augusta, his priestess. In addition, the senators decreeed that Livia should be accompanied by a lictor whenever she performed her priestly functions. She herself gave a million sesterces to a certain Numerius Atticus, a senator and former praetor who claimed that he had seen Augustus ascending into the heavens in precisely the same manner in which Proculus had once claimed to have seen Romulus. The Senate voted a shrine in his honor, and this was built by Livia and Tiberius. Other shines were built in many other places; in some cases communities built them voluntarily, but in others they had to be forced. In addition, the house at Nola where Augustus had died was made a precinct dedicated to his sacred honor. While his shrine was being built in Rome the Senate placed a golden image of him on a couch in the temple of Mars and paid to it all the honors they would later give to his statue. They also voted him other honors: his image was not to be carried in funeral processions, the consuls were to celebrate his birthday with games like those held in honor of Mars, and the tribunes, because they were sacrosanct, were to sponsor these Augustan Games.

Imperial Madness: Suetonius, *Gaius Caligula* 22, 24, 25.

It is well-known that the Julio-Claudian emperors of Rome tended toward behavioral and psychological extremes. The reasons for this may be disputed, but it cannot be denied that the excesses of these imperial personalities had a negative effect upon the Principate, making of it something much different from what Augustus must have envisioned. One of the worst offenders was Gaius (12-41 A.D.), more commonly known as Caligula after the small military boots he wore as a child. Most notable about his four-year reign (37-41) are his quarrels with the Senate, his inclination toward autocracy and the extravagant honors which he claimed for himself. The following passage from Suetonius illustrates as well as any other the instability of Rome's third emperor.

So much for Caligula the Emperor. We must now turn to Caligula the Monster. He took for himself various titles such as "Pious," "Child of the Camp," "Father of the Army," and "Greatest and Best of Caesars." Once, at the dinner table when some foreign kings who had come to pay homage to him were arguing about which of them had the noblest ancestry, he exploded, shouting a line from Homer: "No, let there be but one master and one king!" At that moment he came close to taking a crown for himself and doing away with the fiction that Rome was a republic. But when he had been reminded that he had already achieved a higher rank than any prince or king he decided instead to claim divine status. He ordered that all especially sacred or artistically acclaimed statues of the gods should be brought to Rome from Greece and that their heads should be removed and replaced with his own.

After this Caligula extended a part of the Palace out as far as the Forum and made the temple of Castor and Pollux its vestibule. He would often stand there, between the statues of the divine brothers, ready to be adored by those who came to worship. Some of them addressed him as "Latian Jupiter." He built a temple dedicated to his own divinity and filled it with priests and the most expensive sacrificial animals. It also contained a life-sized golden statue of the emperor which was dressed each day in clothes identical to those which the emperor was wearing. The richest citizens of Rome used all their influence to become priests there. The sacrificial victims were flamingoes, peacocks, black

63

grouse, guinea-hens and pheasants, each offered up only on a particular day of the month.

On nights when the moon was full and bright he would always call upon her to join him in bed, and during the daytime he would have secret conversations with the statue of Capitoline Jupiter, alternately whispering to him and putting his ear to the god's mouth. Sometimes he would raise his voice in anger, and on one occasion he was overheard saying to the god in a threatening voice: "If you will not raise me up into heaven I will throw you down into hell." Caligula later claimed that Jupiter had responded by begging him to share his residence, and so he joined the Capitoline and Palatine hills by building a bridge over the temple of the Divine Augustus. Later, in order to be nearer still, he laid the foundation of a new house in the precincts of the Capitol itself. . . .

He was in the habit of committing incest with his three sisters and at large banquets he placed them in a row beneath him while his wife reclined below. Some say that he raped his sister Drusilla when he was still a child and that their grandmother Antonia, who reared them, once caught them in bed together. Later, when Drusilla was married to Lucius Cassius Longinus, an ex-consul, Caligula took her from him and openly treated her as his lawful wife. When he became ill he made her his heir, leaving to her all his property and the throne as well. When she died he proclaimed a period of public mourning during which it was a capital offense to bathe or eat with one's parents, wife or children. He was so overcome with grief that he suddenly fled the city by night, rode through Campania, crossed to Syracuse, and then returned to Rome just as hurriedly as he had left and without stopping to cut his hair or shave his beard. After this, whenever he had to take an important oath, he would always swear it by the divinity of Drusilla, even when he was out among the people or at some military function. He did not have the same affection for his other two sisters, nor did he show them much respect. In fact, he often prostituted them to his favorites. This is why, at the trial of Aemilius Lepidus, he was so quick to condemn them as adulteresses and participants in the plots against him, producing letters in their handwriting (which he obtained by fraud and seduction) and dedicating to Mars the Avenger, with an explanatory note, the three swords with which they had hoped to kill him.

It is difficult to say which was the most disgraceful: how he arranged his marriages, how he ended them, or the kind of husband he was. At the wedding of Livia Orestilla and Gaius Piso he ordered the bride taken to his own home, and then in a few days divorced her. Two years later he banished her because he suspected that she had gone back to Piso. There are others who say that at the wedding banquet he told Piso, who was reclining across the table from him, "Don't touch my wife," and then carried her away, later issuing a statement that he had taken a wife in the manner of Romulus and Augustus. When someone said that the grandmother of Lollia Paulina had once been a beauty, he suddenly ordered her home from Greece where her husband, Gaius Memmius, was governor. He married her, but then quickly divorced her with orders never to have sexual intercourse again. Caesonia was neither young nor beautiful, had three daughters by another man, and was recklessly extravagant and promiscuous; yet he loved her with a burning passion, and faithfully as well. He used to show her off to his soldiers, having her ride beside him wearing a cloak and helmet and bearing a shield, and for his friends he would display her nude. He did not dignify her with the title of wife until she had borne him a child whose birth he announced at the same time as his marriage to its mother. He named the child Julia Drusilla and carried her about to all the temples of the goddesses until he at last set her in the lap of Minerva, making her responsible for supervising the child's upbringing. Nothing so convinced him that she was indeed his natural child as her vile temper: while still a baby she would try to scratch out the eyes of her little playmates.

Claudius is Proclaimed Emperor:
Suetonius, *Claudius* 10

The proclamation of Claudius as emperor by the Praetorian Guard in 41 A.D. is a significant event in Roman history for it represents the first of many transactions in which the imperial office was bought and sold by the Roman military. By becoming Rome's king-makers, the guardsmen initiated a dangerous practice that was often repeated in later years with tragic consequences for the empire.

After spending most of his life under these or similar circumstances, Claudius finally became emperor at the age of fifty as the result of a surprising turn of events. When Claudius, along with the other courtiers, had been ordered by the assassins to disperse on the pretext that Gaius wanted to be alone, he retired to a section of the palace known as Hermaeum; but soon afterward, when he heard about the murder of the emperor, he crept in terror to a nearby balcony and hid himself behind the door curtains. A guardsman who happened to wander in that direction saw his exposed feet and, wanting to identify the man in hiding, pulled him out and recognized him immediately. Frightened, he threw himself at his feet and saluted him as emperor. Then he took him to his fellow guardsmen, who were angry and did not know how to handle the situation. Nevertheless, they placed Claudius in a litter and, since all the palace slaves had fled, took their turns carrying him to their camp where he arrived in a state of terror and despair. Anyone who saw him lamented his sad condition as if he were an innocent victim being led to his death. After he entered the safety of the camp he spent the night among the guards. Although he felt that there was no immediate danger to his life he saw little chance of succeeding Gaius since the consuls, with the support of the Senate and the regular army, had occupied the Forum and the Capitol and were determined to restore the constitution. In fact, when a tribune of the people summoned Claudius to the Senate house to discuss the situation, he replied that he was in detention and unable to comply. The Senate was paralyzed by its slow procedures and unable to take action because of divisions among its members. Meanwhile, the people had surrounded the Senate building and were shouting their wish that Claudius should be their new emperor. Therefore, Claudius had the guards acclaim him emperor and swear allegiance to him, promising every man fifteen thousand sesterces as a reward. This act made Claudius the first of the Caesars to buy the loyalty of his troops with money.

Catastrophe in Fidenae: Tacitus, *Annals* 4.62–63

In 27 A.D. an enterprising freedman named Atilius staged a program of gladiatorial contests at Fidenae, a small town not far from Rome. Unfortunately, the promoter cared more for profit than public safety. The amphitheater he built for the occasion collapsed under the weight of the many spectators who attended the event and as a result fifty thousand people were killed or injured. Public catastrophes such as this were not uncommon in the cities of the Empire, for the government did little to establish and enforce building codes, provide for the prevention and extinguishing of fires, and the like.

During the year of the consulship of Marcus Licinius and Lucius Calpurnius there was an unexpected disaster which brought in an instant the destruction of a full-scale war. A certain ex-slave named Atilius began construction of an amphitheater at Fidenae in which he intended to stage a gladiatorial show. He failed to lay a solid foundation, however, and to strengthen the wooden superstructure with beams of sufficient strength, for he had very little money and even less concern for public safety. He was, in fact, interested only in sordid profit. Crowds of those who loved such events flocked to the site, for they had been denied them during the reign of Tiberius. Men and women of all ages came, for Fidenae is close to Rome, and their numbers made the catastrophe even worse. The structure was packed with spectators when, with a violent shaking, it collapsed both outwards and inwards, burying a huge crowd of spectators and bystanders. Those who were instantly crushed to death were the lucky ones, for they escaped the torture suffered by those whose mangled bodies remained alive and who in the following hours saw in the light of day their dying wives and children and heard by night their screams and groans. News of the disaster soon attracted crowds of agitated neighbors and grieving relatives, brothers and fathers. Even those whose friends and relatives were away from town for one reason or another were alarmed on their account, for as long as some of the bodies remained unidentified it seemed to them possible that their loved ones were among the dead.

As soon as they began to clear the wreckage away, the crowd rushed in to embrace and kiss the corpses. In some cases disfigured bodies were claimed by more than one party, and fights broke out over the rights to them. In all, fifty thousand people were maimed or killed in the disaster. The Senate decreed that in the future no one with a fortune of less than four hundred thousand sesterces should be allowed to put on a gladiatorial show and that no amphitheater should be built on ground whose stability has not been demonstrated. Atilius was banished. Immediately after the disaster the nobles opened their homes and made medicines and physicians available to everyone, regardless of social class. Thus, even in that dreadful moment Rome lived up to the standard of our ancestors, who after a great battle lavished their wealth and personal attention on the wounded.

The Education of the Young Orator:
Quintilian, *Institutes of Oratory* 1.1.12–20 and 1.2.1–8

Quintilian (*ca.* 35-100) was a native of Spain who received his education at Rome, where he became a distinguished rhetorician, scholar, teacher and lawyer. He was the first rhetorician to establish a public school in Rome and receive payment from the state. His only extant work is the *Institutes of Oratory*, a treatise in twelve books which addresses not only the training of an orator, but also such related topics as educational theory, literary criticism, and the technical aspects of style and rhetoric. Like Cicero, Quintilian believed that oratory, the presentation of ideas using dignified and polished speech, served a vital function in the state. He also maintained that an orator must be a "good man," that is, one whose good character prompts him to serve the state rather than his own interests. Quintilian's interest in the matter of character is particularly evident in the advice he gives on the education of the young.

I believe that a boy's education should begin with the study of Greek, since he will master Latin, our own language, whether we teach it to him or not, and because Latin derives from Greek. Yet I would not want this principle to be so strictly applied that a student should for a long time speak or learn only Greek, as is often the case. This practice creates many problems relating to pronunciation and idiom since foreign intonation creeps into Latin pronunciation and the Latin language is affected by the constant usage of Greek colloquialisms which stubbornly resurface even though the language being spoken is Latin. Thus, in my view Latin should be taught concurrently with Greek rather than after either a short or a long period of instruction in Greek alone, for when the same attention is given to both languages neither will be an obstacle in learning the other. . . .

Some have thought that the education of boys should not begin until they have reached the age of seven, since before then, they say, children are unable to understand what they are taught or to actually do the work of learning. Many writers say that Hesiod held to this view, at least writers who lived before

Aristophanes the grammarian, for he was the first to deny that Hesiod wrote the *Hypothecae,* in which this view is found. Other writers have given the same advice, and these include Eratosthenes. But I agree with those other authorities, such as Chrysippus, who say that no part of a child's life should be devoid of education. Chrysippus, for example, though he thinks that children should be entrusted to nurses for the first three years, nevertheless believes that they may be instructed to good effect even by them. Indeed, why should we think that young children, who are clearly affected by moral influences, are somehow unable to learn anything from the other influences to which they are subject? I recognize, of course, that in the whole span of his first seven years a child will not learn as much as he might in a single year after the age of seven, yet those who are of the view which I have described appear to have greater concern for teachers than for learners. What else, once they have learned to speak, will children do better than learn? Is it possible that they simply do nothing? Or why should we disparage what is learned, however little it may be, prior to the age of seven? The proficiency of a young child may be minimal, yet the child who is given an education will learn more during the year in which he would otherwise have learned less, and the gains made by this kind of advancement, if continued year after year, will accrue to the point of being a considerable benefit by the time the boy passes from infancy to youth. This principle should also be applied in later years so that a boy begins the study of every necessary subject as soon as he is able to gain the slightest advantage from his labor. Let us not waste, then, even the earliest years in the life of a child, so much the less because the dynamics of learning depend on memory, which not only exists in children but functions better in the first years of life than it does later on.

Now, I am not entirely unaware of the differences between children of various ages, and I do not mean to suggest that, in the case of the very young, we should push them hard or demand a great deal. Rather, it is extremely important to avoid these very things so that the child will not come to dislike a subject he is not yet old enough to love and carry this bitterness into later life. Let his instruction be pleasant for him. Ask him questions and give him praise. Never let him feel pleased with himself when he is ignorant of something he should know, and on those occasions when he seems unwilling to learn seek to arouse his envy by offering instruction to some other student. Encourage him to set goals and to enjoy the satisfaction of achieving them, and allow him to develop his powers by promising him the kinds of rewards which young children prize.

When a boy has grown up a bit it is time for him to leave the nursery behind and begin his formal education. Thus, it is appropriate for us at this point to consider whether it is preferable to educate the child privately at home or to entrust him to those I call public instructors at some large educational institution.

I am aware that public education has been endorsed by most experts on learning and by those leaders who have been most influential in shaping the character of the most important states. Nevertheless, it would be foolish to ignore the fact that there are others who say that a private education is better than a public one. These persons make two important points in support of their position. First, they argue that the close association of young people is something which should be avoided for the sake of their moral development, for they are in a formative stage when they are most likely to develop serious character flaws. I cannot deny the truth of this, for public education has often had disastrous results. Second, they assert that, no matter who a boy's teacher is, he will certainly give more of his time and energy to a pupil in a private class of one than he will to any student in a larger class. Their first point is worthy of serious consideration, for if it could be demonstrated that public schools are at the same time morally damaging and educationally superior I would place virtue above the acquisition of even the greatest skill in oratory. And yet I maintain that the two are inseparable, for I am convinced that no one can become a good orator who is not already a good man and, even if a bad man could become a good orator, I would not want him to.

While I agree with those who say that the schools sometimes corrupt the morals of students, it is also true that morals can be corrupted at home. And just as we have many examples of the corruption of morals both at school and at home, we also have numerous instances of the maintenance of good character in both of these environments. In fact, it is the character of the individual student and the level of his commitment to his education that really make the difference. If he has a natural inclination toward evil or negligence as he develops in his early years, private education will provide him with as many opportunities to sin as he will find in a public setting; his tutor may be of questionable character, and his contact with bad household slaves may be just as dangerous as his association with well-to-do companions in a school. But if he inclines naturally toward virtue and his parents truly care about his upbringing they should find for him a teacher of the highest moral character. In fact, wise parents will make the selection of such a teacher a matter of the highest priority. They will also insist on a rigorous course of study for their son and find for him some good friend or faithful freedman to serve as his companion and guardian. The constant companionship of such a person will have beneficial effects on the character even on the character of boys whose development has been fraught with difficulties.

How easy it is to address these concerns, and yet we are often guilty of ruining the character of our children. We spoil them from the day they are born. The soft way in which we rear them, which we confuse with kindness, destroys both their minds and their bodies. What luxury will not be coveted by a man who crawled on purple as a baby? Even before they learn to speak our children can identify scarlet and demand the finest quality purple. We educate their palates before we teach them to speak. They grow up being carried about in litters; if they touch the ground they hang from the hands of the attendants who support them on either side. We delight in hearing them use bad language and reward them with laughter and kisses when they utter expressions so profane that the most vulgar Alexandrian page would not let them pass his lips. We should not be surprised by their behavior, for we teach them to be this way. Our chidren hear us using ugly words and see us with our mistresses and favorites. Our dinner parties resound with dirty songs and our children's eyes behold things of which we should be ashamed even to speak. This is how habits are born, and habits become part of our nature. Our poor children are taught these things before they have the maturity to know that they are morally offensive. As a result, they become luxurious and effeminate and, instead of learning vice at school, they teach it there.

On Orators: Tacitus, *Dialogue on Oratory* 36

Few peoples have attached greater importance to rhetorical skill than the ancient Romans, who considered it absolutely essential to success in public life and the distinctive mark of the educated man. One of those who called attention to the signicance of oratory in public life was the historian Tacitus. In the following excerpt from his *Dialogue on Oratory* he describes the role of orators in the early history of Rome and laments the passing of that age in which the greatest power was concentrated in the hands of those who were the greatest speakers.

Great eloquence is like a flame: it must have fuel to burn and it grows fiercer and brighter when it is fanned.

This principle explains the development of oratory in Rome in ancient times, for although contemporary orators have won all the influence it is possible to win in a world that is stable, peaceful and prosperous, their predecessors had even greater opportunities to have an impact on society when, amidst the social unrest and confusion resulting from the absence of a strong ruler's guiding hand, a speaker's wisdom was measured by his ability to impart it to a bewildered populace. This explains the endless succession of laws proposed by the champions of the people, the speeches of officials who seemed to pass whole nights on the speaker's platform, the prosecutions of influential citizens accused of crimes, the consequent family feuds which lasted for generations, the factions among the aristocrats and the never-ending conflict between the Senate and the common people. All of this tore the state apart, but it also gave orators a chance to speak and to earn great rewards by speaking. In those days eloquence brought easier access to high office, more power than one's colleagues, greater influence with government leaders, more authority in the Senate and greater recognition and fame among the common people. The great orators of old were men who counted even foreign nations among their many clients and who were honored by provincial governors as they left Rome to take up their posts and courted by them on their return. They were men who seemed able to become praetors and consuls whenever they wished and held power even when they were out of office thanks to their ability to sway the Senate and the people by their counsel and authority. They were men who believed that without eloquence it was impossible either to win or keep a distinguished and important position within the state. And it is no wonder that they did, given the fact that they were often called upon to appear and speak before the people, though they did not always wish to do so, that they needed to support their proposals in the Senate with persuasive oral arguments, that if brought into disrepute by some charge they had to defend themselves, and that in criminal trials it was necessary for evidence to be presented verbally and in person rather than by affidavit. Thus, eloquence not only opened the way to great rewards but was also an absolute necessity. It was a great and glorious thing to have the reputation of being a good speaker, but to be silent and tongue-tied was a disgrace.

The Advantages of Roman Rule:
Tacitus, *Histories* 4.74

The Romans always represented themselves as peacemakers to the provincials whose lands were occupied by Roman armies. In the case of the Gauls, the Romans justified their presence by explaining that Gaul would he plagued by constant war among the Gallic and Germanic tribes were it not for the stabilizing influence of the legions. This was the view expressed by Petilius Cerialis, a Roman general who put down a revolt of the Gauls in 70 A.D. Cerialis also pointed to the other advantages of Roman rule in a speech which, although certainly reflecting the attitudes of Roman commanders, was probably invented by Tacitus. A portion of his address appears below.

"There were always kings and wars in Gaul until you submitted to our laws. And although you have frequently provoked us, we have never exercised any of our rights as victors other than to require you to pay the cost of preserving the peace; for peace among different peoples cannot be maintained without soldiers, soldiers cannot be maintained without pay, and their pay must come from taxes. But apart from this we make no real distinctions between ourselves and you. You even command our legions and govern this and other provinces. You are not excluded from any of the privileges that we enjoy. You live far from Rome, but you enjoy all the blessings of the rule of our good emperors just as much as we do; cruel emperors are a danger to those who are closest to them. You should learn to accept the extravagance and greed of bad rulers just as you accept famine, excessive rain and other natural calamities. As long as there are men there will be vices, but vices do not last forever, and in the end times of vice are balanced by periods of good government. Do you think that you will have a milder government if Tutor and Classicus [the leaders of the revolt] are in power? Do you think that they will be able to provide armies to keep out the Germans and Britons for less tribute than you are paying us? Do you think that anything but war among the nations could be the result if (may the gods forbid it!) you drive the Romans out? The structure of our Empire has been strengthened by eight hundred years of good fortune and discipline and it cannot be torn apart without bringing down those who would destroy it. You, especially, are in great danger, for you have gold and other forms of natural wealth, and these are the chief causes of war. Therefore, love peace, cherish it, and the city of Rome in which all of us, conquerors and conquered alike, have an equal share. Let the lessons of good fortune and bad teach you not to prefer defiance and destruction to obedience and security."

An Invitation to Dinner: Pliny the Younger, *Letters* 1.15

In the following letter the younger Pliny feigns anger at his friend Septicius Clarus, who had broken his promise to come to dinner at Pliny's house in order to feast elsewhere on more expensive and exotic fare. Teasingly threatening to charge his friend for the cost of the dinner he had prepared for him, the wealthy but slightly puritanical Pliny describes a rather plain menu of the sort one would find served in the average Roman home. It is interesting to note how much Pliny had looked forward to the conversation and exchange of ideas that always accompanied a good dinner.

Who do you think you are, accepting my invitation to dinner and then not showing up? All right, here's your fine: you'll have to pay for the entire cost of the dinner, and that's no small sum! Everything was ready—a head of lettuce for each of us, three snails, two eggs, cakes, honeyed wine with snow (you'll have to pay for the snow, too, since it melted right there in your dish), olives, beets, cucumbers, onions and a thousand other items no less delightful. You would have heard comic actors or a reader or a harpist or (such is my generosity) perhaps all three. But you wanted to go where they were having oysters, sow's womb, sea urchins and Spanish dancing girls. You'll pay for this, though I'm not sure how. It really was a cruel thing you did; to me, yes, and even to yourself. We could have had such a good time laughing and learning together. You can dine more sumptuously at other men's houses, but nowhere in such a free and easy way as at mine. Come on, have dinner with me just once. And then, if you still prefer dining elsewhere, you can give me excuses whenever I give you invitations.

Pliny the Matchmaker: Pliny the Younger, *Letters* 1.14

One of the traditional rights and responsibilities of Roman fathers was to arrange suitable marriages for their children. Because marriage was an institution used to maintain and even advance one's social, political and economic position in Rome, the selection of a spouse could not be made on the basis of sentiment alone. The following letter from Pliny to his friend Junius Mauricus gives us a good idea of the specific interests of a wealthy man who was seeking to arrange a marriage for his deceased brother's daughter.

You have asked me to be on the lookout for a husband for your brother's daughter. This is a responsibility for which I am well suited, for you know how much I loved and admired that most remarkable man, how he encouraged me in my youth and how he used to praise me in a way that made me seem worthy of the nice things he said. You could not give me a task which I would consider more important or welcome, nor could I take on a responsibility more honorable than that of choosing a young man worthy of being the father of Arulenus Rusticus' grandchildren.

It would have taken me a very long time to find such a man if Minicius Acilianus had not been available. It is as if fate has given him to us. He loves me in that friendly way that one young man loves another (he is a few years younger than I am), but he respects me as if I were his elder. In fact, he wants to be molded and educated by me just as I was by you and your brother.

Acilianus comes from Brixia, one of those towns in our part of Italy which still preserves and practices the modesty, frugality and all the other rustic virtues of former times. His father is Minicius Macrinus, who has remained a leading member of the equestrian order because he has no wish for a higher place in society. The deified Emperor Vespasian wanted to make him a praetor, but he was always quite firm in preferring a life of quiet dignity to the life we live (or, should I say, to a life of striving for political power?). His maternal grandmother, Serrana Procula, comes from the town of Patavium which, as you know, has a reputation for propriety; but Serrana is a model of propriety even for the Patavians. His uncle is Publius Acilius, a man who has few equals when it comes to dignity, wisdom and honesty. In fact, it would be impossible to discover a trait in his family which you would not be happy to find in your own.

Acilianus himself has a great deal of energy and self-discipline. He is also modest. He has already served with distinction in the offices of quaestor, tribune and practor, and so you would not need to assist him in his campaigns. He has a handsome face and his complexion is healthy and ruddy. Indeed, he has the overall attractiveness and grace of someone from the senatorial order. I mention these things only because I think a girl who has kept her virginity until her wedding day has a right to expect something in return.

Should I also mention that his father is quite wealthy? When I pause to consider the qualities which I suspect you are looking for in a son-in-law for your late brother I realize that the answer is "no." But then, when I think about modern morals and the laws which place great importance [as far as membership in the equestrian and senatorial orders is concerned] on a man's wealth, I must conclude that I should at least mention his wealth. And of course money is also an important consideration if we are arranging a marriage which may produce children.

You might think that my affection for Acilianus has led me to exaggerate his virtues, but I swear to you on my honor that my description of him doesn't do him justice. I certainly love the young man very much, just as he deserves, but I would not burden someone I love with excessive praise.

A Widower: Pliny the Younger, *Letters 8.5*

The following letter from Pliny to Geminus tells of the death of a mutual friend's wife. The couple's marriage had clearly been a good one, and Pliny seems to have believed that this may have been due in no small part to the respect the wife had for her husband. Nevertheless, she had other good qualities which demanded recognition and respect. Our literary and epigraphic sources provide us with many reports of genuine love and high regard shared by married couples in Rome.

Our friend Macrinus has suffered a terrible blow. He has lost his wife, a truly remarkable woman, one who would have been considered especially virtuous even in former times. They were married for thirty-nine years, and in all that time they never had a quarrel or exchanged harsh words. She treated him with great respect, and she deserved much respect herself, for she seemed to have taken all that was good from each stage of life and combined these qualities in her own character. At least Macrinus has the consolation of knowing that he was able to keep such a treasure for so long, although this also makes his loss even harder to bear, for the more we enjoy someone the more we miss her when she is gone. I will keep worrying about my dear friend until he is able to take his mind off her a bit and allow his wound to heal, and nothing will heal it but his acceptance of reality, the passing of time and plenty of tears.

Imperial Correspondence: Pliny the Younger, *Letters* 10

Pliny the Younger (*ca.* 61-114) was the nephew of the famous writer Pliny the Elder. Born into a wealthy family, Pliny received an excellent education and had begun an extremely successful career as a lawyer by the time he was eighteen. His career reached its zenith under the Emperor Trajan (98-117), who nominated him for a consulship in 100. He became augur in 103 and, about 111, governor of Bithynia in Asia Minor. During the course of his career Pliny wrote numerous letters which were collected in ten books. Book X, which contains Pliny's correspondence with Trajan, is a valuable source of information about the policies and procedures of Roman rule in the provinces.

33

Pliny to the Emperor Trajan

While I was off in another part of the province a great fire broke out in Nicomedia which destroyed many private homes and two public buildings (the Elders' Club and the Temple of Isis), although there is a road which separates them. From the very beginning it was fanned by strong winds, but it would not have spread so far had it not been for the indifference of the people who simply stood there, content to watch the disaster unfold. To make matters worse, there is not a single siphon, water bucket or any other piece of fire-fighting equipment in the entire city. I have ordered that these things should now be procured.

Will you, Sir, consider the possibility of forming a fire brigade of no more than 150 members? I will make sure that only true firefighters are admitted and that no one abuses the privileges of membership. It will not be difficult to monitor such a small group.

34

Trajan to Pliny

So, you have been thinking of creating a fire brigade at Nicomedia like those which can be found in other cities. We must remember, Pliny, that organizations like the one you are proposing have been responsible for political disturbances in your province, and especially in the cities. Citizen groups quickly turn into political organizations no matter what name they go by or for what purpose they were originally formed. It will be much better for us to supply the firefighting equipment directly to the owners of the burning properties and to instruct them in its use. If they require additional help they can ask for volunteers from the crowds which gather.

37

Pliny to the Emperor Trajan

Sir, the people of Nicomedia spent 3,318,000 sesterces on an aqueduct which was never completed and was eventually torn down. They then requested and received a grant of 200,000 sesterces for another one, but they abandoned it as well. Now, after having wasted such tremendous sums, they are going to have to spend even more money if they are to have a water supply.

I myself have inspected the spring which could, according to the original plan, fill an aqueduct that would supply the entire city with pure water. Only a few arches are still standing, but new ones could be built from the blocks of stone used in the first two projects. And I think that still others should be made of brick, which is easier to work with and cheaper.

At the moment, however, it is essential that you send us an architect or an engineer trained in aqueduct construction so that we do not fail a third time. Let me assure you that the finished aqueduct will be efficient, beautiful and a credit to your reign.

38

Trajan to Pliny

We must make sure that Nicomedia has an adequate water supply, and I am sure that you will set to work on this matter with all due diligence. But in the name of Jupiter make sure that you put just as much effort into finding out who should be held accountable for all the money that Nicomedia has wasted. It's possible that someone has made a killing by starting and then abandoning these aqueducts. Let me know the results of your investigation.

45

Pliny to the Emperor Trajan

Is there a grace period during which permits for the use of the Imperial Postal Service remain valid after their expiration dates? If so, how long is it? Please write to me and free me from doubt. I am anxious not to allow any illegal activity or, on the other hand, to hold up important correspondence.

46

Trajan to Pliny

Postal permits which have expired should not be used. That is why I make it a matter of policy to send out new permits to all the provinces before the old ones expire.

88

Pliny to the Emperor Trajan

I pray, Sir, that this birthday and many others still to come will bring you the greatest happiness and that you will enjoy health and strength as you enhance your already immortal fame and glorious reputation with ever new achievements.

89

Trajan to Pliny

Thank you, my dear Pliny, for your prayers that I will have many more birthdays made happy by the continued good fortune of our country.

Caracalla's Extortions: Dio Cassius, *Roman History* 78

The death of the Emperor Marcus Aurelius in 180 brought the end of the Pax Romana. His son and heir, Commodus, was a recklessly extravagant and unworthy successor, and by the reign of Septimius Severus (193-211) it was clear that no emperor could rule Rome without the support of the army. On his deathbed, in fact, Severus is said to have urged his sons to win the favor of the soldiers by enriching them and to despise all other men. The following excerpt from the *Roman History* of Dio Cassius describes the efforts of Marcus Aurelius Antoninus, better known as Caracalla, (211-217), to act on his father's advice. Besides granting citizenship to virtually all free men within the empire in order to increase tax revenues, Caracalla stripped the rich of their wealth. Dio Cassius, himself a senator, gives us a sense of the disgust and resentment with which those who were victimized by Caracalla viewed the emperor's policies.

Antoninus spent a great deal of money on the soldiers and was able to surround himself with a powerful military force by making all kinds of excuses and arguing that Rome's many wars made this necessary. At the same time, he went out of his way to rob and grind down everyone else, especially the senators. For example, he was always demanding gold crowns, claiming that he had defeated some enemy or other. Now, I am not saying that the actual making of the crowns was terribly expensive (after all, how much can a crown cost?); rather, I am pointing to the huge amounts of money which were constantly demanded of the cities for the so-called "coronations" of the emperor. Then there were the goods which we had to provide to him in great quantities and on all kinds of occasions without receiving any compensation and, sometimes, at great cost to ourselves. He would either give these to his soldiers or sell them off. He used to demand gifts from wealthy individuals and the cities and, in addition to these, there were the taxes, both the new ones which he levied and the ten percent tax which he established in place of the old five percent tax on manumitted slaves, bequests, and gifts in general, for he did away with the right of succession and the exemption from taxes which had previously been enjoyed by heirs who were closely related to the deceased.

When Antoninus made all people within his empire citizens of Rome he gave them, at least nominally, a great honor; but his real purpose was to increase tax revenues, for non-citizens were exempt from most taxes. Apart from the taxes and extortions which I have already mentioned, he used to make us build all sorts of expensive houses for him whenever he left Rome and luxurious roadhouses for him to use in the middle of even the very shortest journeys. He never used any of these, and he never even laid eyes on some of them. We also built theaters and hunting lodges and race tracks wherever he spent the winter or planned on spending it, and always without the smallest contribution from him. All of these were promptly destroyed, for it seems that the only reason he had for ordering us to build them was to strip us of our wealth.

The emperor spent money on his soldiers, as I have already said, and also on wild animals and horses, for he was always killing them in great numbers, both wild and domestic. He made us supply most of them, although he did buy a few himself. On one occasion he killed a hundred boars with his own hands. . . . During his reign he so viciously ravaged the fortunes of those he ruled that one day at the race track the Romans shouted in unison: "We'll strip the living to death, and then we'll bury the dead." In fact, he often used to say: "No one in the world should have money but me, for I want to give it to the soldiers." Once, when Julia reproved him for spending so much money on the soldiers and said, "we no longer have any source of revenue, neither just nor unjust," he showed her his sword and said, "Cheer up, mother, for as long as we have this we will never run out of money."

Maximinus Ravages Rome:
Herodian, *History* 7.3

The Emperor Maximinus (235-38), who had been made a centurion by his predecessor, Septimius Severus, was the first man to rise from the lowest ranks of the army to the imperial throne. Originally a Thracian peasant, he had no real education or administrative experience. In order to meet the immense expense of maintaining the military and running the state Maximinus robbed the urban middle class. The following account of his extortions is from the *History* of Herodian, a Syrian Greek who served as an official in the imperial bureaucracy.

These, then, were the military exploits of Maximinus. His achievements would have won him glory if he had not been so terrifyingly ruthless in his treatment of his associates and his subjects. What sense was there in his destruction of foreign barbarians when, at the same time, he was conducting an even greater slaughter back home in Rome and in the provinces? Why should we attach any value to the booty he captured from the enemy when be was also stripping his own people of every last bit of their property? During his reign informers were given complete freedom, and even encouragement, to harm people and stir up trouble by calling attention to crimes committed by a person's parents or grandparents which had happened to go unnoticed. Whenever a person was summoned to court on an informer's testimony he was immediately found guilty and all of his property was confiscated. The tyrant pretended that he needed a constant supply of money for his soldiers, but his greed was so great that it was very common to see a man who was wealthy one day reduced to poverty the next. His ears were always open to slanderous charges and neither the age nor the position of the accused mattered to him. There were many provincial governors and military commanders, men who held the honorable office of consul or had received military honors, whom he had arrested on trifling, petty charges. He would order these men to come to him alone and by chariot, from the East, the West, the South—wherever they happened to be—to Pannonia [in modern Hungary] where he was staying. Then, after subjecting them to insults and torture, he would punish them with exile or death.

As long as these actions affected only individuals and the tragedies suffered were confined to private households the people of the cities and the provinces were not alarmed by them. This was because the misfortunes of the wealthy are of no interest to the common people, although there are certain evil and mean-spirited people who envy the powerful and prosperous and gain pleasure from their unhappiness. But when Maximinus had impoverished most of the distinguished families of Rome he decided that what he had done was insignificant and not enough to satisfy his needs. And so he turned to the public monies which were to be used for the public food supply, distribution to the poor, theaters and festivals and expropriated them for his own use. Money offerings from the temples, statues of the gods, tokens of the honor of the heroes, decorations from public buildings, various ornaments from around the city, and anything that could be used for making coins—all these he melted down. But the thing that most upset the people was that, even though there was no fighting going on anywhere and no one was bearing arms, Rome was very much a city under siege. Some citizens set their hands to the work of opposing the emperor and established guards around the temples, ready to be cut down before the altars rather than allow their country to be devastated. In fact, from that time on a rage against Maximinus began to build among the people of the empire, and especially in the cities. Even the soldiers could no longer support him in his actions, for their families and friends reproached them, claiming that it was with their help that Maximinus was abusing them.

These are the reasons why the masses of the empire were filled with hatred for Maximinus and ready to revolt against him.

A Christian View of Diocletian and Maximian: Lactantius, *On the Deaths of the Persecutors* 7–8

Lactantius (*ca.* 250-317 A.D.), called by some "the Christian Cicero," was a native of Africa who converted to Christianity as an adult and served as a professor of rhetoric until Diocletian's persecution of Christianity ended his academic career. His famous work *On the Deaths of the Persecutors* was intended to illustrate the corruption of those who persecuted the Christians and the means by which God exacted his vengeance on them. In the excerpt below Lactantius attacks Diocletian, for whose reforms and administrative ability he had little regard, and Maximian, who ruled jointly with Diocletian within the tetrachy, first as Caesar and then as Augustus.

Diocletian, that inventor of crimes and mastermind of evil, although he destroyed everything else, could not resist laying his offensive hands even on God. He ruined the Empire both by avarice and cowardice, for he chose three other men to rule jointly with him and, in doing so, he divided it into four parts with the result that armies now increased in number and each of the four co-rulers strove to have far more soldiers under his command than earlier rulers had had in the days when emperors ruled singly. Before long there were many more individuals on the government payroll than there were taxpayers. Tax assessments grew to be so enormous that farmers abandoned their farms, which reverted to wilderness. And, in order that a mood of fear and insecurity should spread everywhere, the provinces of the Empire were subdivided into miniscule administrative units with numerous governors and countless other officers of inferior rank stationed in every region and in almost every city. Procurators of various ranks and deputies of prefects were everywhere. These officials rarely dealt with civil matters but were often involved in condemnations and proscriptions. Their exactions of countless taxes were perpetual, rather than merely frequent, and they caused unendurable sufferings.

It is likely that the hardships associated with the maintenance of the army might have been endured, but the insatiably greedy Diocletian would not allow these to diminish his treasury in the slightest. Thus, he was always collecting extra taxes and "gifts" in order to keep intact those funds which he had already accumulated. When his extortions had pushed prices to the ceiling he attempted to fix them at that level by decree. As a result, much blood was shed for the most trifling of things. People no longer dared to offer anything for sale, so that an even greater and more lamentable scarcity of goods ensued. Bare necessity finally forced the abrogation of the decree, but only after the masses had suffered terribly.

The emperor had an uncontrollable passion for building, and so the people of the provinces were required to pay additional taxes for the payment of the construction workers and artisans and the purchase of carts and all the other necessities associated with building projects. There were many of these: basilicas, circuses, mints, armories, a palace for his wife in one place and a palace for his daughter somewhere else. At one point Diocletian ordered a large section of his capital of Nicomedia to be razed and its population evacuated —men, women and children driven out of their homes as if the city had been captured by an enemy. When it had been rebuilt at the cost of the destruction of the provinces, he claimed that the work had not been done properly and ordered it done again according to a different plan. In accordance with his wishes the buildings were either torn down or remodeled, and without any guarantee that they would not have to be torn down yet again! It was by such foolish means that he continually struggled to make Nicomedia as magnificent as Rome.

I will not say much about the many people who died because of their possessions or fortunes since such deaths were so common in those days that their frequency made them appear almost normal. It was one of Diocletian's most outstanding characteristics that whenever he saw a very fine field or an unusually beautiful house he promptly made some false accusation against its owner, who would then be executed. It seemed that he could not steal without also shedding blood.

And what can we say of his co-emperor Maximian, who was called Herculius? He was much like him, for the two could not have remained such faithful friends had they not been alike in mind, will and judgment. They differed only in that, while Diocletian was more greedy than aggressive, Maximian was more aggressive than greedy—but aggressive in doing what is evil, and not what is good. He was the ruler of Italy, the very heart of the Empire, and Africa and Spain, its two richest provinces, and yet he was careless in protecting the wealth in the city of Rome itself. Whenever he required funds there were senators willing to provide witnesses who, by offering false testimony against their colleagues, caused their eyes to be torn out [and their property confiscated]. In this way the bloody treasury was filled with ill-gotten wealth.

Maximian had a great passion not only for young men, a hateful and despicable thing, but also for the daughters of Rome's leading families.

Wherever he went girls would be torn from the arms of their parents the moment he was taken by the whim to have them. He considered the happiness he found in his powerful office to be based on these things and was content as long as nothing was denied his passion and evil desire.

The Breakdown of the Empire:
Salvian, *On the Governance of God*, 5.4–7

The Christian priest Salvian of Marseilles (*ca.* 400-470) was an eyewitness to the chaotic conditions which accompanied the end of Roman rule in Gaul. In his *De Gubernatione Dei* he presented a vivid description of the breakdown of the Roman administrative system and expressed his disgust with a Roman government which had become so corrupt that life among the barbarians was preferable to living under its sway. In the selection below Salvian describes the plight of the Bagaudae, a group of peasants in northern Spain and Gaul who revolted against the Roman government in the late fourth and early fifth centuries.

For what cities are there, or even municipalities and villages, in which there are not as many tyrants as *curiales* [*i.e.*, members of the municipal councils]? Of course, it may be that they are not true tyrants but only brigands who take that title because they think it connotes power and honor. After all, most robbers are boastful and like to be considered more fierce than they really are. But in any case, as I said before, there is no place left where the lifeblood of widows and orphans is not drained by the men who control the cities. The holy men are victimized as well and ought to be considered with the widows and orphans since they are either unwilling to protect themselves out of devotion to their vows or are unable to save themselves because of their simplicity and humility. No widow, orphan or holy man is safe. Indeed, except for the robbers themselves, only the very powerful are safe from the plunder, destruction and brigandage which are spreading everywhere. The world has come to such an evil pass that only the wicked can be certain of their security. . . .

Meanwhile, the poor are being robbed, the widows groan, and the orphans are trampled underfoot—so much so that many of them, including those of good birth with a liberal education, have sought refuge with the barbarians in order to escape the sufferings and persecutions in the cities and towns. There, among the barbarians, they hope to regain their dignity as Romans, for they cannot bear the barbarous indignities they endure among the Romans. These Romans differ in customs and language from the barbarians to whom they flee and are also unused to the nauseating odor and filth of the latter's bodies and clothing, yet they prefer the strange life they live among them to the injustice that is rampant in their homeland.

That is why Romans everywhere are crossing into the lands of the Goths and the Bagaudae and other tribes and why they never regret their decision to do so. These days Roman citizenship, which was once so highly valued and dearly bought, is joyfully repudiated and shunned and is considered not only worthless but even abhorrent. And what greater proof can be offered of the wickedness of the Romans than that there are many upright and noble men whose status as citizens of Rome should have been a source of pride and honor who have been driven so far by the cruelty of Roman injustice that they no longer wish to be Romans?

I must now speak of the Bagaudae, who were robbed, oppressed and murdered by evil and bloodthirsty judges. They lost both the rights of Roman citizenship and the honor of the Roman name. Yet [despite their innocence] we Romans say that they brought their misfortunes on themselves. We give them a name that recalls their downfall. We call them rebels even though we ourselves forced them to rebel. We call them criminals even though we were the ones who forced them into crime.

For how else did they become Bagaudae except by our wickedness, the injustice of our magistrates and the proscription and pillage of those men who have used the assessments of public tax to their own benefit and made the tax levies a source of personal wealth? Instead of governing their subjects they devoured them like wild beasts. They not only fed on their possessions, as ordinary brigands would do, but on their blood and torn flesh as well.

And so it happened that men strangled and nearly killed by cruel extortions began to live as barbarians since they were not permitted to be Romans. They were satisfied to be what they were not, since they were not permitted to be what they were. They had no choice but to do whatever they could to save their lives, for they had already lost their liberty. . . .

And now, what is the only desire of those poor souls who are frequently, even constantly subjected to destruction by the public tax levies, who are menaced by the unceasing threat of proscription, who must abandon their homes in order to avoid being tortured in them, who must even go into exile to escape torture? . . . In the districts taken over by the barbarians the one desire of all the Romans is that they should never again find themselves under Roman rule. In such places it is the one and general prayer of the Roman people that they will be allowed to continue the lives they lead among the barbarians.

II
The Romans
at War

The Battle of Cannae: Livy, *History* 22.44–51

In 216 B.C. the Romans transferred the command of their army from Fabius Maximus to two inexperienced consuls, L. Aemilius Paullus and C. Terentius Varro, who led their troops against Hannibal at Cannae on the plain of Apulia. The result was a catastrophic defeat for the Romans, whose roughly 48,000 infantry and 6,000 cavalry were nearly annihilated by the Carthaginians. Hannibal's victory can be explained in part by his use of Greek military tactics which enabled him to surround and destroy the Romans with a numerically weaker force. The following account of the battle is from Livy's history of the early Republic.

The Roman consuls who were pursuing the Carthaginians did their best in reconnoitering the roads. After they arrived at Cannae, where they could clearly see the enemy positions, they proceeded to fortify two camps which they built at approximately the same difference from each other as those at Geronium, thus dividing their armies as they had before. The river Aufidus flowed between the two camps and was accessible at certain spots to water-carriers from each, though not without opposition; but it was the smaller camp on the south side of the river that had easier access to the water, since the enemy had not posted troops there to guard it.

It was Hannibal's hope that the Roman consuls could be enticed to fight on ground ideally suited to a cavalry engagement, since his cavalry was his invincible weapon. Thus, he arrayed his forces and dispatched his Numidian horse with orders to provoke the Romans by small, rapid attacks. This caused yet another eruption of strife and discord among the soldiers in camp and dissension between the consuls. Paullus threw the recklessness of Sempronius and Flaminius in Varro's face and Varro replied that Fabius was a perfect example of the kind of general who must hide his fear and lack of spirit. He called on gods and men to witness that it was not his fault that Hannibal had made his way into Italy, for his hands had been tied by the actions of his colleague and his eager soldiers had been denied the chance to fight. Paullus answered that if the legions were recklessly led into an ill-advised battle and defeated he would be entirely without blame for the loss though he would share in its consequences. He added that Varro would have to make certain that the

94

boldness of the Romans' tongues was matched by the boldness of their deeds in battle.

While the Romans were wasting time quarreling instead of making plans for the coming battle, Hannibal began pulling back the greater part of his forces from the positions they had held for most of the day and dispatched his Numidians across the river to attack the Romans who had come from the smaller camp to fetch water. No sooner had they appeared on the far bank than their shouts and screams sent the disorganized water-carriers running back to the camp in a panic, and they continued their attack until they came to the unit stationed in front of the rampart, thus nearly reaching the camp itself. The fact that one of their camps had been threatened by a small band of irregulars seemed so completely outrageous to the Romans that the soldiers in the main camp would have immediately crossed the river and attacked the enemy had it not been for the fact that Paullus was in command at that moment.

On the following day, however, it was Varro's turn to command and he acted as expected; he mobilized his troops, gave the order for battle without consulting his colleague and led his men across the river. Paullus was absolutely opposed to this plan of action but he had no choice other than to follow Varro and give him his support; remaining in the camp was not an option.

Once they had crossed the river the Romans joined with the troops in the smaller camp and formed their line of battle. On the right wing, close to the river, they placed the cavalry, and next to them the legions. On the outside of the left wing they placed the cavalry of the allies and, next to them, so that they were in contact with the legions, the allied footsoldiers. The front line was comprised of slingers and light-armed auxiliaries. The consuls were in comand of the wings, Varro of the left and Paullus of the right. Geminus Servilius was given command of the center.

At daybreak Hannibal crossed the river with the main body of his army after sending ahead of him the Baliares and the other light-armed troops. He then placed his units in the line of battle in the same order in which he had brought them over. He positioned the Gallic and Spanish cavalry on the left wing near the river, put the Numidian cavalry on the right and created a secure center by arranging his foot soldiers so that the Gauls and Spaniards were flanked on both sides by Africans. One might have mistaken the Africans for Roman soldiers, for they were armed mostly with the weapons the Carthaginians had won from the Romans as spoils of war, some at Trebia but the majority at Lake Trasimene. The Gauls and Spaniards had shields which were almost identical, but their swords were very different; those of the Gauls were very long and unpointed while the blades of the Spaniards, who preferred to pierce rather than strike, were short and had sharp points. These tribes were more frightening than the others because of their huge size and the ways in which they exhibited themselves; the Gauls fought naked from the navel up, while the Spaniards took their positions wearing purple-bordered linen tunics that shone with a dazzling whiteness. The Carthaginian line of battle was comprised of a total of forty thousand infantry and ten thousand cavalry. Hasdrubal commanded the left wing, Maharbal gave orders on the right, and Hannibal, assisted by his brother Mago, took charge of the center.

The battleline of the Romans faced south while that of the Carthaginians looked north. Both sides benefited from the fact that the rising sun shone obliquely on them, although we do not know whether they positioned themselves as they did by design or by chance. Unfortunately for the Romans, a wind called Volturnus by the local people began to blow clouds of dust into their faces which made it dificult for them to see.

When finally the war cry was raised the auxiliary forces rushed to attack and the battle began with an engagement of the light-armed troops. Then the Gallic and Spanish cavalry which formed the left wing of the Carthaginians joined battle with the right wing of the Romans. This cavalry engagement was a very unusual one. The two sides were forced to attack each other head-on, there being no room for flanking maneuvers since the river shut them in on one side and the concentration of foot soldiers limited their movement on the other. Both sides pushed straight ahead, and when their horses were so jammed together that they could no longer move their riders began grappling with their enemies and pulling them from their saddles. Before long most of them had been unhorsed and were fighting on foot in a fierce struggle which did not last long, for the Romans were soon defeated and abandoned the battlefield.

As this preliminary engagement was coming to an end the regular infantry went into action. At first the two sides seemed to be evenly matched in strength and spirit, but then the Romans, after trying many times to advance, finally began to push back the thin wedge-shaped formation projecting from the Carthaginian line with their own dense line. The Romans pressed their attack as the Gauls and Spaniards fell back in panic and confusion, and they continued to advance without opposition through crowds of fleeing soldiers until they reached the center of the Carthaginian line and, finally, the African auxiliaries. These had been used to hold the two wings, which had been drawn back, while the center, where the Gauls and Spaniards had been positioned, projected a bit from the rest of the line. When this wedge had been driven back far enough that it was even with the rest of the Carthaginian line, and as it yielded even further so as to form a kind of hollow, the Africans began a flanking movement on both sides. The Romans foolishly rushed in between them, and as they did the Africans extended their wings into crescent-shaped formations and surrounded their enemy.

From this moment on the Romans, whose success against the Gauls and Spaniards had gained them no advantage, were now forced to begin a new fight with the Africans. But in this they were handicapped by two factors. Not only were they surrounded by the enemy, but they were by now tired men who were pitted against soldiers who were fresh and vigorous.

By this time the Roman left wing, where the cavalry of the allies had been positioned across from the Numidian cavalry, had also become engaged in the fighting, though because of a Carthaginian stratagem the action there was slow in developing. About five hundred of the Numidians, pretending that they wanted to desert, rode over to the Roman lines with their shields slung behind their backs and carrying, along with their regular weapons, swords concealed under their tunics. They quickly dismounted and threw their shields and javelins to the ground and were then taken to a position behind the Roman line and told to remain there. They obeyed this order for the time being, but as soon as the Romans around them had turned their attention back to the battle they grabbed the shields which were lying about everywhere among the heaps of the dead and attacked the Romans from behind, striking their backs and cutting their hamstrings in a slaughter that was made particularly appalling by the panic and confusion it caused in the Roman lines.

It was as these developments were occurring—a rout on the Roman left wing and a noble but hopeless struggle at the center of the line—that Hasdrubal, who was in command in that part of the field, withdrew the Numidians from the center, where they were not fighting particularly well on foot and against men they met face to face, and sent them off in pursuit of the scattered fugitives. He also sent in the Gauls and Spaniards to assist the Africans, who were by now worn out by work more aptly called slaughtering than fighting.

Elsewhere in the field, Paullus had been critically wounded at the beginning of the battle by a stone thrown by the enemy's slingers. In spite of his condition he made repeated attacks on the center of Hannibal's line, always keeping his men in close formation and in a few instances actually succeeding in making things work for the Romans. He was guarded by a force of cavalry, but his condition eventually worsened to the point where he was unable to control his horse and, as a result, he and the men guarding him were forced to dismount. When word of this development reached Hannibal the Carthaginian commander realized that the Romans were finished and remarked that Paullus might as well have handed his men over to him in chains. The dismounted horsemen continued to fight although they knew they would be beaten. They chose to die where they stood rather than to run away, and the triumphant Carthaginians, angered by their continued resistance, cut them down without mercy since they could not push them back. But in the end the Romans were routed. Only a few escaped by turning their backs and running, although they were exhausted and wounded.

Thus, the entire army of the Romans was now broken and in disarray. Some of the fleeing soldiers who had the strength managed to find and mount horses in the hope of escaping. One of these was the military tribune Gnaeus

Lentulus. As he was riding by he caught sight of Paullus sitting on a stone and bleeding from his wounds. "Lucius Aemilius," he cried, "heaven knows that you alone among the Romans are not to blame for what has happened here today. Please, while you still have some strength left, take my horse and save yourself. I will help you mount him and offer you protection. The battle has been a catastrophe. Don't make it even worse by adding to it the death of a consul." "May the gods bless you for your courage," replied Paullus, "but there is still a little time for you to escape. Get going, and tell the Senate to turn its attention to Rome and to fortify its defenses before the victorious Carthaginians arrive. Also, give a personal message to Quintus Fabius. Tell him I never forgot his advice while I lived and that even in the hour of my death I still remember it. As for me, I would rather die here in this field surrounded by the bodies of my men. I would not want to stand trial a second time after my consulship expires, nor would I wish to testify against my consular colleague, thus defending myself by putting the blame on another man." While the two men were conversing a group of fleeing soldiers ran by with some Numidians in close pursuit. In the confusion Paullus was killed under a volley of spears. Lentulus managed to escape on his horse.

By this time the battle was complete. Seven thousand Romans managed to make their way back to the smaller camp and ten thousand to the larger one. Another two thousand took refuge in the village of Cannae itself, but since it had no defenses they were quickly surrounded by the Carthaginian cavalry under Carthalo. Varro was able to reach Venusia with fifty horsemen by staying away from the fleeing soldiers, either by chance or by design.

It has been said that as many as 45,500 foot soldiers and 2,700 horsemen lost their lives at Cannae, roughly half of them citizens and half allies. Among the dead were the quaestors of the two consuls, Lucius Atilius and Lucius Furius Bibaculus, twenty-nine military tribunes and numerous ex-consuls and men who had been praetors or aediles. Gnaeus Servilius Geminus was killed, as was Marcus Minucius, who had been master of the horse the previous year and consul several years before that. Also among the dead were eighty senators or men who had held offices which would have made them eligible for election to the Senate; these had served in the legions as volunteers. They say that three thousand foot soldiers and 2,700 cavalry were taken prisoner.

This, then, is the story of Cannae, a military disaster as notable as the defeat [of the Romans by the Gauls in 390 B.C.] on the Allia. In fact, the losses sustained at Cannae were greater, though the consequences were not as serious since Hannibal failed to follow up on his victory. The disaster at Allia resulted in the loss of Rome but not that of the army. At Cannae, however, the consul who escaped managed to get away with a mere fifty men, leaving virtually all the rest to share the fate of Paullus.

In the two Roman camps the soldiers were without leaders and had only a few weapons. The men in the large camp sent a messenger to ask those in the small one to come over and join them during the night, when the Carthaginians would be fast asleep after a hard day's fighting and feasting afterward. Then, the messenger suggested, they could proceed together to Canusium. But this proposal was not very well received by some in the small camp who asked why their compatriots weren't willing to accomplish their purpose by simply coming over to them. They were aware that the field between the two camps was full of Carthaginians and that the men who had sent the messenger preferred to risk the lives of others rather than their own. Others in the small camp approved of the plan but lacked the resolve to carry it out. At last the military tribune Publius Sempronius Tuditanus roused them to action. He shouted, "Do you really intend to allow yourselves to be taken prisoner by a brutal and greedy enemy? Do you really want to give the Carthaginians the opportunity to humiliate you and exalt themselves by allowing them to set your ransom after making you tell them whether you are a citizen of Rome or a Latin ally? You will not—not if you are fellow citizens of Lucius Aemilius the consul, who chose to die nobly rather than to live in dishonor, and of the heroes whose bodies lie in heaps around him. Let us leave quickly, before the night is over and more enemy soliders come to block our escape. We'll fight our way through the undisciplined crowd of men now shouting at our gates. With a bit of courage and a good sword a man can cut through any line, no matter how dense. Why, we'll be able to pass through the rabble outside as easily as if there were no one there to oppose us. So come on, all of you who want to save yourselves and your country as well, and follow me!"

Having said this, he drew his sword and led his fellow soldiers, in wedge formation, straight into the midst of the enemy. The Numidians threw their javelins at them on their right side, where they were vulnerable, but by shifting their shields to the right six hundred of them were able to make their way to the large camp. Then, without delay, the combined forces set out for Canusium and arrived there safely. This operation was by no means planned; it was the product of the courage, impulses and luck of the men involved rather than the result of strategic planning.

The triumphant Hannibal, in the meantime, was surrounded by his officers, who offered him their congratulations on the victory and urged him to allow himself and his exhausted soldiers to rest until the next morning. But Maharbal, the commander of the cavalry, argued that they should not waste time in inaction. "My general," he said, "so that you will realize the true significance of today's victory, let me inform you that in five days you will dine in triumph in the Capitol! I will lead the way with my cavalry. The Romans will not notice us until we are at their gates. All you need to do is follow us."

As attractive as this idea seemed to Hannibal, it was also too fantastic for him to believe at that moment. Thus, while praising Maharbal for his enthusiasm, he also told him he needed time to consider his plan. Maharbal replied, "Truly, the gods do not shower all their gifts on any one man! Hannibal, you know how to win a battle but you do not know how to exploit your victory." It is generally acknowledged that Hannibal's decision to delay saved the city of Rome and the empire.

At daybreak the following morning the Carthaginians went out to collect the spoils of the battle and examine the carnage, a horrible spectacle, as it turned out, even for them to see. The bodies of thousands of Roman soldiers lay scattered all over the battlefield. Foot soldiers were mingled with cavalry, for they had been brought together in the changing phases of the battle and as they sought to escape. Here and there among the dead a wounded and bloody man brought back to consciousness by the cold of morning would try to stagger up over his comrades only to be killed quickly by a blow from the enemy. Others were found still alive who had had their hamstrings and thighs cut from behind as they fled. They now bared their throats, begging the victors to spill what little blood was left in their veins. Still others had dug holes and buried their heads in them, hoping to die by suffocation. But the strangest of all these sights was that of a Numidian soldier who was pulled alive from beneath the body of a Roman, though with his nose and ears mutilated. The Roman, when he was no longer able to use his sword, had died in a frenzied rage, tearing his enemy to pieces with his teeth.

Discipline in the Roman Army:
Polybius, *Universal History* 6.37–38

Writing in the second century B.C., decades before the professionalization of the Roman army by Gaius Marius, Polybius described the means by which the commanders of its citizen army kept order and encouraged heroism among the troops. Readers will recognize in the excerpt below the origin of the term "decimation," this being one of the techniques used by the Romans to enforce discipline.

A court-martial composed of all the tribunes immediately meets to try [the soldier accused of not keeping watch correctly], and if they find him guilty he is beaten to death. The execution takes place as follows. The tribune lightly taps the condemned man with a cudgel, whereupon the rest of the soldiers fall upon him, striking him with clubs and stones. In most cases he dies there within the camp, but even those who manage to escape are not saved by doing so. How could they be? They are not allowed to return to their homes, and no member of such a man's family would dare to let him back into the house. Thus, the lives of those who fall into this misfortune are completely ruined. The *optio* [lieutenant] and *decurio* [sergeant] of the squadron are punished in the same way if they fail to give the right orders at the right time to the patrols and *decurio* of the squadron scheduled to take the next watch. Because of the extreme severity and the inevitability of this punishment soldiers of the Roman army keep their night watches very carefully.

The soldiers take orders from the tribunes and the tribunes from the consuls. A tribune (or, in the case of the allies, a prefect) has the authority to impose fines, accept sureties and order a flogging. The punishment of death by beating is inflicted on anyone who steals something from the camp, gives false testimony, sexually defiles his body, or has already been punished three times for the same offense. The following are considered unmanly and disgraceful in a soldier: lying to the tribune about one's bravery on the battlefield in order to gain distinction, abandoning one's post in a covering force because of fear, and throwing down any of one's weapons on the battlefield because of fear. For this reason men who are assigned to a covering force often face certain death; because of their fear of punishment they will remain at their posts even though they are vastly outnumbered. Similarly, soldiers who have lost a shield or sword or some other weapon will often cast themselves into the midst of the enemy hoping that they will either find what they lost or escape, by dying, the disgrace and insults from their own families which would otherwise await them.

If the same thing happens to a large force of soldiers and entire maniples [units of up to 300 men] flee from their posts under pressure from the enemy, the officers choose not to beat to death all those who are guilty but use instead a method of punishment which is both effective and terrifying. The tribune calls the legion together and brings the guilty soldiers up to the front. He gives them a severe reprimand and then chooses by lot some five or eight or twenty of the offenders, selecting about a tenth of the men who had shown themselves guilty of cowardice. Those on whom the lot falls are beaten mercilessly in the manner I have already described. The rest are put on rations of barley instead of wheat and are ordered to stay outside the camp in some place which has no defenses. Since the danger and fear of drawing one of the fatal lots is the same for all of the men (since there is no way to determine on whom it may fall), and since the public humiliation of being put on barley rations is shared by all alike, the Romans have devised the best possible means both for inspiring fear and eliminating cowardice.

They also have an excellent method of encouraging the young soldiers to face danger. After a battle during which some of them have shown unusual courage, the general assembles the troops and calls to the front the men he thinks demonstrated exceptional bravery. First he praises each of them individually, describing each man's gallantry in battle and anything else he considers worthy of mention. After this he distributes rewards. A man who has wounded an enemy receives a spear. A man who has killed and stripped an enemy receives a cup if he is in the infantry and horse-trappings if he is in the cavalry (although originally the reward was just a spear). These gifts are not given to men who have wounded or stripped an enemy in the normal course of a battle or during the storming of a city but to soldiers who voluntarily and deliberately put themselves in danger during a skirmish or some similar situation in which it was not necessary to engage in single combat. The first man to climb over the wall in the assault on a city is rewarded with a crown of gold. Similarly, those who have protected or saved one of Rome's citizens or allies are honored with gifts from the consul, and the men they saved give golden crowns to their rescuers of their own free will (or, if they do not, they are forced to give them by order of the tribunes who judge the case). In addition, a man who has been saved in this way reverences his savior for the rest of his life and must treat him as if he were his father.

By making use of incentives such as these the Romans not only inspire the men who actually see and hear the rewards ceremony to emulate their brave comrades, but also those who remain at home. This is because the men who receive awards, in addition to enjoying great fame in the army and at home, are also honored in religious processions when they return from the wars, for during these no one is allowed to wear decorations except those who have received honors for bravery from the consuls. Further, it is customary for them to hang up their trophies in the most conspicuous places in their houses where they are looked upon as tokens and proofs of their valor. In view of the fact that so much importance is given to the matter of punishments and rewards in the military it is no wonder that the Romans bring every war they enter to a brilliant and successful conclusion.

The Struggle for Syracuse:
Plutarch, *Marcellus* 14–19

The Greek city of Syracuse, founded by Corinthian colonists in the eighth century B.C., became one of the leading military powers of the western Mediterranean after its victory over Carthage at Himera in 480 BC. and, later, one of the region's most important cultural centers. By the third century, however, Syracuse had lost much of its influence and was no match for the Romans, who conquered it in 211 B.C. The heroic defense of the city was organized by the brilliant Greek scientist Archimedes, whose efforts to save it were described by Plutarch in his biography of the Roman general Marcellus.

Then Marcellus left with his entire army and marched against Syracuse. He encamped near the city and sent ambassadors to explain to the Syracusans what had happened at Leontini. But this action did not bring any results; the Syracusans were not persuaded since the partisans of Hippocrates were now in control of the affairs of the city. Then Marcellus attacked Syracuse by land and sea simultaneously with Appius in command of the land forces while he himself approached with sixty quinqueremes full of all kinds of arms and missiles. He constructed an engine on a great platform made of eight vessels chained together and advanced toward the rampart, counting on the great quantity and excellence of his preparations and on his own personal glory. But all this posed no threat to Archimedes and his machines. This great man did not view his inventions as serious work; most of them were for him nothing more than mere games of geometry. He had constructed them before the war in compliance with King Hiero's desire and appeal that he turn from the theoretical to the concrete and somehow mix his abstract knowledge with something tangible, thus rendering his theories, through practical applications, more comprehensible to the masses of the people.

   The first pioneers of this highly-prized and renowned science of mechanics were Eudoxus and Archytas, who cleverly employed it to illustrate geometric principles and to solve by means of practical experiments and actual instruments problems which were not easily understood by logical and geometric demonstrations. Such was the problem, for example, of finding the two mean lines of proportion frequently required in constructing geometric figures. . . . Plato, however, was indignant at this practice and severely reproached them for corrupting and destroying the good of geometry by abandoning abstract and intellectual notions and becoming involved with material bodies, which demand much degrading manual labor. So, its reputation fallen, mechanics became separated from geometry and, scorned for a long time by philosophy, it became one of the military arts. However, Archimedes wrote to King Hiero, his friend and relative, that with a given force it is possible to move any given weight. And it is said that, relying on the strength of his demonstration, he even boasted that if he had another earth to stand upon he could move this one. Hiero, in amazement, begged him to put his theory into practice and to show him some great mass moved by a small force. Archimedes took a three-masted ship from the royal navy which had just been drawn out of the docks with great effort and the labor of many men and, placing in this vessel many passengers and the usual cargo, he sat some distance away and without any great effort, but by calmly pulling with his hand the end of the pulley, dragged the ship toward him smoothly and evenly, as if it were sailing in the sea. The king marveled at this demonstration and, having grasped the power of the art, convinced Archimedes to construct for him machines for all kinds of siege operations, offensive and defensive. The king never used these machines, however, since he spent most of his life in peaceful and literary pursuits, but now they were ready to be used by the Syracusans, their inventor himself being there along with them. As the Romans attacked the city on two sides at once, the Syracusans were at first struck with fear, thinking that they could not possibly resist such violence and force. But when Archimedes fired his engines he hurled on the land forces of the Romans all kinds of missiles and stones of huge size which landed with an unbelievable noise and violence that no man could withstand; for they crushed those upon whom they fell in heaps and threw their ranks into confusion. Some of the ships were suddenly seized by poles thrust from the walls and plunged to the bottom of the sea by the great weights which the Syracusans dropped on them from above; other ships they caught by iron hands or beaks resembling those of cranes and, lifting them up into the air by their bows, the Syracusans set them upright on their sterns and plunged them into the water; or, by using engines worked inside the city, they drew some ships out of the water, whirled them about, and dashed them against the cliffs and steep rocks found under the walls, inflicting heavy casualties on their crews. Frequently a ship would be lifted out of the sea into the air and—a horrible sight to behold as it swayed back and forth until the crew were thrown out or overcome with slingshots—it would crash, empty of men, into the walls, or would fall into the sea when the beaks were released.

The engine that Marcellus was bringing up on the platform, which was called a *sambuca* [harp] because it bore some resemblance to that musical instrument, was hit while still at some distance from the walls by a stone weighing ten talents [about 830 pounds] and then by a second and a third which fell with such great noise and force that the platform on which it stood was damaged, the result being that its fastenings loosened and it was completely dislodged from its base. Marcellus, not knowing what to do, promptly withdrew his fleet and ordered his land forces to retreat.

Then, in a war council, the Romans decided to assault the city walls again, this time by night, if possible; for the stretched cords which Archimedes used to fire his missiles, they thought, required long distances to be effective and would be entirely useless if fired at short range since the missiles would fly over the heads of the soldiers without causing them any harm. But Archimedes, in anticipation of just such an eventuality, had long before prepared engines effective at any distance, short or long, and shorter missiles; and from a series of small openings pierced through the wall, which were numerous and well-spaced, short-range engines invisible to the enemy and known as "scorpions" were waiting to be fired. As the Romans attacked, thinking that they would not be detected, they found themselves instantly exposed to a shower of darts and other missiles, and when stones fell upon them from above and they were shot with arrows from all parts of the wall they retreated. But then, as they were going away, missiles of a longer range were fired on them in their retreat, causing many casualties among the men and the collision of many ships; the Romans were unable to retaliate in any way against the enemy. Since most of the engines under the wall had been constructed by Archimedes, and since thousands of darts were falling on them from invisible hands, they thought they were fighting against the gods! Marcellus escaped the danger unscathed, however and, deriding his own technicians and engineers, he asked them, "Are we to quit fighting this geometrical Briareus who, to our shame, is playing games with our ships, using them as goblets to draw water out of the sea, and who is surpassing the legendary hundred-handed giants in hurling against us so many darts at once?" And, in fact, all the other Syracusans constituted the body of the organism created by Archimedes; he was the soul and mind that moved and directed everything. For all other arms were laid aside and the city used only his weapons for its defense and security. Finally, realizing that the Romans had become so afraid that if they merely saw a rope or a little beam over the wall they would turn and run away shouting that Archimedes was bringing some engine to fire at them, Marcellus abstained from all combat and assault operations, counting on a long siege to reduce the city. Archimedes possessed so elevated and profound a mind and had acquired such a wealth of scientific knowledge that although these inventions gave him a reputation of an intelligence not human, but divine, he did not want to leave behind him any writings on these matters. He considered mechanics and, in general, all the arts that touched on the needs of everyday life, as base and ignoble, and devoted his zeal only to those pure speculations whose beauty and excellence are not affected by material needs—speculations which cannot be compared to any others, and in which the proof rivals the subject, the one providing grandeur and beauty, the other accuracy and a supernatural power. For it is not possible to find in all of geometry more difficult and abstract propositions explained on simpler and clearer principles than in his work. Some attribute this to his natural genius, others to his excessive industry thanks to which each of his works seems to have been accomplished easily and without labor. For no one could discover through his own efforts the solutions to his problems, though as one studies them he is made to think that he himself would have found them, so smoothly and rapidly he leads one along the path of proof. Thus, one cannot doubt what has been said about Archimedes, that he was always bewitched by some familiar and domestic siren so that he would forget to eat his food and neglect the care of his person, that when forcibly dragged to be bathed and to have his body anointed and perfumed he would draw geometrical figures in the ashes of the fire, and that when his body was oiled he would trace diagrams on it with his finger, for he was prey to an extreme passion and was truly possessed by the Muses. He was the discoverer of many admirable things, and it is said that he had begged his friends and relatives to place on his tomb, after his death, a sphere enclosing a cylinder, and to indicate on it the proportion of the volumes of the containing solid to the contained.

Caesar Invades Britain: Caesar, *Gallic War* 4.20–38

Julius Caesar made two unsuccessful attempts (55-54 B.C.) to gain a foothold in Britain, which was eventually occupied by the Romans in 43 A.D. during the reign of Claudius. The following excerpt is from Caesar's own account of his first campaign in Britain in his *Gallic War*.

The summer was almost over, and winter arives early in Gaul because it lies so far to the north. Nevertheless, Caesar was determined to go to Britain, for he recalled that in nearly all of his Gallic campaigns the Gauls had received assistance from the peoples there. He thought that even though the remaining season was too short for a large-scale military action it would still be worthwhile to visit the island, observe its peoples and learn something about the landscape and its harbors and landing-places. The Gauls have no knowledge of any of these things since it is only their traders who have occasion to visit Britain and these are familiar only with the coast which faces Gaul. This explains why Caesar, although he spoke with traders from many parts of Gaul, could not learn anything from them about the size of the island, the strength of its native peoples, their customs in war or harbors which might accommodate a large force.

Anxious to have such information in hand before undertaking an expedition, Caesar sent a galley under the command of Gaius Volusenus, whom he considered the right man for the job, to explore the island and report to him as soon as possible. Meanwhile, Caesar himself marched with his entire army to the country of the Morini, from which one can make the shortest crossing to Britain, and ordered ships to gather there from all the neighboring regions. To these he added the fleet which he had built the summer before for the Venetian campaign. But his plans were leaked, and when traders reported them to the Britons several tribes of the island dispatched envoys to Caesar with promises of hostages and orders to tell him they would submit to Rome. Caesar granted them an audience, offered them a generous arrangement and advised them to keep their word. Then he sent them back to their island along with Commius, whom he had placed on the throne of the Atrebates after subduing them. Caesar was impressed by the courage, resourcefulness and loyalty of this man who was also highly regarded by the Britons. He instructed him to visit as many tribes as possible in order to persuade them to accept the protection of Rome and to announce to them his imminent arrival. Meanwhile, Volusenus surveyed the country as best he could without putting his life in danger by actually disembarking and thereby making himself vulnerable to attack. After four days he returned to report his findings to Caesar.

While Caesar was assembling his fleet in the country of the Morini, ambassadors representing a large part of that tribe came to him asking forgiveness for making war on Rome and blaming their previous behavior on their barbarism and ignorance of Roman ways. They promised that henceforth they would obey his commands. Caesar considered this a very fortunate offer, for he did not want to leave an enemy in his rear and there was little time left in the season to undertake another campaign; besides, the expedition to Britain was much more important to him than the subjugation of small Gallic tribes. Thus, he asked for large number of hostages and when he had received them he took the tribe under his protection.

Eventually, about eighty transports were found and assembled. These, he thought, were enough to move two legions. He combined them with the warships and assigned command of the vessels to his quaestor, his lieutenant-generals and the auxiliary officers. Another eighteen transports were about eight miles up the coast where they had been prevented by contrary winds from joining the assembled fleet; these Caesar assigned to the cavalry. The rest of his army he placed under the command of the lieutenant-generals Sabinus and Cotta with instructions to proceed against the Menapii and the regions of the Morini which had not sent ambassadors to him. He also ordered Publius Sulpicius Rufus, another lieutenant-general, to guard the harbor and gave him a force sufficient for its defense.

When these arrangements had been made, Caesar took advantage of favorable weather and set sail one night at about midnight. The cavalry was to ride to the farther harbor, embark there and follow him. They were quite slow in this, however, and so Caesar arrived in Britain at about nine in the morning with only the first group of ships. From his position offshore he could see the enemy spread out atop cliffs steep enough to allow them to hurl missiles straight down onto the narrow beach. He decided, therefore, that this was too dangerous a place to make a landing and lay at anchor until three o'clock in the afternoon in order to give the rest of his fleet time to join him. As he waited he called together the generals and military tribunes, reported to them what he had learned from Volusenus and explained his plans for action. He warned them that the requirements of warfare, and especially at sea where conditions are constantly changing and events unfold rapidly, made the immediate execution of all commands absolutely necessary. When he had dismissed his officers he observed that both wind and tide were favorable and gave the signal for weighing anchor. Then he sailed on about seven miles and brought his ships to a beach that was level and open.

The natives recognized what the Romans intended and sent out their cavalry and charioteers to meet them, as is their custom in war. The rest of their forces followed close behind, and together they attempted to prevent us from landing. There were, in fact, several factors which made disembarkation difficult for the Romans. The ships were large and could not be run ashore except in deep water. The troops, who were unfamiliar with the place, had to jump from the ships while carrying their heavy weapons, keep their balance in the surf and fight an enemy who knew the terrain, stood on dry land or just a little water, and fearlessly threw their missiles and urged on their well-trained horses. Our men were inexperienced in fighting battles of this kind and so they were frightened and showed none of the energy and enthusiasm they usually display when fighting on solid ground.

When Caesar saw this he ordered the galleys, whose appearance was unfamiliar to the Britons and which were more maneuverable than the transports, to be pulled out to sea a little and then rowed at high speed onto the beach on either side of the enemy. Once there, Caesar supposed, the men on their decks could drive the Britons off with slings, bows and artillery. This tactic proved very effective, for the natives were frightened by the peculiar shape of the galleys, the motion and the oars and the strange war machines. They stopped fighting and then pulled back a little. Our men were still hanging back because of the depth of the water, but then the standard-bearer of the Tenth Legion, after praying to the gods for success, cried out, "Jump, comrades, unless you want to betray our eagle to the enemy. I, for one, will do my duty to my country and my commander." Then he leaped down from the ship and headed toward the enemy carrying the eagle. When our soliders saw this they urged each other not to allow themselves to be disgraced and jumped from the ship all at once. The men in the other ships followed suit and advanced toward the enemy.

Both sides fought well, although our soldiers became greatly confused as they could not maintain their ranks and follow their proper standards. Indeed, they attached themselves to the first standard they came upon as they jumped from the ships. But the enemy knew all the shallows, and as soon as they saw our men leaving the ships they spurred their horses along the shore to attack them while they were still wading through the water. In some cases large bands of them would surround smaller groups of our own men while in others they would hurl their spears at the exposed right flank of our entire landing party. When Caesar saw what was happening he ordered the small boats carried on the warships and the boats used for scouting to be manned with soldiers and dispatched them to assist those of our men who were in trouble. Once all of our soldiers had reached dry land they attacked the Britons and routed them. They were unable to chase them as they retreated, though, because the cavalry had not been able to stay on course and reach the island. Thus, in this respect Caesar's success fell short of perfection.

When the defeated Britons had recovered from the battle they sent envoys to Caesar to sue for peace, promising that they would give him hostages and obey his commands. With them came Commius the Atrebatian who, as we have already seen, Caesar had sent into Britain. When he landed there and began delivering Caesar's message they had seized him and bound him in chains, but now they were sending him back, blaming his mistreatment on the ignorant common people and begging Caesar to forgive them. Caesar protested their unprovoked attack, especially because they had made it after they had of their own accord sent an embassy across the channel to ask for peace, but he agreed to pardon their ignorance and demanded hostages. Some of these were handed over to him on the spot, but the rest, they said, would have to be gathered from distant regions and would be delivered within a few days. Meanwhile, the Britons were told to return to their farms and the leaders of the various tribes began to flock to Caesar's camp from every direction in order to put themselves and their people under his protection.

And so peace was established. Four days after Caesar arrived in Britain the eighteen ships which were were transporting our cavalry set sail from the northern port aided by a gentle wind. But just as they came within sight of the camp a violent storm developed which made it impossible for them to stay on course; some were blown back to the very port from which they had started while others, facing great hazards, were able to make their way westward to the lower part of the island. They dropped anchor there, but when the storm continued into the night and they began to take on water they were forced to put out to sea and return to the Continent.

It happened that there was a full moon that night, and consequently a very high tide, though the Romans were unaware of this. The ships in which Caesar had used to cross the channel and then beached began to fill with water while the transports which lay at anchor were battered by the waves as our men looked on helplessly. A number of ships were smashed to bits and others were rendered useless by the loss of cable and other tackle. Naturally, the troops were deeply troubled by this development, for there were no ships to take them back, no materials for repairing the damaged ships, and no provisions for wintering in Britain since everyone had assumed that the army would be returning to Gaul.

When the British chiefs who had gathered at Caesar's camp learned what had happened they met to discuss how they might exploit the situation. Knowing that the Romans had no cavalry or ships or grain, and guessing from the small size of his camp that his forces were modest (the camp was especially small because Caesar had not brought along much equipment), they decided that the best thing for them to do would be to renew hostilities, prevent our men from procuring grain and other supplies, and drag the war into the winter, for they believed that Britain would never again be invaded if they could only manage to defeat this particular Roman army. Thus, the chiefs renewed their agreement of cooperation and began to slip away from the camp and secretly call back into service the men who had returned to their farms.

Even before Caesar had become aware of this the combination of the loss of his ships and the fact that the Britons had stopped delivering hostages led him to suspect that things might turn out as they did. Thus, he took appropriate measures to prepare for whatever might happen. Grain was brought in from the fields each day, timber and bronze from the most severely damaged ships were used to repair the less damaged vessels and additional materials for repair of the ships were ordered from the mainland. The soldiers worked hard, and as a result of their labor all but twelve of the ships were restored to seaworthiness.

One day, while the Romans were still working on their ships, the Seventh Legion was sent on one of its usual missions to collect grain. Nothing unusual had yet occurred; some of the Britons were at work in the fields, some were on their way to our camp and others were returning from it. Then the sentries on duty at the gates informed Caesar that a suspiciously large cloud of dust could be seen in the direction the legion had gone. He realized at once that the Britons were up to some new trick and ordered the cohorts on guard duty to march with him, two other cohorts to replace them at the gates and the rest of his troops to follow him as soon as they had armed themselves. When he had marched some distance he saw that the Seventh Legion was in serious trouble and only barely able to hold its ground. The men were being crowded together and missiles were raining down on them from all sides. The Britons had guessed that the Seventh Legion would come to this district because it was the only one in the region in which the grain had not already been harvested. They had arrived the night before and taken cover in the woods. Then, when our soldiers had set down their arms and were busy reaping, they suddenly attacked, killing some and throwing the rest into confusion and encircling them with their horsemen and chariots.

They employ their chariots in battle in the following way. At first they drive them back and forth across the battlefield hurling their spears, for the terror caused by the horses and the sounds of the wheels is usually enough to throw the ranks of their enemy into confusion. Then, when they have worked their way between the squadrons of their own cavalry, the warriors riding in the chariots jump to the ground and fight on foot. The charioteers then withdraw a short distance from the battlefield and leave their chariots positioned in such a way that the warriors will have a handy means of escape if they are overwhelmed by a superior force. In this way they manage to combine in battle the mobility of cavalry and the steadiness of infantry, and by practicing their technique daily they become so expert that they are able to remain in complete control of their teams as they drive at full gallop down the steepest of slopes, bring them to a stop, and turn in an instant. They run along the pole, stand on the yoke and then, quick as lightning, leap back into the chariot.

These unusual tactics had their desired effect on the Seventh Legion, and so Caesar's rescue mission came just in time. At his approach the enemy quit their assault and our own soldiers recovered their nerve. But Caesar did not think it wise to engage the enemy in battle; instead, he held his position for awhile and then returned to the camp. All our troops were involved in these events, and so the Britons who had been kept working in the fields now took advantage of the opportunity to run away.

Several days of uninterrupted bad weather followed these events, forcing our men to remain in camp and preventing the Britons from attacking. Meanwhile, the natives sent messengers to all parts of the country to spread the word that our forces were small and weak and to describe for them the great opportunities they now had for plunder and securing their freedom forever by driving the Romans out of their camp. In this way they quickly assembled a large force of infantry and cavalry and advanced towards our camp.

Caesar knew that what had happened before would most likely happen again; that is, if the enemy were forced to retreat they would make good use of their speed to escape. However, he had acquired about thirty horsemen whom Commius the Atrebatian had brought over, and so he ordered the legions to form up in front of the camp. Once the battle began the enemy proved unable to resist the relentless attack and turned and took to flight. The Romans chased them as far as they could, killing many of them and burning buildings all over the countryside until they finally returned to the camp.

That same day the Britons sent envoys to ask Caesar for peace. He agreed, but now demanded that they double the number of hostages previously required and insisted that they be delivered to him on the Continent, for the equinox was approaching and he did not wish to expose his damaged ships to the danger of winter storms. It so happened that the weather was favorable for the moment, and so he set sail from the island a little after midnight and reached the Continent safely with his entire fleet, although two of the transports drifted so far to the south that they could not make their assigned ports.

When about three hundred men had disembarked and were on their way to the camp, they were suddenly surrounded by a group of the Morini, with whom Caesar had made peace before departing for Britain. There were not very many of them, but they appeared to be inspired by thoughts of plunder and ordered the Romans to lay down their arms or be killed. When the Romans formed up to defend themselves an enemy battle cry brought a rapid attack by a total of six thousand men. When this was reported to Caesar he dispatched his entire cavalry to assist the threatened troops, whose exceptional bravery enabled them not only to withstand the attack with only a few casualties and even to kill a number of the enemy. As soon as the cavalry appeared the Morini dropped their weapons and fled, suffering very heavy losses as the ran.

The next day Caesar sent Labienus with the legions which he had brought back from Britain to deal with the rebellious Morini. The marshes in which they had taken refuge the previous year were now dried up, and so they had no place in which to hide. As a result, most of them were captured by Labienus. The rest made their way into the very densest parts of the forest, and so Labienus and Cotta, who had earlier led their legions against the Menapii, destroyed all their fields, cut down their grain and burned all their buildings. Then they returned to Caesar and wintered with him and his legions in Belgic territory. Only two of the British tribes sent hostages; the rest broke their word. When it received Caesar's messages concerning these achievements the Roman Senate decreed a public thanksgiving of twenty days.

The Defeat of the Treveri: Caesar, *The Gallic War* 6.1–8

The conquest of Transalpine Gaul was one of the high points in the career of Julius Caesar, for it added to Rome's dominions a territory twice as large as Italy and revealed his genius as a soldier and administrator. The limitless energy, persistence and strategic ability which enabled him to accomplish this outstanding feat are made evident, not surprisingly, in his own description of the campaigns in Gaul, *The Gallic War.* The selection below is a description of the defeat of the Treveri, a powerful Gallic tribe who made a valiant effort to resist Caesar's conquest of their homeland in the Moselle basin.

Caesar had many reasons to suspect that more serious problems would soon surface in Gaul. Thus, he commissioned three of his generals, Marcus Silanus, Gaius Antistius Reginus and Titus Sextius with the task of recruiting new troops. He also dispatched a message to Pompey who, as proconsul, was remaining near Rome in order to fulfil his duties to the state, and asked him to mobilize the soldiers from the northern regions of Italy who had been sworn in during his consulship and send them to him. In Caesar's view it was extremely important to make a lasting impression on the tribesmen by demonstrating that the resources of Italy were sufficient not only to replace quickly men and materials lost in war but to actually increase the size of expeditionary forces which sustained casualties. Motivated by patriotism and friendship, Pompey complied with Caesar's request, the result being that the latter's officers were able to assemble and bring to Gaul by the end of the winter three legions of new soldiers, thus adding to the whole army twice the number of cohorts that had been lost by Sabinus. The speed with which this operation was executed and the strength of the reinforcements showed the Gauls the great capabilities and immense resources of the Romans.

Following the death of Indutiomarus, which was previously discussed, the Treveri transferred command of the tribe to his kin, who repeatedly attempted to gain the support of the German tribes in their immediate vicinity by promising to give them bonuses of money. When these efforts failed they approached more distant tribes and sealed alliances with those who responded to their overtures by exchanging oaths with them and offering hostages to assure them that the bonuses would be paid. They also succeeded in making Ambiorix a member of their alliance by means of a covenant. All of this was communicated to Caesar, who saw preparations for war being made all around him. The Nervii, Aduatuci, Menapii and all the Germans on this side of the Rhine were uniting under arms, the Senones were ignoring his summons and conspiring with the Carnutes and neighboring tribes, and the Treveri were sending embassies in search of German aid. Caesar, therefore, decided it would be necessary to begin the year's military operations earlier than usual.

Accordingly, before winter had ended he assembled the four nearest legions and attacked the Nervii before they could either muster their forces or flee. Many cattle and prisoners were captured and divided among the troops as booty, the country was devastated and the Nervii were forced to surrender and deliver hostages. When this operation had been completed Caesar led his legions back to their camp. Then, in early spring, he convened one of the councils usually attended by all the Gauls. On this occasion, however, the Senones, Carnutes and Treveri did not attend. Caesar viewed their absence as a sign that a rebellion was about to begin, and in order to show that he considered its suppression a matter of extreme importance he moved the council to Lutetia, a small town of the Parisii. The latter lived in a region next to that of the Senones and in the past these two peoples had formed a single state; however, it was generally believed that the Parisii had not been involved in the Senones' dealings with the other rebellious tribes. On the same day that the decision to move the council was made Caesar departed with his legions and soon reached the land of the Senones by forced marches.

When he heard that Caesar was coming, Acco, the leader of the uprising, ordered the people to gather in their strongholds. But before they could manage to do so they were informed that the Romans had already arrived. Thus, they had no choice but to abandon their plan and send deputies to beg Caesar's pardon. The Aedui, the traditional protectors of the tribe, introduced them to Caesar and acted as their advocates. He readily granted the Aedui the pardon they requested and accepted the excuses they offered, for he thought that the summer season should be devoted to the coming war and not to judicial investigations in the provinces. However, he did demand a hundred hostages who were entrusted to the Aedui for safekeeping. Similarly, the Carnutes sent an embassy and hostages to Caesar when he was in their region, employing as their advocates the Remi, whose vassals they were. They received the same treatment as the Senones. Caesar then adjourned the council and ordered the various member tribes to supply him with cavalry.

These parts of Gaul having been pacified, Caesar now devoted himself to the war against the Treveri and Ambiorix. He ordered Cavarinus and the cavalry of the Senones to march with him, for he was afraid that his hot temper or the enmity he had earned might cause trouble within the tribe. Then he tried to guess which strategy Ambiorix might employ, for he was convinced that the man had no intention of fighting a pitched battle. Near the territory of the Eburones lived the Menapii, who were protected by a vast and unbroken expanse of marshes and forests. They alone among the Gauls had never sent ambassadors to Caesar to sue for peace, and he knew that Ambiorix had established relations with them and that they had become friends with the Germans through the agency of the Treveri. Caesar considered it prudent to deprive Ambiorix of these allies before launching his attack against him, for he was afraid that in desperation his enemy might seek to hide among the Menapii or join the German tribes across the Rhine. Therefore, he sent the heavy equipment of the whole army to Labienus in the country of the Treveri and ordered two legions to begin marching there while he himself set out for the territory of the Menapii with five lightly-equipped legions. As for the Menapii, they did not muster an army but, relying on the natural defenses of their land, took their possessions and sought refuge in the forests and marshes.

Caesar divided his forces, giving the command of some units to Gaius Fabius, a lieutenant-general, and that of others to Marcus Crassus, a quarter-master-general. Then, after causeways had been quickly constructed, he approached the Menapii with his three divisions, burning farms and villages and capturing many cattle and human beings. This action was so effective that the Menapii had no choice but to send representatives to Caesar asking for peace. He accepted their hostages and warned them that he would once again consider them his enemies if they allowed either Ambiorix or his deputies within their borders. Once these matters had been settled Caesar set out for the land of the Treveri, leaving behind Commius the Atrebate and some cavalry to keep the peace among the Menapii.

Meanwhile, the Treveri had been mustering large forces of infantry and cavalry and were making plans to attack Labienus, who with a single legion had spent the winter in their land. They were within a two-day march of his camp when they heard that the two legions sent there by Caesar had arrived; subsequently, they encamped fifteen miles away and decided to wait for the arrival of German reinforcements before taking further action. When Labienus learned of this he wondered if it might not be possible to lure the reckless Gauls into battle before the arrival of the Germans. Leaving behind five cohorts to guard his camp and equipment, he marched toward the enemy with twenty-five cohorts and a large force of cavalry and established a camp a mile away from their own. A river with steep banks and difficult to cross separated him from the enemy, but he had no intention of crossing it himself and did not expect the enemy to attempt such an undertaking either. The Gauls' expectations of receiving reinforcements were increasing every day, and Labienus let it be known publicly that since the Germans were said to be approaching he would not risk his own safety and that of his army but would strike camp and withdraw from his position early the next morning. News of this soon reached the enemy, for some of the Gauls serving in Labienus' cavalry quite naturally sympathized with their compatriots across the river. During the night Labienus summoned the military tribunes and senior centurions and revealed to them the plan he had devised. Then, hoping to make the enemy think that fear and panic had broken out in the camp, he ordered it to be struck with more noise and confusion than is usual, so that the Roman departure was as deafening as a rout. Since the two camps were located so near to each other news of the activity in the Roman camp was reported to the Gauls by their scouts before dawn.

The Gauls now urged one another not to let the booty they had been counting on escape them, for since the Romans appeared to be in a panic they thought it would be foolish to waste time waiting for the Germans and an embarrassment for their large army to shrink from attacking such a small group of men, and especially men who were hampered by baggage in their retreat. And so no sooner had the Romans left their camp than the Gauls bravely crossed the river to engage them on unfavorable ground. This is exactly what Labienus had expected, and in order to draw the entire enemy army across the river he cooly continued to pretend that he was marching away. Then, after sending his baggage a short distance ahead and placing it on high ground, he told his soldiers, "Men, this is your chance. You have the enemy trapped in a position where it is difficult for him to maneuver. Give me evidence now of the same courage you have so often demonstrated when fighting under our leader Caesar. Imagine that he is present and watching you with his own eyes." At the same time he commanded them to turn toward the enemy and deploy themselves in a battle line and placed his cavalry, with the exception of a few squadrons sent to protect the baggage, on the flanks. The Romans at once raised the battle cry and threw their spears at the enemy. When the Gauls saw our soldiers, who they had thought were in flight, advance to the attack, they lost their nerve and fled in a panic into the nearby woods. Labienus pursued them with his cavalry, killed many of them and took a large number of prisoners. A few days later the tribe surrendered to him, for the Germans who were coming to assist them had turned back as soon as they heard that the Treveri had been routed. The family of Indutiomarus, who had instigated the revolt, followed the Germans and fled the country. Gingetorix, who had always remained loyal to the Romans, as we have already seen, was now given civil and military authority over the Treveri.

The Battle of Pharsalus: Caesar, *Civil Wars* 3.88–99

In 48 B.C., a year after returning from Gaul and seizing the city of Rome, Caesar followed his rival Pompey into Greece and met him in battle at Pharsalus in Thessaly. The outcome was a resounding victory for Caesar, whose army of no more than twenty-two thousand defeated an enemy force roughly twice that size. The victory has been explained by some as the result of Caesar's military genius and by others as that of Pompey's poor strategy. Whatever the reason, Pompey fled to Egypt where he was treacherously murdered by Ptolemy XIII. The only surviving member of the First Triumvirate, Caesar had now only to eliminate lesser enemies before making himself the master of the Roman world. The selection below is from Caesar's own account of the Battle of Pharsalus in his *Civil Wars*.

As Caesar approached Pompey's camp he observed that the latter had drawn up his troops in the following order. Two legions, the First and the Third, were on the left wing. These were the units the Senate had ordered Caesar to hand over to Pompey at the beginning of the civil wars. Pompey himself took his position on the left wing while Scipio and the Syrian legions held the center. On the right wing were the Cilician legion and the Spanish cohorts which, as we have already seen, were brought over by Afranius. Pompey believed that these were the best of the units under his command; he placed all of the others between the center and the wings. These forces amounted to one hundred and ten cohorts numbering forty-five thousand men, including two thousand reserves who had gone over to Pompey's side because he had given them rewards for their distinguished service in his past campaigns. He scattered these all along his line and assigned to seven remaining cohorts the responsibility for guarding the camp and nearby forts. There was a river with steep banks which offered protection to his right wing, and so he was free to use all of his cavalry, archers and slingers to protect the left wing.

As was his custom, Caesar placed the Tenth Legion on his right wing and the Ninth on his left, though the latter had sustained heavy losses in the fighting at Dyrrachium. To it he added the Eighth Legion, in effect forming one legion from two, and gave orders that they were to support each other. His line was made up of eighty cohorts numbering twenty-two thousand men.

Seven cohorts were assigned to guard the camp. Antony was given command of the left wing, Sulla of the right, and Gnaeus Domitius gave orders in the center. Caesar himself took a position directly opposite Pompey. Then, taking note of the way in which Pompey's forces were arrayed and fearing that his own right wing might be overpowered by the other's cavalry, he quickly withdrew one cohort from each legion of the third line and formed a fourth line which he stationed opposite Pompey's cavalry. After explaining his purpose to these units and reminding them that the outcome of the battle would depend on their valor, he ordered the third line and the entire army not to commence hostilities until he personally gave the signal with a flag.

It was Caesar's custom to exhort his troops before battle, and on this day he spoke to them of his constant concern for their welfare and reminded them of the many occasions on which they had seen him seek peace. He recalled his negotiations through Vatinius, the pleas for understanding which he addressed to Scipio through Aulus Clodius, and his attempts at Oricum to persuade Libo to establish a dialogue with Pompey. It had never been his desire, he said, to waste the blood of soldiers or to deprive the Republic of either of the two armies engaged in this conflict. When he had finished speaking the soldiers showed their enthusiasm by clamoring for battle, and Caesar gave the signal with a trumpet.

Among Caesar's men there was a veteran, an extremely courageous man named Gaius Crastinus, who as a senior centurion had seen service the year before with the Tenth Legion. When he heard the trumpet sound he cried, "Follow me, my comrades, and serve your general now as well as you have always served him. This is our last battle. When the day is done Caesar will have recovered his dignity and we will have our freedom!" Then, looking back at Caesar, he added, "My general, whether I live or die today my actions will be worthy of your gratitude." Having said this he led the attack from the right wing with some one hundred and twenty volunteers from the same cohort close behind him.

There was just enough space between the two armies to allow each to charge. But Pompey had ordered his men to await Caesar's attack without moving from their positions and to allow his line to break apart. They say he did so on the advice of Gaius Triarius and that his objective was to minimize the impact of Caesar's attack and loosen his formation, thus giving the Pompeians, still maintaining their ranks, the chance to charge an enemy in disarray. Moreover, Pompey believed that the enemy's missiles would be less effective if his soldiers remained in position instead of running forward to meet them and that Caesar's soldiers would be exhausted from running the entire distance to Pompey's lines. It is our opinion, however, that Pompey acted unwisely in this, for there is a certain spirit of excitement and aggression in men which is heightened in the heat of battle, and it is the duty of a commander not to suppress this spirit but to exploit it. Indeed, the ancient practices of sounding trumpets in all directions and having the whole army raise a battle cry are very sensible for, as even the ancients knew, they both terrify the enemy and incite in our own men a thirst for battle.

When the order for battle was given our soldiers charged with their javelins ready to be hurled. But when they noticed that the Pompeians were not advancing against them their training and experience gave them the good sense to stop in the center of the field so as not to make contact with the enemy when their strength was sapped. After a few moments they charged again, threw their javelins and quickly drew their swords, as Caesar had ordered. Pompey's men were up to the challenge. They withstood the volley of javelins, maintained their ranks under our attack, hurled their javelins and drew their swords as their cavalry charged and their archers moved forward. Our own cavalry were unable to check the attack and were eventually forced to retreat, a move that encouraged Pompey's horsemen, now in squadrons, to intensify their efforts and begin to encircle the open flank of our line. But Caesar noticed this development and signaled the men of the fourth line, which consisted of six cohorts. They quickly advanced and charged the enemy cavalry with such force that not a single rider managed to hold his position; the entire force retreated, not only abandoning the battlefield but fleeing to the highest hills in the region. The flight of the cavalry had disastrous consequences for the archers and slingers who were left behind. Helpless and unprotected, they were all killed by our men. Meanwhile, our cohorts surrounded Pompey's left wing, which had continued to resist, and attacked it from the rear.

It was at this time that Caesar commanded his third line to attack, for this unit had remained out of the action until now. With these new and vigorous forces now replacing our weary soldiers, and with our attack from the rear, Pompey's men could no longer hold their ground but turned and ran en masse. In his exhortations before the battle Caesar had predicted that victory would come from the performance of the fourth line positioned across from Pompey's cavalry, and he proved to be correct. For these were the very cohorts which repelled the initial charge of cavalry, slew the archers and slingers, surrounded the left wing of the Pompeian line and then began the rout. When Pompey saw that his cavalry had been forced to flee and that the most reliable part of his army was in a panic he lost heart and left the battlefield himself. Riding off to his camp, he shouted to the men guarding the praetorian gate in a voice loud enough for everyone to hear, "Guard the camp, and defend it well in case you are attacked. I will visit the other gates and encourage the men protecting the camp." Then he went to his headquarters, fearful of the outcome of the battle but willing to wait for its conclusion.

When the fleeing Pompeians had been forced to withdraw behind their walls, Caesar, reasoning that they should not be given a chance to recover from their fright, advised his soldiers to take advantage of their good fortune and storm the camp. They were nearly exhausted from the battle and the heat of the sun, for they had fought until noon, but were ready nevertheless to obey his every command. The camp was energetically defended by the cohorts which had been left to guard it, and in particular by the Thracian and other barbarian auxiliaries. As for those who had fled the battle, they were weary and demoralized; the majority of them had thrown away their weapons and standards and were now far more interested in continuing their flight than in defending Pompey's camp. In the end the defenders were unable to resist the onslaught of our forces; tired and wounded, they abandoned their posts and followed their centurions and tribunes in the hope of finding refuge in the nearby hills.

In Pompey's camp one could see arbors, great quantities of silver plate and soldiers' lodgings layered with freshly cut turf or, in the case of Lucius, Lentulus and others, protected from the sun by ivy. There were many other signs of excessive luxury and confidence of victory, so that one might have supposed these were men so little disturbed by the possibility of defeat that they gave themselves over entirely to self-indulgence. Ironically, these same soldiers had accused Caesar's ill-equipped and long-suffering army of living in luxury, despite the fact that it always lacked necessities. While our soldiers were spreading throughout the camp Pompey found a horse, tore off his military insignia and rode out the rear gate in the direction of Larissa. But he did not stop there. Meeting up with some of his men he rode day and night with an escort of thirty until he reached the coast, where he made his escape on a grain ship. They say he complained repeatedly about the failure of his plans and speculated that he might have been betrayed since the very part of his army on which he had counted for victory had been that which began the retreat.

Once Caesar gained possession of the camp he urged his men to finish the task at hand rather than abandon themselves to plunder. They obeyed him and set about building earthworks around the hill on which the Pompeians had taken refuge. Meanwhile, the latter had become uncomfortable due to the lack of water in their hilly retreat and were now preparing to move their entire force along the ridge in the direction of Larissa. When Caesar saw this he decided to divide his forces. Commanding some of the legions to remain in Pompey's former camp and others to go back to his own fortifications, he took four legions along an easier route and after marching six miles overtook the enemy and drew up his line for battle. When they saw him the Pompeians halted on a hill which was bordered at its foot by a river. Caesar gave orders and encouragement to his troops who, although they were worn out by the unbroken labor of an entire day, managed to built an entrenchment between the river and the mountain, thus denying the enemy access to water during the night. When they had finished this work the Pompeins sent messengers to Caesar with offers of surrender. A few of senatorial rank, however, managed to escape under cover of darkness.

Early the next morning Caesar commanded the Pompeians in the hills to come down to the plain and hand over their weapons. They complied, falling to the ground and begging him with outstretched arms and tearful eyes to spare their lives. He put them at ease with a few words about his leniency, gave them guarantees of safety and then turned them over to his troops with instructions that they should not be injured or have their property taken from them. After this Caesar sent the legions back to camp for a rest, replaced them with the fresh troops that had been standing guard there, and arrived with them in Larissa that same day.

At the Battle of Pharsalus Caesar lost fewer than two hundred soldiers from the rank and file and about thirty courageous centurions. One of them, Crastinus, who we mentioned earlier, fought gallantly and died from a sword-thrust in the face. This man's statement before the beginning of the battle was fully justified, for Caesar thought his bravery in battle was extraordinary and concluded that he was deeply indebted to him. It appears that about fifteen thousand of the enemy wre killed and that more than twenty-four thousand surrendered, including the cohorts left to guard the Pompeian camp who gave themselves up to Sulla. Many others sought refuge in various cities in the region. One hundred and eighty of the enemy's standards and nine captured eagles were presented to Caesar.

Resisting Roman Rule: Josephus, *Jewish War* 2.352–400

The Romans found governing Judea a difficult business. Not only were the Jews unappreciative of the Roman presence in their land, they were also extremely sensitive to any Roman show of disrespect for their religious beliefs or interference with the practice of their faith. Rome did make some concessions, such as exempting the Jews from emperor-worship, but there were also flagrant offenses against Jewish sensibilities, Caligula's attempt to place a statue of himself in the Temple at Jerusalem being a good example.

Jewish discontent increased until open rebellion broke out in 66 A.D. only to end four years later with Roman victory and the destruction of Jerusalem. In his account of the rebellion the historian Flavius Josephus recorded the speech of Herod Agrippa II, who argued before the outbreak of the rebellion that the Jews would have no chance against Rome. The following excerpt from his address explains why many inhabitants of the empire believed that any attempt to resist the might of Rome was doomed.

"I admit that the ministers of Rome are unbearably harsh, but does it follow that all the Romans are persecuting you? Even Caesar? Yet it is against them, and against him, that you are going to make war! It was not on their orders that an unscrupulous governor was sent to us from Rome, and western eyes cannot observe events in the East. In fact, it is not easy for the people of Rome even to get news from our part of the world. It would be absurd to go to war against an entire nation because of the petty offenses of one man, especially when that nation does not even know of our complaints! The injustices for which we hold them responsible can quickly be set right; the same Roman procurator [*i.e.,* governor] will not be here forever, and his successors are sure to be more reasonable. But war, once it begins, cannot easily be stopped or fought to its conclusion without disaster . . . .

"Where are the men, where are the weapons on which you will rely? Where is the fleet you will use to sweep the Roman seas? Where is the treasury to pay for your campaigns? Do you think you are going to war with Egyptians or Arabs? Are you going to ignore the might of Rome and not consider your own weakness? Haven't our own forces been defeated time and again even by our neighbors, while theirs have been victorious all over the world? And even the world is not big enough to satisfy their ambition; the Euphrates is not far enough to the East, or the Danube to the North, or Libya and its southern deserts to the South, or Cadiz to the West. No, they have sought a new world beyond the Ocean, carrying their arms as far as the previously unknown land of Britain. What is the matter with you? Do you think you are richer than the Gauls, stronger than the Germans, more clever than the Greeks, more numerous than all the peoples of the world? What makes you think that you can defy the power of Rome?

"'It is a hard thing to be enslaved,' you will say. How much harder for the Greeks who, though they are the noblest people under the sun and occupy such vast territory, are still subservient to the *fasces* of the Romans. So are the Macedonians, who have a better right than you to demand their freedom. And what about the five hundred cities of Asia? Don't they, without a garrison, bow down before a single governor and the consular *fasces*? Need I mention the Heniochi, the Colehians, and the Taurian race, the peoples of the Bosporus, the Black Sea and the Sea of Azov? There was a time when they did not recognize even one of their own as master, but now they are held in subjection to three thousand soldiers, while forty warships keep the peace on a sea once wild and filled with pirates. What just demands for liberty could be made by Bithynia, Cappadocia, Pamphylia, Lycia and Cilicia, and yet they pay their tribute willingly.

"And then there are the Thracians, who are spread over a country five days' march in width and seven in length, a country more rugged and more easily defended than your own and whose freezing climate repels invaders—and yet they obey the orders of two thousand Roman guards. The Illyrians, their neighbors, live in a land that reaches from Dalmatia to the Danube border, and yet they are dominated by only two legions. In fact, the Illyrians combine forces with the Romans to fight off the raiding Dacians. And then there are the Dalmatians, who have struggled so often for liberty and whose many defeats have only led them to struggle again—now they live peacefully under a single Roman legion.

"If any people ought to be tempted to revolt by their special advantages it is the Gauls, who have such tremendous natural defenses: on the East the Alps, on the North the Rhine, on the South the Pyrenees, and on the West the Ocean. And yet, even though they are surrounded by such defenses, and despite the fact that they number three hundred and five tribes occupying a land so rich that they fill the whole world with their products, they are willing to nourish Rome with their wealth and take whatever the Romans portion out to them from the riches of their own homeland. They tolerate this situation not because they are weak-spirited or an inferior race (they fought for eighty years to preserve their freedom), but because they are in awe of the might of Rome and its good fortune, which wins more victories for the Romans than their arms. That is why the Gauls submit to twelve hundred soldiers though they have almost as many cities!

"And then the Spaniards—the gold they take from their soil could not save them, nor could the vast expanse of land and sea that separates them from the Romans, nor the tribes of Lusitania [*i.e.,* Portugal] and Cantabria [*i.e.,* north coastal Spain] with their zest for war, nor the neighboring Ocean that terrifies even the natives. No, the Romans reduced Spain to slavery, carrying their arms across the cloudy Pyrenees and as far as the Pillars of Hercules. A single legion now suffices to guard this remote nation of stubborn fighters.

"Which of you has not heard of the Germans? I am sure you have seen their magnificent figures many times, for the Romans have German slaves everywhere. These people live in a vast country. Their pride is even stronger than their bodies, and they have souls that despise death. When enraged they are fiercer than the most savage animal. Yet the Rhine contains their violence and the Romans have mastered them with eight legions, enslaving the captives while the rest of them flee for safety.

"Consider the defenses of the Britons, you who have such faith in the walls of Jerusalem. They are surrounded by the Ocean and they dwell on an island as big as the part of the world in which we live; yet the Romans crossed the sea and enslaved them, and four legions now keep the peace on that huge island. But why should I go on, when even the Parthians, that most warlike of peoples, the rulers of so many nations and a race protected by powerful armies, send hostages to the Romans and can be seen in Italy, those aristocrats of the East, submitting in the name of peace. Almost every nation under the sun bows before the might of Rome. . . .

"Some of you may think that your war will be fought on special terms, and that when the Romans have won they will treat you kindly. They will not. They will make you an example to the world by burning Jerusalem to the ground and annihilating your entire race. Even if some of you were to survive you would never find refuge, since there isn't a single nation that isn't either ruled by Rome or afraid that it will be. And the danger is not only a threat to us, but also to those who live in other cities, for there is not a city anywhere that doesn't count Jews among its population. If you go to war they too will be massacred by your enemy, and because of the foolishness of a few men every city will be wet with Jewish blood. . . ."

They Create a Desert and Call it Peace: Tacitus, *Agricola* 29–31

In 98 A.D. the Roman historian Tacitus wrote a biography of his father-in-law Cnaeus Julius Agricola, who had once served as governor of Britain. From Britain Agricola advanced into Scotland where he established Roman outposts which protected his province from the attacks of the highlanders. This interesting work describes not only the character of Agricola and the Roman conquest of Britain, but also illustrates many of the aspects of Roman imperialism. For example, the speech of Calgacus, a Caledonian chieftain who was eventually subdued by the Romans, clearly reflects the sentiments of the vanquished toward their Roman masters and the noble proclamations of the propagandists of the Pax Romana.

Early in the summer Agricola suffered a personal tragedy in the loss of a son born just a year before, a loss which he bore neither with the showy affectations of strength often displayed by brave men nor, on the other hand, with tears such as those which bereaved women shed. In his grief he found a source of strength in war. Sending ahead a fleet to make raids at various places and thereby raise a general alarm, he advanced with a lightly armed force which included in its ranks a few brave Britons who had proved their loyalty through years of peace. He brought this force as far as the Grampian mountains, where the enemy had taken its stand; for the Britons had not been the least bit discouraged by the outcome of the last battle and had made up their minds that they would now either get their revenge or be enslaved. Convinced at last that they should stand united against their common foe, their treaties and negotiations now resulted in the convergence of the whole strength of their various tribes. More than thirty thousand men had already assembled and more were on the way—young men from all over the country and older warriors who were still strong and vigorous, men who had earned fame in war and decorated themselves with their own tokens of battle. Meanwhile, one of the many leaders, a man superior to the rest in bravery and in birth, Calgacus by name, spoke to the battle-hungry multitude:

"Whenever I reflect on the cause of this war and the difficulties of our present situation, I am convinced that this day and this unity we have achieved will be the beginning of a struggle which will bring the freedom of all Britain.

Slavery is something unknown to us, there are no lands behind us to which we can retreat, and even the sea offers us no possibility of escape since the Roman fleet threatens us there. And so in war and battle, in which the brave find glory, even cowards will now find safety. The occasional success of others in resisting the Romans has until now given us reason to hope that we, because we are the most famous people in Britain and live in the very heart of it, might remain out of sight of the conquered shores and keep our eyes unpolluted by the sight of slavery there. We who live at the extreme limits of the earth and of freedom in this distant sanctuary of British glory have so far found protection in it. But now even the most remote confines of Britain are being reached, and those yet unreached seem ever more marvelous. But there are no other nations beyond us, nothing but waves and rocks and the even more terrible Romans from whom the oppressed vainly seek to escape by obedience and submission. These bandits of the world plunder the lands of the wealthy and despoil those of the poor. Rapacious when their enemy is rich, hungry for dominion when he is poor, they have not been satisfied though they have ranged across the world from East to West. They are unique among all peoples in that they covet the rich and the poor with equal enthusiasm. They give the name of empire to their robbery, slaughter and plunder; they create a desert and call it peace.

It is a law of nature that a man's children and kin should be his most precious possessions, but conscription tears them away from us and makes them slaves in foreign lands. If our wives and children manage to avoid being raped by the Romans they are still dishonored by pretending to regard them as our friends and guests. The Romans take our possessions and our money as tribute and they steal our harvests for their own granaries. They even destroy our bodies as we labor under lashes and insults to cut down forests and clear swamps. Those who are born to be slaves are sold once and for all; thereafter they are fed by their masters. But Britain must daily purchase and feed her own enslaved people. And just as the newest slave in the house is always the object of the cruelty of the others, so we who are the newest and most contemptible slaves in a world long accustomed to slavery are destined for destruction. We have no productive lands, no mines, no harbors in good repair for the sake of which we might be spared. Conquerors are not fond of subjects like ourselves who are brave and high-spirited; besides, remoteness and isolation, though they offer a measure of protection, also arouse suspicion. And so you have no hope of receiving mercy. Take courage, then, whether your motive be safety or glory. Under a woman's leadership the Brigantes succeeded in burning down a Roman colony and stormed an army camp; had their success not made them careless they might have liberated the entire country. We are a strong, un-conquered people, committed to preserving our freedom. Let us show in our first clash with the Romans what heroes Caledonia has kept back for this fight."

They received Calgacus' speech with enthusiasm and, as is the custom among the barbarians, with songs, shouts and discordant cries. Then one could see the men forming for battle, the glittering of their weapons, and the boldest of the warriors taking their places in the front lines.

III
Literature

Roman Comedy: Plautus, *The Braggart Warrior* Act 1, Scene 1

The most famous playwright of the Roman Republic was Plautus, a writer of comedies who was born *ca.* 255 Sarsina, a town on the border of Umbria. Like Terence, who followed half a century later, Plautus adapted Greek plays written in the fourth and third centuries B.C. in the tradition of New Comedy. Many critics charge that he practiced *contaminatio,* the combining of two Greek plays into a single Latin comedy. *The Braggart Warrior,* a delightful play enlivened by plenty of farce, ribaldry, deception and mistaken identity, is almost certainly an example of this practice. The play focuses on Pyrgopolynices, an insufferably vain soldier who considers himself the ultimate conqueror—in the bedroom as well as on the battlefield. Much of the action concerns the efforts of the friends and lover of a courtesan he has stolen to rescue her from the boastful soldier. In the beginning of the play Artotrogus, Pyrgopolynices' lackey, artfully calls attention to the foolishness of his vainglorious master.

Enter Pyrgopolynices from his house, followed by Artotrogus and some orderlies carrying a shield

PYRGOPOLYNICES

Make sure that you polish my shield so that it shines more brightly than the sun. In the heat of battle I want its brilliance to dazzle the eyes of my enemies.

looking at his sword

Poor sword! I wish I could console you. You must be very unhappy, hanging by my side so long without seeing any action. I know how eager you are to cut some enemy to pieces. But wait! Where is Artotrogus?

ARTOTROGUS

Right here, sir, standing next to a man as bold and blessed as a prince. Why, even Mars himself wouldn't dream he's half the soldier you are, or compare his own exploits with yours.

PYRGOPOLYNICES

Who was the fellow I saved in the Battle of Weevil Plains, where the commander was Bumblebattle Bigshotsoldier, the grandson on Neptune?

ARTOTROGUS

I remember, sir. You must mean the one with the golden armor, the one whose legions you puffed away with a single breath, just as the wind blows away leaves or a thatched roof.

PYRGOPOLYNICES

Oh, that was nothing, nothing at all.

ARTOTROGUS

Nothing? Good heavens, sir! Nothing, I suppose, next to all the other deeds I could mention—*(aside)* that you never did!

to the audience, with disgust

If anyone has ever seen a bigger liar or a more fatuous braggart he can have me for his own, and I'll make sure he gets my papers. Still, he *does* make a great olive salad.

PYRGOPOLYNICES

looking around

Where are you?

ARTOTROGUS

Right here, sir! Say, what about that elephant in India? You smashed his forearm with nothing but your fist!

PYRGOPOLYNICES

Forearm?

ARTOTROGUS

Front leg, I mean.

PYRGOPOLYNICES

It was just an accidental slap, actually.

ARTOTROGUS

It must have been. If you had hit him on purpose your arm would have gone clean through him, hide, flesh, bones and all.

PYRGOPOLYNICES

Come on now, enough of this.

ARTOTROGUS

You're right, sir. There's no point in describing your adventures to me—I already know all about them.

to the audience, with disgust

It's my belly that makes me suffer like this. If I don't lend him my ears my teeth won't have anything to chew on. I have to go along with everything he says.

PYRGOPOLYNICES

What was it I was about to say?

ARTOTROGUS

Aha! I know what it was! Good heavens, sir, you did it! I remember that you did it!

PYRGOPOLYNICES

Did what?

ARTOTROGUS

slightly embarrassed

Uh, whatever it was you did, sir.

PYRGOPOLYNICES

Have you got a —

ARTOTROGUS

interrupting

A writing tablet? Yes, I do. And a stylus too.

PYRGOPOLYNICES

You know me like a book!

ARTOTROGUS

I ought to, sir. It's my duty to know you inside and out and to anticipate your desires even before you are aware of them yourself.

PYRGOPOLYNICES

with feigned indifference

So you remember, eh? Well then, tell me what you remember.

ARTOTROGUS

Well, let's see. There were a hundred and fifty Cilicians, a hundred Scythians, thirty Sardinians, sixty Macedonians—that's how many you killed in one day, sir.

PYRGOPOLYNICES

But how many have I killed altogether?

ARTOTROGUS

Seven thousand, sir.

PYRGOPOLYNICES

That's right! You've counted them correctly.

ARTOTROGUS

And without a tally sheet! I committed every one of them to memory.

PYRGOPOLYNICES

My goodness, that's very impressive.

ARTOTROGUS

Thinking about food helps.

PYRGOPOLYNICES

If you keep behaving yourself you'll eat to your heart's content. There'll always be a place for you at my table.

ARTOTROGUS

hoping for more praise

And what about that time in Cappadocia when you would have killed five hundred men with a single stroke if your sword hadn't been dull.

PYRGOPOLYNICES

They were only foot soldiers, so I let them live.

ARTOTROGUS

Why should I tell you what the whole world already knows, that you are the one and only Pyrgopolynices, a man unsurpassed in bravery and good looks? Women love you, sir, and I can't say that I blame them, considering that you're so handsome. Why, do you remember those girls who caught me by the cloak yesterday?

PYRGOPOLYNICES

trying to hide his interest

Yes. What did they say to you?

ARTOTROGUS

They kept asking me questions about you. One of them wondered if you were Achilles. "No," I said, "he's his brother." Another one said, "Mmmm, he's so handsome. And he has such fine manners and gorgeous hair. I envy the women who get to sleep with him."

PYRGOPOLYNICES

Did they really say those things about me?

ARTOTROGUS

Of course they did, and they begged me to bring you back to the same spot today so that they might watch you, as though you were a one-man parade.

PYRGOPOLYNICES

It's hard to be so handsome.

ARTOTROGUS

It must be, sir. The women really are a bother, always begging and pleading for a chance to see you. They bother me so much that I barely have time to attend to all your needs.

PYRGOPOLYNICES

Well, it seems that it's time for us to be off to the Forum so that I can pay the new recruits I enlisted yesterday. King Seleucus himself asked me if I would do him the favor of signing up some new soldiers. I've decided to devote the whole day to the king.

ARTOTROGUS

Let's go then.

PYRGOPOLYNICES

to his orderlies

Come along, men.

He strides off grandly toward the Forum, Artotrogus and the orderlies making fun of him as they follow.

The Poet of Love and Anguish:
Catullus, *Epigrams*

The Roman poet Gaius Valerius Catullus (*ca.* 84-54 B.C.)
was born into a wealthy family at Verona. When he was about
twenty-two he came to Rome where he joined a circle of leading
social and political pesonalities. One of these was Julius Caesar,
whom Catullus ridiculed in some of his epigrams. Another was
the woman Catullus called by the pseudonym Lesbia. Tradition
identifies her as Clodia, the wife of Q. Caecilius Metellus and
a notoriously promiscuous socialite with whom the young poet
fell in love shortly after his arrival in Rome. Perhaps the most
striking feature of Catullus' poems is their deeply personal
nature. In them we find his reflections on many of the events
and relationships which filled his brief but intense life with
delight, conflict, poignancy and despair. Though some have been
disturbed by his frequent obscenity, Catullus wrote with an
honesty and eloquence which have earned him recognition as
one of Rome's greatest poets.

2

Hello there, sparrow, my girl's little pet.
She plays with you, cuddles you, lets you
nuzzle her finger, then pokes you to make
you bite if she thinks a little trick will
take her mind off the sorrow that never
really goes away.
I wish I could play with you like that
and ease the pain that's tearing me apart.

3

Weep with me, you Loves and Cupids,
and all of you beautiful people.
My Lesbia's sparrow is dead—
her darling pet sparrow.
She loved him more than anything;
he was as sweet as honey,

and he knew her as well as
she knew her own mother.
He never left her lap,
just hopped back and forth
chirping for her alone.
Now he's on his way down that
dark road from which they say
no one ever returns.
A curse on you, you damned darkness!
How could you have taken
such a pretty little sparrow away?
And you, you miserable sparrow,
it's all because of you that my Lesbia's
eyes are swollen, red and full of tears.

5

Let's live it up, my Lesbia, and love,
and not give a damn what cranky old farts
might say about us.
Other suns may set and then rise again,
but once our short light goes out there'll be
nothing left for us but sleep and endless night.
So give me some kisses: first a thousand,
then a hundred, then another thousand,
a second hundred, a thousand more,
and then another hundred.
And when our kisses reach many thousands
we'll lose count of them all, so that
no envious soul will give us the evil eye
when he learns how many kisses we've kissed.

39

Egnatius has white teeth,
and so he's always smiling.
Go to court when the defendant's
lawyer has got everyone sobbing—
he's smiling.
At the funeral of a young boy, when the
bereaved mother is grieving for her only child—
he's smiling.
Whatever the occasion, wherever he is,

whatever he's doing—
he's smiling.
It's a sickness, really, and not a very pretty one.
So let me give you some advice, my dear Egnatius:
even if you were a Roman or a Sabine, a Tiburtine,
a piggish Umbrian or a bloated Etruscan, a dark,
big-toothed Lanuvian, a Transpadane (like me)
or anyone else who brushes his teeth with
good clean water, I still would not want to
see you smiling so much, since there's
nothing more stupid than a stupid smile.
But you're Spanish, and everyone knows that over
there in Spain you people brush your teeth
and gums with pee,
so that the brighter your smile is,
the more urine we know you've been drinking.

52

What's stopping you, Catullus?
Why not just die?
There's Nonius (that degenerate!)
sitting in a curule chair,
and we've got that liar Vatinius
for a consul.
So what's stopping your, Catullus?
Why not just die?

69

There's no point in wondering why
women aren't willing to sleep with you,
Rufus, though you buy them
fancy dresses and sparkling stones.
There's an ugly rumor going around
that says there's a wild goat living
under your armpits, and they're all
scared of him and his stench.
After all, he's not the kind of animal
a nice girl ought to be sleeping with.
So get rid of that stinking nose-slayer
or just stop wondering why women run away.

70

My woman says there's no one she'd rather marry
than me, not even if Jupiter himself wanted her.
That's what she says, but what a woman says
to an eager lover might as well be written
on wind and running water.

75

My head's been screwed up
so bad because of you, Lesbia,
so ruined by devotion,
that I couldn't like you
if you were the best of women,
or stop loving you, no matter
how much you hurt me.

85

I hate her and I love her.
Why? I don't know,
but it's the way I feel,
and it's killing me.

92

Lesbia's always cursing me,
she can't stop putting me down,
and yet I know she loves me.
How? I'm the same way:
I curse her up and down,
turn around, and say I love her.

101

I've come through many lands and seas
to get to this sad ceremony, my brother,
to give you these last rites for the dead
and stand here talking to your silent ashes.
Fate is cruel; she should never have
taken you from me!
But here, I've brought these gifts
according to the ancient custom.
Take them, wet with all my tears,
and forever, brother, hail and farewell.

Roman Destiny: Virgil, *Aeneid* 1.254–296

The Roman poet Virgil (70-19 B.C.) was a prolific writer, but he is best known for his *Aeneid,* an epic poem which describes how, after the fall of Troy, the hero Aeneas led a band of surviving Trojans in their search for a new home. After several unsuccessful attempts to settle at various sites in the eastern Mediterranean, destiny brought them to Italy. The idea that the Roman people were descended from the Trojans did not originate with Virgil. Tradition, based largely on Book XX of Homer's *Iliad,* had long held that Aeneas had brought a remnant of his nation to Latium, where they built the city of Lavinium and where, some three hundred years later, Romulus established the city of Rome. Virgil's great achievement was to shape this legend into a national epic which glorified the heritage and destiny of the Romans. Among those who approved of the work was Augustus, the poet's patron, who found in it considerable praise of his own person and achievements. Although the dying Virgil had requested that the unfinished poem be destroyed, the emperor ordered its publication.

Early in the *Aeneid* the Trojans suffer as they wander over the seas enduring many hardships. Venus, Aeneas' mother, appeals to Jupiter to bring an end to their ordeal. The following passage relates Jupiter's reassuring response to his daughter. Note that references to Caesar are to Augustus (Gaius Julius Caesar Octavianus) and that Venus is called Cytherea after the Greek island where she was said to have been born from sea foam.

Smiling down on her with the smile
that stills the sea and sky,
the Father of gods and men lightly kissed
his daughter and began to speak:
Fear not, Cytherea. Take comfort,
for your people's destiny remains the same.
You will see the city walls of Lavinium
just as I promised, and exalt great-souled

Aeneas to the limit of heaven's brightest stars.
I have not changed my mind.
No, and let me tell you
—for I know doubts are always gnawing at you—
let me show you what lies hidden in
the secret scrolls of fate:
Aeneas will wage massive war in Italy,
crushing its fierce tribes and
building city walls and a new way of life
till a third summer sees him ruling in Latium
and three winters have passed since
his conquest of the Rutulians.
His son Ascanius—now surnamed Iulus,
though before Ilium fell his name was Ilus—
Ascanius shall reign thirty years,
through all their cycles of months,
and move his throne from Lavinium
to strongly fortified Alba Longa.
Here for three hundred years
a line of kings sprung from Hector will rule
until the queen-priestess Ilia,
pregnant by Mars, bears his twin sons.
One of them, Romulus, nurtured by a she-wolf
and joyfully wearing her tawny pelt,
will come to power, found a city for Mars
and call its people Romans, after his own name.
For them I set no limits of space or time.
Empire without end I give them.
Even Juno, whose bitterness now stirs sea,
land and sky into turmoil, will change her ways
and join me in cherishing the Romans,
lords of the earth, the toga-wearing people.
This is my will.
With the passing of ages the time will come
when the sons of Troy will enslave Thessaly
and glorious Mycenae, and rule in conquered Argos.
From their illustrious line will come a Caesar
—Julius his name, handed down from great Iulus—
whose dominion will be bounded only by the tides,
his fame only by the stars.
The day will come when you will raise him to heaven,
laden with the spoils of the East, where he will

receive the prayers of men just as you do.
The harsh years of war will end then,
and violence will soften into peace.
Ancient Fides and Vesta, Romulus and Remus,
his brother, shall make the laws.
The grim iron Gates of War will be locked
and inside unholy Fury will sit enthroned
on savage weapons, his hands enchained behind him
by a hundred brazen shackles, roaring horribly
with his blood-stained mouth.

A Poet of the Augustan Age:
Horace: *Odes* and *Epodes*

One of the greatest of Roman poets, Horace was born in 65 B.C. in Apulia and died in 8 A.D. His father was an Italian freedman whose personal success and ambition for his son explain the expensive education Horace received in Rome under the grammarian Orbilius. Following additional study in Athens and service with Brutus' army at Philippi, Horace returned to Rome where he was fortunate enough to meet Virgil, who introduced him to his future patron, Maecenas.

Horace is sometimes spoken of as a court poet who slavishly supported every aspect of Augustus' reform program. Such a description is misleading, however, for the poet had already completed much of his work by the beginning of the principate and mentioned Augustus in only a few of his works. Nevertheless, it is clear that his sentiments were for the most part in line with the emperor's. Thus, although he found occasions on which to praise the pleasures of love and wine, he preferred to emphasize the importance of moderation, simplicity and the other virtues associated with the old Roman morality that Augustus tried to revitalize.

Epode 2

Happy is he who tills his ancestral fields,
plodding behind his oxen, free from debt
and far from business cares.
A man like the most ancient of men,
he is no soldier who rises for slaughter
at the trumpet's call,
no sailor trembling out on the angry sea.
He has no love for the Forum or the society
of the powerful in their sumptuous homes.
He is one who finds his pleasure in wedding
hardy vines to supporting poplars
and watching his herd of lowing cattle
graze in some secluded dale.

In his skilled hands the pruning-knife
cuts away the barren branch and
grafts a fruitful one in its place.
He stores away his pressed honey in clean jars
and shears the gentle sheep.
When autumn comes to crown the fields
with ripened fruit
he rejoices as he gathers in the grafted pears
and harvests grapes in clusters of deepest purple
with which to honor you, Priapus,
and you, Silvanus, protector of boundaries.
How pleasant for him to lie under
an ancient ilex tree, or often on the tufted grass,
while nearby the rippling stream purls on
between high banks.
Birds chatter in the forest, and the splashing
waters of crystal springs invite him to easy sleep.
In winter, when the Thunderer sends
crashing rain and chilling snow,
he takes his hounds to chase
savage boars into waiting snares
or stretches wide his nets for the hungry thrush
and his noose for the timid hare and foreign crane—
the very best of prizes.
Who would not forget even the pain
that unhappy love can bring
while he enjoys pleasures such as these?
And if some modest woman helps him care
for their home and sweet children,
like a Sabine wife or the suntanned mate of
a strapping Apulian; if she
piles the firewood high upon the blessed hearth,
preparing for her weary husband's return;
if she closes the fertile flock within
its wattled pen to drain their swelling udders
and draws new wine from the jar
to serve with simple home-cooked fare,
then nothing could please me more—
not Lucrine oysters, or even turbot or *scarus,*
should winter thunder down on eastern waves
and drive them to our shores.
Neither African fowl nor Indian pheasant

would warm my belly more than
olives picked from the choicest branches,
the meadow-loving sorrel, health-giving mallows,
a lamb slaughtered at the feast of Terminus
or a kid snatched from the prowling wolf.
What joy, while feasting so splendidly,
to see sheep hurrying home from their pasture,
weary oxen returning from the fields, dragging
the upturned plowshares with their languid necks,
and the many slaves born in your own wealthy house
gathered around the shining images of the ancestors
who watch over your house.

These were the words of the moneylender Alfius
when he was a day away from keeping his vow
to give up loansharking for farming.
But his second thoughts got the better of him:
he called in his funds on the fifteenth
but was back in business on the first.

Ode 1.38

I detest these silly Persian niceties, my boy.
Imagine: wreaths bound with linden bark
and desperate searches for late-blooming roses.
It's best to wear wreaths of simple myrtle,
for then our garlands will suit us well
as you pour the wine, slave, and I drink it,
under the vine-filled trellis.

Ode 3.14

Citizens! They said that Caesar, like Hercules,
sought the laurels whose price is death,
but now he returns to his household gods
as victor from the coast of Spain.
Let his wife, rejoicing in her peerless husband,
offer sacrifice to the just gods and then
come forward, and also the sister of our
distinguished leader and, wearing garlands
of the freshest blossoms, the mothers of
virgins and soldier-sons whose lives he has saved.
Let no ill-omened words pass your lips,

you boys and still unmarried girls.
This day will be for me a day of celebration
free from black cares,
for as long as Caesar rules the earth I shall
never fear revolution or death by violence.
Go find perfume, boy, and garlands,
and a jar of wine that remembers the Marsian War
(if any jar escaped intact the violence
of the roving Spartacus).
And tell sweet-voiced Neaera to quickly
tie a ribbon in her chestnut hair
and to ignore that nasty janitor
if he tries to stop her as she leaves.
I would not have endured such instults
when Plancus was consul and I was an ardent youth.
But my graying hair has calmed the fire spirit
of one who once went looking for trouble.

Echo and Narcissus: Ovid, *Metamorphoses* 3.339–510

About 8 A.D. Ovid published his *Metamorphoses,* fifteen books of verse in dactylic hexameter which recount some two hundred and fifty of the most famous myths of the ancient world. In the following excerpt Ovid tells how Narcissus, the son of of the river-god Cephisus and the nymph Liriope, was loved by the nymph Echo but fell in love instead with the reflection of his own image. This well-known story was a favorite in antiquity and is typical in its intent both to entertain and to offer moral instruction.

And so Tiresias grew famous throughout the
towns of Boeotia for the perfect prophecies he
gave to all who asked. The first to put the seer's
powers to the test was the water-nymph Liriope,
whom the river-god Cephisus had once raped,
catching and holding her fast in the twists
and turns of his winding course.
When her time came the lovely nymph
bore her child, a baby boy adorable from
the very first, and named him Narcissus.
She asked the prophet if he would live
to enjoy a good old age, and the seer said,
"Yes, if he never comes to know himself."
For years the prophecy seemed to make no sense,
but then the boy's death, the way he died
and his weird love proved that it was true.

When Narcissus reached his sixteenth year
he seemed equally boy and man. Many were the
girls who wanted him, and young men too,
but the proud heart within his slender body
would allow no girl or boy to touch him.
One day he had driven a frightened deer into
a net when a nymph named Echo saw him—
queer-voiced Echo, who must speak when others

speak and hold her tongue when they do not.
She had a body then, as well as a voice,
but then as now the talkative girl could
only repeat the very last words of all she heard.
It was Juno who had made her so, for there
had been many times when the Queen of Heaven
might have caught Jove with the nymphs in
the mountains if garrulous Echo had not held her
in converstion until they finished their love-making.
When Juno learned the truth she said,
"The tongue you used to trick me will lose
its power now, that voice of yours will
be able to utter only the briefest sounds."
She made good on her threat: the nymph can only
mimic voices and echo the last words she hears.

When she saw Narcissus wandering in the forest,
Echo burned for him. She followed him in secret,
and as she came closer her passion flared and
grew hotter, as when a torch is lit the sulphur
smeared upon the tip leaps to blaze bright
within the flame that sets it alight.
She longed to go to him, to win him with
seductive speech, but her nature kept her silent
until at last he gave her a word to repeat.
It happened that Narcissus became separated
from his friends and began to shout,
"Is anyone here?" and Echo answered, "Here!"
Astonished, the boy looked all around and cried
in a louder voice, "Come here!"
"Come here!" she shouted after him.
He looked behind him and, seeing no one,
he called again, "Why run away?"
only to hear his question returned as a reply.
He stopped then, confused by her voice,
and said, "Come, join me!"
Never more eager to give her answer,
Echo shouted, "Come, join me!"
and to make the words come true she rushed from
the forest to throw her arms around the boy's neck.
But he ran from her, and as he fled he cried,
"Keep your hands off me! Stay away!

I'll die before I'll let you hold me!"
And all Echo could say was "I'll let you hold me!"
Spurned and humiliated, she ran back to the
forest to hide herself among the leafy trees and
make her home inside lonely caves.
Her love came with her, and feeding on the pain
of her rejection it left her grieving through
sleepless nights until she began to waste away.
Living on nothing but sorrow, she grew dry and
began to shrivel. Soon there was nothing left
of her but voice and bones, and in the end
she was only voice, her bones having turned to stone.
Echo still hides in those woods and goes unseen
up in the hills, but all those who call for her
will hear her voice—it is her voice that lives.

Narcissus had scorned others too,
nymphs of the hills and springs, boys and men,
until one unhappy youth raised his hands to heaven
praying, "Let Narcissus love and go unloved,
let him fail as I have failed!"
and Nemesis granted his just prayer.

There was a pool whose silver-clear waters
no shepherd brought his herd to drink
nor mountain goat ever tasted.
No bird, nor beast nor falling branch
ever disturbed its stillness.
Grass grew thick and green all around it,
nourished by the moisture, and the surrounding
trees protected it from the sun's warm rays.
To this very place Narcissus came,
hot and weary from hunting, and lay down,
enchanted by the cool and green.
He bent down to drink, but as he did another thirst
arose within him, for in the water he saw a face
and fell in love, believing the reflection
mirrored there was real. Spellbound, he lay
as motionless as a statue of Parian marble,
staring at himself. He saw eyes that shone
like stars, curls worthy of Bacchus or Apollo,
an ivory neck, a beautiful face, smooth cheeks

and snowy skin with just a hint of rosy blush.
Marveling at the very things that made him marvelous,
he foolishly desired and was desired, sought
and was sought, burned with the love he felt
and was burned by it too.
Time after time he tried to kiss the face
he saw reflected on the cheating water.
Again and again he plunged his arms into the pool,
trying in vain to embrace the neck he saw.
Not realizing what he adored, he adored himself.
Foolish boy! Why did you seek in vain to
grasp a fleeting image?
That which you tried to hold was nowhere, nothing,
a phantom that vanished when you blinked your eyes.
Intangible, it had no existence of its own;
it came with you, stayed with you,
and would have left with you, too—
if you could have left.

Nothing could drag him from that place,
neither hunger nor thirst nor sleep.
He lay there on the grass, gazing endlessly
on the the false image with eyes that longed
but were left unsatisfied. Then, standing,
he raised his arms toward the surrounding trees
and cried, "Trees! Forest! Has there ever been
a love so cruel? Surely you know, for it is
deep within your shadows that lovers have
always found their hiding-places. Tell me,
in all your long centuries have you ever seen
anyone suffer as I am suffering?
I see, and love the one I see, but when I reach
to touch him he is not there.
No ocean lies between us, no long highway,
no towering mountain range or fortress walls.
Only a thin sheet of water keeps us apart,
and being so close to him makes my suffering worse.
He wants me too, I know, for each time I try
to kiss him through the clear water
he strains to meet my kiss with his own.
There is so little between us, I can't believe
that we cannot touch each other.

Listen to me, whoever you are, come out of there!
Why are you so elusive, beautiful boy?
Where do you go when I reach for you?
Does my age offend you? My looks?
That cannot be; nymphs have fallen in love
with me because I am young and handsome.
Besides, I see hope and friendship in your eyes.
When I reach for you, you try to embrace me as well.
You smile at me when I smile at you.
You weep when I weep, nod when I nod,
and when I speak I see your own lips moving,
though I've never heard the words you've spoken.

Wait! Now I understand!
The image on the water is my own!
I burn with love for myself, the flames I
feel fueled by my own beauty.
What should I do? Love? Be loved?
How can love even be possible when in myself
I already have the one I desire?
My wealth makes me poor!
If only I could leave my body!
And here is a strange wish from a lover:
If only my beloved would go away!
I am young, but this sorrow will soon kill me.
Death will take away my grief, and so I do not fear it,
though I wish the one I love might live.
But he will not: two lovers sharing a single soul
will die a single death.

Having said this he turned again to the pool
and stared like a madman at the face there,
but the tears he shed sent ripples across
the water and the image was disturbed.
He saw it fading and cried, "Don't go!
Don't leave me, cruel lover! We cannot touch,
but I can look at you, at least, and let
my madness feed on the sight of your face."
In agony, he ripped his tunic and with his
cold white fists he beat his chest until
it turned a rosy hue, like that of an apple
that is part red, part white,

or the deepening red of ripening grapes.
When the water stilled he saw his reflection again,
but now the sight was too much for him.
Just as wax melts before a fire
and morning frost turns to dew beneath the sun,
Narcissus slowly softened and melted away,
consumed by the love that burned within him.
Nothing remains of him now, no trace of his
rosy-white color, his vigor, his good looks
or the body that Echo had once loved.
She watched as he was dying, and though
she was still angry and resentful she wept for him.
Each time he cried "Alas!" she said the same,
and when he beat his chest she repeated those
small sounds of grief.
When, still staring into the water, he said,
"I loved you, beautiful boy, but in vain,"
those words, reverberating, filled the place.
And when at last he said, "Goodbye,"
Echo said "Goodbye" to him.
Then he laid his tired head upon the green grass
and death closed the bright eyes
that had once loved their master's beauty.
Below, in the underworld, Narcissus saw himself
in the waters of the Styx.
His sisters, the Naiads, wept and shaved their
heads for their beloved brother.
The Dryads mourned as well, and sad Echo
answered their sobs with her own.
They built a funeral pyre for him,
but when they set their torches to it
they saw that there was nothing left of him.
They found instead a flower whose golden center
was encircled by petals of purest white.

Instruction in Seduction: Ovid, *Art of Love* 1.35-175

The Roman poet Ovid (43 B.C.-18 A.D.) was one of the most popular poets of antiquity. Among his most famous works is the *Ars Amatoria* or *Art of Love,* a sophisticated guide to seduction in which the poet represents himself as the divinely appointed *praeceptor amoris,* or "professor of love." The first two books teach men how to find and keep a mistress while a third explains to women how to keep a man's affection. Ovid claimed that his instructions were meant for those intent on seducing only women of questionable virtue and therefore did not encourage immorality. Augustus, who was attempting to reform the morals of Rome, did not agree and sentenced him to banishment at Tomis on the west coast of the Black Sea, where he spent the rest of his life in exile.

First, my young soldier, my dear trainee,
you must strive to find
a girl you can really love.
Once you've found her you'll have to win
her heart, and then you'll want
to make sure your love will endure.
This is my subject, these are my limits,
this is the race I will run.
While you are single and on your own,
pick out the girl to whom you can say,
"You are the one I love!"
You'll have to look hard for her—
the girl of your dreams isn't going
to fall from heaven into your arms.
The hunter knows where to spread his nets
for the stag and the hidden places
where the wild boar lurks.
The fowler knows the bushes and thickets
and the fisherman the spots where
fish may be caught.
You, too, if you would find lasting love,

must learn where to find your prey.
I will not ask you to cross the sea.
No, a short walk will do.
It's true that Perseus found his dark
Andromeda in India, and Paris seized
Helen in faraway Greece,
but Rome boasts so many lovelies that
you'll find yourself exclaiming,
"All the world's beauty is right here!"
All the cornfields of Gargara, all of Methymna's
vineyards, all the fish of the sea, the
birds of the air, the stars of the sky,
all these are nothing next to the number of
girls in Rome.
Remember, this is Venus' town.
Do you like the really young ones just beginning
to bloom? We have more than you can handle.
Are ripe young women your desire? There are
thousands from which to choose.
Care for someone a bit older and wiser?
Believe me, we have whole battalions of *them*.
Here's the idea: When the sun is high stroll down
some shady colonnade—Pompey's, perhaps,
or Octavia's, dedicated to her dear departed Marcellus.
Livia's portico is a fine one, adorned by those
fine old paintings, and don't forget that of the Danaids,
those unhappy, murderous wives. . . .

Be sure not to overlook the races, for the
Circus is large and full of opportunities.
You won't need suggestive finger signals or
covert winks and nods, not in that crowd.
Go ahead, you can squeeze in next to any girl
you like. No one will stop you from getting
close to someone pretty in the seats at the track.
You'll need a good opening line.
Try asking her, "Whose horses are those?"—
and put money down on whatever horse she plays.
When the ivory images of the gods come by in
stately procession, clap and cheer for Venus,
Queen of Love.
It may happen that some dust will fall on

your girl's breast. If it does, lightly brush it away.
No dust? It doesn't matter. Brush it off anyway.
Don't let such a minor detail stop you.
If her cloak should touch the ground you should
reach down to rescue her hem. Your reward
may be a peek of ankle, or even knee.
Keep on eye on the man sitting behind you.
Don't let him press his knees into
her tender back.
Girls are easily swayed by such small attentions.
Plumping up her cushion will impress her,
and she'll be absolutely enchanted if you
fan her or slip a stool beneath her feet.
That's the way love happens at the track.

Trimalchio's Feast: Petronius, *Satyricon* 29–36

Although some scholars still question his identity, it is probable that the Petronius who wrote the *Satyricon* is identical with the Gaius Petronius described by Tacitus as a confidant of Nero who was later dismissed from the emperor's court and ordered to commit suicide. His *Satyricon,* which has been preserved only in fragmentary form, is a picaresque novel in which Petronius ridicules the new class of rich men who had risen from humble beginnings to challenge with their wealth the old Roman aristocracy. The novel recounts the adventures, mostly in southern Italy, of three disreputable freedmen: Encolpius (the narrator), Ascyltus and Giton. They run into trouble with the authorities, have love affairs and abandon themselves to a variety of other pleasures. Of the latter, the most famous is a feast at the home of Trimalchio, an ex-slave turned millionaire whose vulgar and ostentatious behavior are meant to exemplify the morals and manners of the *nouveaux riches* of the early Empire.

As I was staring in amazement at all this I almost fell backwards and broke my leg. There on the left side of the entrance to the colonnade, not far from the porter's station, was a painting of a huge dog with a chain around its neck. Over it in large letters was written:

BEWARE OF THE DOG

My friends laughed at me, but I pulled myself together and went over to look at the whole wall. On it was a mural of a slave market. There were slaves with prices posted above their heads; then Trimalchio himself, holding a white staff and being escorted into Rome by Minerva; then a painting of him studying accounting and yet another of Trimalchio as a steward. The artist had executed the work in great detail and with explanatory captions under each part of it. At the end of the colonnade Mercury was shown pulling Trimalchio up by the chin to a platform where Fortune sat with her overflowing cornucopia and the three Fates spinning their golden threads.

I also observed in the colonnade a number of runners practicing with their coach. There was a large cabinet in a corner which had been put to use as a shrine, for it held silver statues of the household gods, a marble image of Venus, and a marvelous gold box in which I was told were contained the first whiskers ever shaved from the master's face. I asked the porter about some of the other paintings and he told me that one depicted the *Iliad,* another the *Odyssey,* and another the gladiatorial games sponsored by Laenas.

We didn't have time to look at much else there, for by now we had arrived at the entrance to the dining room, where an accountant sat examining ledgers. Here I saw something I really liked: *fasces* [the symbols of magisterial authority] were fastened to each of the doorposts, and over the entrance was the inscription:

PRESENTED TO C. POMPEIUS TRIMALCHIO
PRIEST OF THE CULT OF AUGUSTUS
BY HIS STEWARD CINNAMUS

Beneath this same inscription hung two lamps, and there were two plaques, one on each doorpost. One of them said:

ON DECEMBER 30 AND 31
OUR GAIUS
WENT *OUT* TO DINNER

The other depicted the phases of the moon and the seven heavenly bodies. Studs of various colors marked lucky and unlucky days.

When we had seen enough of these interesting things we tried to walk into the dining room, but one of the slaves screamed: "Right foot first!" We stopped right away, of course, not wanting to enter the room in the wrong way. Then, trying again, we were stopped by another slave who threw himself at our feet and begged us to help him escape punishment by flogging. He said he hadn't done anythng seriously wrong: he had been guarding the steward's clothes at the baths when someone stole them—a loss of not even ten sesterces. We backed away again and went to ask the steward, who was counting gold, to forgive him. He raised his head in pompous fashion and said, "It's not that he lost anything truly valuable. It's just that the miserable creature is so damned careless. Those clothes were a birthday present from a client, a dinner outfit of genuine Tyrian purple. Of course, they *had* been worn and washed before, so what the heck? Go ahead, tell him he's off the hook."

We thanked him profusely for his kindness, and when we finally *did* enter the dining room the same slave ran over to us and, to our astonishment, covered us from head to toe with grateful kisses. "You'll soon know to whom you've been so kind." he said. "This waiter will make you a nice gift of the master's wine."

We finally took our places and immediately slaves from Alexandria attended us, pouring iced water on our hands. Others followed who took our feet and gave us pedicures. They were not silent as they performed this disagreeable work but sang the entire time. I found myself wondering if there might be other singers on the staff and, in order to find out, I asked for a drink. A boy promptly complied, singing in a shrill voice as he served me. And it turned out that every single slave who was asked to perform some service did so with a song. Thus, one had the impression of being at a musical comedy rather than in the dining room of a respectable man.

The slaves now brought in some extraordinarily fine *hors d'oeuvres,* for by this time all of us had taken our seats except Trimalchio. He had not yet appeared although, oddly enough, the place of honor had been reserved for him. One of the objects placed before us was a young donkey made of Corinthian bronze which sat on a large tray and carried two panniers on its back, one filled with green olives and the other with black ones. It was flanked by two pieces of plate with Trimalchio's name and the weight of their silver engraved on their rims. There were also some small iron frames shaped like bridges which held dormice seasoned with honey and poppy seed. Steaming-hot sausages were placed on a silver grill beneath which dark plums and red pomegranates were arranged in such a way as to give the impression of flames burning over charcoal.

As we were enjoying these elegant dishes Trimalchio was carried in to the sound of music and placed on a pile of well-stuffed pillows. It was such a comical scene that we almost laughed in spite of our efforts to keep silent. His cropped head protruded from a scarlet robe and around his well-muffled neck he had tucked a napkin with a broad purple stripe and dangling tassels. On the pinkie finger of his left hand he wore a huge gold ring. There was another, smaller one on his fourth finger which looked like solid gold but was actually studded with little iron stars. In order to show off even more of his jewelry, Trimalchio had bared his right arm and adorned it with a large gold bracelet and an ivory circlet fastened with glittering metal.

As he sat picking his teeth with a silver toothpick, Trimalchio spoke to his guests: "My friends, I'm not quite ready for dinner yet, but I don't want to make you wait any longer. So I've left my other amusements for your sake. But I hope you won't mind if I finish my game before I eat." Immediately a boy appeared with a board made of juniper wood and dice made of glass. I also noticed another touch of luxury: instead of the ordinary black and white game pieces, Trimalchio played with gold and silver coins. While he was absorbed in his playing, and we were still sampling the *hors d'oeuvres,* a tray was brought in with a basket on it. In the basket sat a hen carved from wood, her wings spread about her as though sitting on a brood. Two slaves ran up and, as the orchestra struck up a tune, they began searching the straw under her and digging out peahen's eggs, which they gave to the guests.

Trimalchio turned away from his game and said: "My friends, I gave an order for that bird to be set on some peahen's eggs. By Hercules, I hope they are not starting to hatch! Let's see if they are still soft enough to eat."

We picked up our "eggs," which were quite heavy and made of a thick, molded pastry, and cracked them. I would gladly have thrown mine away, for it seemed to me to have a well-formed chick in it. But I heard another guest who had been there before say that there would be something good inside. I felt inside with my fingers and found a delicate little birdie in the middle of a peppered yolk.

By this time Trimalchio had had enough of his game. He asked to be served all the dishes previously enjoyed by his guests and loudly offered everyone a cup of honeyed wine. Then, without warning, the orchestra blared and a troupe of singing waiters entered and cleared the dishes and *hors d'oeuvres* from the tables. In the ensuing confusion, however, a silver dish accidentally fell to the floor and was quickly picked up by a slave. Observing this incident, Trimalchio ordered that the boy's ears be boxed and the dish thrown back to the ground. Another slave came in with a broom and began to sweep up the dish and the rest of the mess. Two long-haired Ethiopians followed him carrying small leather bottles like those used to sprinkle sand at the circus. From these they poured wine over our hands. No one ever offered us water.

We enthusiastically complimented our host on these fine arrangements. "The god of war is fair," he said, "and so I gave instructions that each of my guests should have his own table. Besides, these smelly slaves will be less offensive if we don't sit so close together."

Wine bottles sealed with great care were then brought out to us. Around their necks hung labels which said:

GENUINE FALERNIAN WINE
BOTTLED IN THE CONSULSHIP OF OPIMIUS
ONE HUNDRED YEARS OLD

While we were reading the labels Trimalchio clapped his hands and exclaimed, "What a pity that a bottle of wine should live longer than a man! Let's drink, then, for wine is life, and I'm serving you real Opimian. I didn't serve stuff this good yesterday, when my guests had more class."

While we were drinking and enjoying this luxurious hospitality a slave came in carrying a silver skeleton which was constructed in such a way that its joints could be bent and turned in all directions. After he had dropped it on

162

the table and made it assume different postures by manipulating the joints, Trimalchio recited a poem he had composed:

> Our lives last but a brief span,
> So let's enjoy them while we can,
> For death will reduce us to this.

While we applauded his performance more food was brought in. Although this course was not as sumptuous as the previous one, it was so unusual that we couldn't take our eyes off it. It was served on a deep round tray whose edges were decorated with the twelve signs of the Zodiac. Over each of these was placed a delicacy related to the sign. There were butter beans over Aries the Ram, beef over Taurus the Bull, testicles and kidneys over the Twins, a garland over Cancer the Crab, an African fig over Leo the Lion, a sow's udder over Virgo the Virgin, a balancing scale with a tart in one pan and a cake in the other over Libra the Scales, a lobster over Scorpio, a bull's eye over Sagittarius the Archer, a fish with horns over Capricorn, a goose over Aquarius the water-bearer and two mullets over Pisces the Fishes. The center of the tray contained a honeycomb set on a bed of herbs arranged to look like grassy turf. A young Egyptian slave walked around serving bread from a silver oven and wailing a show tune from *The Asafaetida Man.*

Noticing that we were reluctant to eat this less elegant fare, Trimalchio said: "Come on, eat! These are only appetizers!" Instantly, four slaves rushed into the room. Dancing to a tune played by the orchestra, they removed the top of the tray and revealed another beneath it. In it lay fat fowls, sows' udders and a hare with wings attached to make it look like Pegasus. At its corners stood little gravy boats in the shape of the satyr Marsyas. From their phalli we poured streams of spicy sauce on fish which seemed to swim in a nearby "pond" on the tray. The slaves now began to applaud and we joined them as we turned with enthusiasm to the enjoyment of these exquisite delicacies. Trimalchio, who was as pleased as the rest of us by this ingenious display, now ordered a slave to come and carve. He stepped up promptly and began slicing the meat. His hands moved to the rhythm of the orchestra so that he gave the impression of a gladiator performing to the accompaniment of organ music while Trimalchio chanted insistently: "Carve -er, Carve -er, Carve -er!" I suspected that this repetition was an inside joke and so I asked the fellow sitting to my left for an explanation, since he had been there many times before. "The fellow doing the carving is named Carver," he said, "and so every time Trimalchio calls his name he is also telling him what to do: 'carve her.'"

Satire: Martial, *Epigrams*

Born and educated in Spain, Martial (*ca.* 40-104) spent the better part of his life in Rome where he gained recognition, though not wealth, as a writer of satirical epigrams. Because he was familiar with the whole of Roman society, from the imperial household down to the class of slaves, Martial was well qualified to comment on all of its peculiar features. His epigrams—delightful portraits of the rich and poor, the powerful and the helpless, the virtuous and the vile—give us an exciting and colorful glimpse of life in ancient Rome.

1.1

Here I am,
the one you read,
the one you ask for.
It's me, Martial,
known throughout the
world for my clever
little books of epigrams.
While I live and breathe
my learned readers honor
me with a glory few poets
enjoy even long after
they have turned to dust.

1.32

I don't like you, Sabidius,
though I'm not sure why.
I only know that I just
don't like you.

2.38

Here, Linus, in case you'd like
to know, is what I like best
about my farm: whenever I am
there, you are not.

2.80

Fannius committed suicide
in order to escape his enemies.
Is it crazy, or isn't it,
to die in order to avoid being killed?

3.14

Tuccius, starving, set out
for Rome from Spain,
but hearing how small the
grain dole was he
went back home again.

3.61

Cinna, you clod, you say you're
not asking me for much.
All right then, it's not much
I'm refusing you.

4.12

Thais, you're not ashamed that
you never say no to anyone.
Be, at least, ashamed of this:
that you never say no to any*thing.*

4.24

Lycoris seems to outlive
all her friends.
I wish she'd get to know
my wife.

4.49

Believe me, Flaccus,
anyone who says that epigrams
are nothing more than silly
little verses doesn't know
what he's talking about.
What's really silly are
those poems about the horrid

banquets of Tereus and Thyestes
(who ate their own children),
Icarus and his melting wings,
and the Cyclops and his Sicilian sheep.
You won't find such long-winded
foolishness in any of my poems.
My Muse doesn't go in for
that kind of tragic schlock.
Still, as the saying goes,
"All men praise these works,
marvel at them, adore them."
And its true—they praise them,
but they *read* mine!

5.73

You ask, Theodorus, why I never send you
copies of my books, though you're always
begging me to see them. For good reason:
I'm afraid you'll send me some of yours!

5.9

I was feeling ill, and so Symmachus
the physician made a house call to see me.
He had a bunch of medical students in tow,
and every one of them gave me the once
over with ice-cold hands.
Before you came by I was ill, Symmachus,
but now I'm *sick*.

5.83

The poor will always be poor,
Aemilianus, only the rich prosper.

6.31

Charidemus, you know that your wife's
been doing it with the family doctor,
and yet you don't say a thing.
You must not want to die of natural causes.

You're a fink and a liar,
a cheat and a pimp.
You're a pervert and a lousy
gladiator trainer, too.
I don't get it, Vacerra:
how come you aren't rich?

Downtown Rome: Juvenal, *Satire* 3

Juvenal, perhaps the greatest of the Roman satiric poets, flourished in the early years of the second century A.D. We know very little about him aside from the few autobiographical details he included in his poems and some brief references to him in the epigrams of his friend Martial. These suggest that he lived as an impoverished and virtually unrecognized poet who did not begin publishing his work until he had reached middle age. Tradition says that as a youth he was banished for mocking a court official, perhaps by Domitian whom he clearly despised.

Juvenal wrote with an angry pen, attacking with bitterness and derision all the peoples and practices that made Rome a city he could not love. Bribery, sycophancy, poverty, soldiers, women, homosexuals, gluttons, nobles, Greeks, Syrians, Egyptians—all of these were among the objects of the poet's scorn. Many were his targets in his third satire, which appears below.

Though saddened by the departure of my old friend,
I have to hand it to him for
deciding to move to Cumae and raise by one
the population of the Sibyl's town.
Ah, Cumae! Gateway to Baiae, a charming retreat
on a pleasant shore.
Why, I myself would prefer a desert isle off that coast
to a street in downtown Rome.
Where could we ever find a place more miserable,
more lonely than Rome?
Rome, where we live in unending dread of fires
and collapsing roofs and a thousand other perils,
where poets never stop mouthing their verses
all through the hot, dead days of August.

While they load his things on a little wagon,
my friend waits by the Porta Capena,
that dripping gate beneath the ancient aqueduct
where old king Numa used to come by night
to meet his goddess.
But now the place

(sacred spring, grove, shrine and all)
is rented out to Jews with nothing but baskets
stuffed with straw for furniture.
Yes, these days even the trees have to pay their way,
and so the Muses have been evicted from their grove
to make room for swarms of low-rent beggars.

Let's go down, then, into the valley of Egeria
and its artificial caves.
How much closer to us might the water nymph be
if her fountain were edged by sweet green grass
instead of this unnatural polished marble!
It was here that my friend Umbricius explained
the reasons for his leaving:

"Since there's no room in this city for an honest man,
no reward for his labor,
because I am poorer today than I was yesterday,
and will have even less tomorrow,
I'm leaving, by God, for Cumae,
where the weary Daedalus finally came to rest his wings.
I'm going while my white hairs are still new
and before I've become stooped with old age,
while Fate still has time left to give me
and I can walk without a cane.
Goodbye Rome, my homeland!
Artorius and Catalus can have you,
and all the rest who remain can go on
making a profit from their black work,
grabbing those easy government contracts
for building temples, maintaining rivers and harbors,
flushing sewers, hauling corpses off to the pyre
and selling slaves.
They're the ones who used to toot their horns
in the road shows, puffing their cheeks
in every town and village.
But nowadays they put on shows of their own,
slaughtering anyone on whom the happy crowd turns thumbs
down and then going off to part-time jobs cleaning toilets.
There's nothing they won't do. Why should there be?
They're the sort Lady Luck pulls out of the gutter
just for laughs.

"What is there for me to do in Rome, anyway?
I'm not a liar; if a book is awful I can't praise
it and beg for a copy.
I'm not an astrologer; I could never predict
for some eager heir the date of his father's demise.
I've never been able to find meaning in frog guts,
and I'll leave to others the job of bringing a wife
gifts and notes from her lover.
I can't condone stealing, so no governor would be
willing to put me on his staff.
Here in Rome I'm useless and unwanted.
To be a success here you've got to be a party
to some dirty business, your soul filled with
burning secrets that must never be told.
No one who confides something harmless
will ever think he owes you anything or give you
even the tiniest gift to keep you quiet,
but a grafter like Verres will show his appreciation
to anyone he knows can turn him in whenever he likes.
Never let the gold that the shady Tagus sweeps down
to the sea become so important that for its sake
you lose sleep over favors you must one day return
or the fact that you are always a threat to
your dangerous friend.

"Now, let me say something about a people our
rich men love but whom I try my best to avoid.
I'm not ashamed to say it:
I can't stand a Rome full of Greeks!
Of course, our city's scum is made of more than Greeks.
For years the Syrian Orontes has been pouring
into the Tiber, dumping its lingo and its manners,
its flutes and harps, tambourines,
and those girls who sell themselves at the Circus.
(Do you like whores wearing painted hats?
Then this is the place!)
These days, Romulus, even your country-bumpkins
think they're Greek, sporting Greeky dinner jackets
trimmed with decathlon medals and wearing
eau de underarm fresh from the gym.
The Greeks themselves come flooding in:
one from high Sicyon, another from Amydon or Andros,

and others still from Samos, Tralles and Alabanda.
They all head for the Esquiline Hill
and the *Mons Viminalis,* worming their way
into the houses of the wealthy in hopes of
one day becoming their masters.
They're quick-witted and impudent, ready with
more slick talk than Isaeus himself could spout.
Look at that fellow over there!
His profession is being whatever you want him to be:
grammarian, orator, geometrician, painter, trainer,
soothsayer, rope-dancer, doctor, magician—
a hungry Greek will do anything.
Tell him to fly and off he goes!
Think of Daedalus. Was he African? Sarmatian?
Thracian? No, he was a Greek born
in the very heart of Athens!

"Why should I be forced out
of my own hometown by these purple-robed dandies?
Is some easterner blown here by the same oriental wind
that brings us our prunes and figs going to sign
his name before mine and lie upon a softer couch?
Does it count for nothing that I was here first,
that as a baby I drank in the Aventine air
and was nourished by Sabine olives?

"The Greeks are master sycophants;
they praise the talk of idiots
and compliment the ugly on their beauty.
They compare the skinny necks of weaklings
to the muscle of Hercules and enthuse
over a singing voice so bad it sounds like
the squawking of a lovesick rooster.
We could try to praise such things,
but we'd never be believed.
What actor could outperform a Greek
in mimicking Thais, a wife, or a naked Doris?
Who would believe it's really a masked actor speaking
and not the woman he's pretending to be?
Yet back home in Greece even the best of them—
Antiochus, Stratocles, Demetrius and Haemus—
could never win a round of applause.

Why? They'd never be noticed, since
everyone is an actor in Greece.
Smile, and your fawning Greek will split his sides
with laughter.
Cry, and he will gush rivers of insincere tears.
Say you're a bit chilly in midwinter and
he'll put on his cloak.
Tell him you're hot and he'll break into a sweat.
We never meet on even terms, he and I;
he always has the advantage
since he's ready day and night to put on
whatever expression he thinks will
be most gratifying to his patron
if the old boy manages to belch nicely,
or piss straight, or drain the contents of
his golden cup in just one breath.

"While I'm on the subject of Greeks,
let's not forget their professors of philosophy
and the crimes they commit under cover of
cap and gown.
I'm thinking of Egnatius the Stoic,
a Hellene born on the banks of the Cydnus,
who, by informing on Barea, ensured
the murder of his friend and disciple.
No, there's no room in this town for
a respectable Roman, not when some Protogenes,
Diphilus or Hermarchus is in charge,
someone who, like all Greeks, is genetically
disinclined to admitting outsiders
into his circle of friends.
Once he has put a drop of Greek poison
into his patron's ear a Roman like me
gets booted out the back door.
Nowhere is it so easy to dump
an old and faithful client.

"Let's not flatter ourselves: a poor man's
labor isn't worth a dime here in Rome,
not even if he's up and dressed in his toga
and on his way to work before dawn
when the praetor is ordering his lictor to run

to the homes of Albina and Modia,
lest some colleague be the first to send his
greetings to those childless and early-rising ladies.
Here in Rome the sons of citizens must give way
before the slaves of the rich,
for they will happily surrender a tribune's pay
to pant atop an aristocratic Calvina or Catiena
while you, if you like the face
of some for-sale floozy, are too enervated by poverty
to ask her down from her chair.
Bring to court in Rome a witness as famed
for his honesty as Scipio, Numa or Metellus
and the first question will be about money
('How many slaves does he own? acres? dessert dishes?')
and the last about character.
A man's credibility rises in proportion
to the amount of cash he has in his strongbox.
A poor man can swear his oath on every altar
from here to Samothrace and they still won't believe him:
'Why should someone with nothing to lose fear the anger
of gods falsely sworn by?'

"If you're poor you're a joke.
They laugh if your cloak is torn and dirty
or if your toga is smudged.
It's funny if your shoes are coming apart
or if they see patches covering the holes.
The worst thing about poverty is
that it makes us the objects of ridicule.
'Get back to the cheap seats!' the ushers shout,
pulling you out of those reserved for *equites*
and making room there for the moneyed sons
of pimps and auctioneers, gladiators and trainers.
It was that brainless Otho's idea that we
should be seated according to our wealth.
And what man ever wins the approval of his prospective
father-in-law if he has less cash than his fiancée?
What poor man ever finds himself heir to a fortune
or is hired as special assistant to an aedile?
We poor Romans should have left town long ago!

"It's hard for a man to rise to the top
when poverty stands in his way,
and nowhere harder than here in Rome.
In Rome they charge you a fortune to rent
the most miserable apartment,
and just as much to fill even the little bellies
of your skinny slaves.
With what you've got left you can only afford
to put scraps upon your plain earthenware dishes.
You're ashamed of them now,
but they would do you proud if suddenly
you found yourself living out in the countryside
where a man is happy with a cloak
of coarse Venetian blue.

"It's true that in most of Italy a man never wears
a toga until he's laid out for burial.
On festival days, when a grassy field
is theater enough for staging a favorite play
and a rustic babe nursing at his mother's breast
is frightened by the gaping mouths
of the actors' pallid masks,
you will see the country folk all dressed alike,
from the front row to the back,
and even the venerable aediles content to wear
tunics of plain white.
But here in Rome we dress ultra chic,
beyond our means and always on credit.
Trying to get ahead, our ambition
leads us into poverty.
No one can deny that everything has its price
in Rome—patrons included:
how much must you pay for the privilege
of greeting Cossus?
how much will it set you back to get
a silent nod from Veiento?
The first sits there getting a shave,
the latter is busy at the altar, dedicating
a lock of his boyfriend's hair.
The great man's house is full of cakes,
but though you're a guest in your patron's home
you'll have to pay for them.

Even your patron's slaves expect a tip
for granting you access to their master's ear.

What resident of cool Praeneste,
or of the wooded Volsinian hills
who in quaint Gabii, what dweller on Tivoli's heights
has ever feared that his house would collapse?
But we Romans live in a city held upright
by the sticks the landlords use
to prop up their tottering tenements
and patch the cracks in their walls,
all the while telling us to sleep soundly
though the beams above our heads are rotten.
I don't enjoy the fires and nightly alarms:
down below your neighbor is calling for water
and moving out his few possessions,
while smoke is already billowing out
of the third story windows,
but you don't know it,
for when the alarm begins on the first floor
the last to know is the man who lives
up in the attic with the nesting doves
and has nothing but roof tiles to keep out the rain.
It happened to Codrus, who roomed up there
sleeping in a bed too small for a midget
and owning nothing more than a cupboard
with six mugs and a pitcher,
a statue of Chiron reclining,
and an old chest full of Greek books
whose inspired pages had been gnawed by barbaric mice.
Codrus had nothing, it's true,
and yet he managed to lose it all.
But the worst part of his misery is this:
although he is destitute and begging for a meal,
no one will give him the favor
of a bite to eat or a roof over his head.

"But if wealthy Asturicus' mansion burns down
you'll find the whole city outraged by the disaster.
The women tear their hair, the nobles wear black,
and the praetors adjourn their courts.
Even before the flames have died

someone shows up with a gift of marble or money,
someone else brings statues, polished and white,
and yet another donates a masterpiece
by Euphranor or Polyclitus
or perhaps an ornament from some Asian temple.
Others give books and bookshelves,
busts of Minerva and silver coin.
This is how the rich man replaces what he has lost
with more and finer things than those
he had before the fire.
Is it any wonder that some suspect
he struck the match himself?

"If you can tear yourself away
from the games at the Circus you can
buy a house in Sora, Fabrateria or Frusino
for what you now pay in Rome to rent
a dark hole for just a year.
Out there in the country you'll have
a little garden and a shallow well
with so much water that you won't need a rope
to fill a bucket for your thirsty plants.
In the country your hoe will be your friend,
and you'll have a garden fit to feast
a hundred vegetarians.
You'll have accomplished something
even if you become nothing more than the master
of one little lizard out there in the boondocks.

"Here in Rome the sick usually die
from lack of sleep.
The food that lies undigested in
their burning stomachs makes them weary,
but who can sleep in a tenement house?
Only the rich can afford a place to sleep.
And that's the problem.
Even a sleepy Drusus or a drowsy sea-calf
would be kept wide-awake by the noise
of the carts rumbling in the narrow streets
and the shouting of the angry drivers
when traffic comes to a standstill.
When a rich man on some business errand

comes along the crowd makes way for him to pass by,
borne high above them in his roomy Liburnian litter.
Inside he can read, write, or even enjoy a catnap
behind the closed window curtains.
And he'll get to his destination before we do,
no matter how we hurry, for we find ourselves
blocked and pressed on every side by the surging throng.
Someone jabs me with an elbow, another pokes me
with a sedan chair pole.
On one side a beam strikes me,
on the other a wine cask bangs my head.
My legs are caked with the thick mud of the street,
strangers trample on my feet and a soldier
grinds his hobnails down on my toe.

"Look at that cloud of smoke
and the clients beneath it,
pushing and shoving to get
their daily handout.
There are a hundred of them,
and each has brought a kitchen slave
loaded down with more pots and pans
than mighty Corbulo himself could carry.
The poor little fellows have to run about the braziers
to fan the flames that warm today's dole.
In the crowd newly-mended tunics are ripped again,
and danger looms as mammoth wagonloads
of fir and pine roll by,
the tottering logs promising death to the people.
What will happen if an axle breaks
beneath that load of Ligurian marble,
dumping a mountain of stone upon the crowd?
What will be left of their bodies?
Who will identify the limbs and bones?
The broken body of a common man disappears
along with his soul.
Meanwhile, back at home, his unwitting household
prepares for his return with the dole,
washing dishes, blowing on the fire,
making a racket with the greasy strigils,
filling the oil flasks and
laying out the towels.

177

While the slaves rush about attending to their tasks
their master is already sitting beside the Styx,
shivering in terror before the ferryman.
But the poor wretch has no hope of ever crossing
the muddy current since he has no copper coin
in his mouth to pay for his passage.

"Consider the many dangers of nighttime in Rome.
Broken pots and leaking jars tossed from high windows
and rooftops come crashing down upon your head
and gashing the pavement.
Only a reckless fool would go out to dinner
without having first made his will,
since each night there's a death for every open window.
You can only hope and pray that the tenement-dwellers
will be content to drop nothing worse than
the rotting contents of their garbage pails.

"Watch out, too, for the ornery drunk
who suffers through the night
because he hasn't had a chance to kill.
Like Achilles mourning his friend,
he tosses back and forth in restless sleep,
unable to find peace until he's
slugged it out in a good brawl.
And yet, no matter how hot and rash
he may be with youth and wine,
he'll always steer clear of the
scarlet-cloaked nobleman who passes by
with a bodyguard bearing torches and brass lamps
that warn him to stay away.
But I have only moonlight to guide me home,
or perhaps the small radiance of a sputtering lamp.
The drunk has nothing but contempt for me,
and so the fight begins
(if something so one-sided can be called a fight).
He blocks my way and tells me to stop.
I do what he says.
What other choice have I got?
He's crazy, and much stronger than I am.
'Where are you from?' he demands.
'Whose cheap wine and beans are

in that bloated gut of yours?
What cobbler's been feeding you chopped leeks
and boiled sheep's jowl?
You'd better answer me, punk,
or I'll jog your tongue with a kick in the shin.
Where do you hang out, anyway?
In some synagogue, I'll bet!'
It doesn't matter whether you answer him or not,
he's going to beat you to a pulp either way.
And then he'll take *you* to court for assault and battery!
That's a poor man's freedom for you:
beaten and cut, he has the right to beg
for permission to go home with a few teeth
left in his head.

"And there are other nighttime terors in Rome.
You can lock up your house and secure
your shop with bars and chains,
but the burglars will get past them and rob you
or some thug will creep in and slit your throat.
When the police are patrolling the Pontine marshes
and the Gallinarian woods
the criminal scum who live there run to safety
in Rome, as if it is their sanctuary.
There's not a furnace or anvil in town
that doesn't groan from the labor
of forging chains for them.
Most of our iron, in fact, ends up as chains,
and it may be that soon we will have none left
for plowshares, hoes and mattocks.
You would be right to say that the happiest of Romans
were those of our ancestors who lived
in the good old days when Rome was governed
by kings and tribunes and was well-served
by a single jail.

"I could give you a hundred other reasons why
I'm leaving, but I have to go.
My cattle are lowing, the sun is sinking,
and my mule-driver is signalling me with his whip.
Goodbye. Please don't forget me.
And if someday you should escape from Rome

to visit Aguinum, your hometown,
I hope you'll send for me.
I'll come to your country wearing my thick boots,
ready to hear your satires if they deem me
worthy of the honor.

IV
Religion

Sacrifices: Cato the Elder, *On Agriculture*, 139–141.

In his treatise *On Agriculture* Marcus Cato (234-149 B.C.), described the religious rites which Roman landowners performed as part of their practice of agriculture. Because the Romans believed that spirits inhabited the land and all that grew there, they sought to give these entities proper recognition. Thus, as the first portion of the excerpt below indicates, it was necessary to make an offering to the proper spirit when thinning a grove. Cato also describes the ritual for purifying land. This involved leading a procession of sacrificial animals around the area. The Latin name for this procession, *suovetaurilia*, is derived from *sus* (pig), *ovis* (sheep) and *taurus* (bull).

When you thin out a grove of trees you should perform the following Roman ritual. Sacrifice a pig and repeat this prayer: "Whether this grove is dedicated to a god or goddess, it is your right, deity, to receive a pig in compensation for the thinning of this sacred grove. For this reason I pray that the sacrifice will be performed correctly, whether I do it or someone whom I have appointed. I humbly pray that in return for this sacrifice you will be good to me and look kindly on me, my house, my family and my children. To this end, receive this pig which I offer you."

If you want to till your field, offer the same sacrifice again and add these words: "for the sake of doing this work." This ritual must be done each day you plow and in the part of the field in which you are working. If you miss a day, or if some public or private holy day should prevent the performance of the ritual, you must perform it later.

Here is the ritual for purifying land. Order the *suovetaurilia* to be led around the area and say these words: "In order that with the help of the gods our work will be successful, I order you, Manius [*i.e.,* probably the name of the landowner's slave or overseer], to purify this land by driving or carrying the *suovetaurilia* around whatever portion of the land you think best." Say a prayer and pour a libation of wine to Janus and Jupiter. Then say this prayer: "Father Mars, I pray that you will be good to me and look kindly on me, my house and my family. To this end, I have ordered this *suovetaurilia* to be led around my field, my land, and my farm. Save us from diseases visible and invisible, ward off barrenness and desolation and protect us from disasters and violence. Let my crops, my grain and my large vineyards be abundant. Keep my shepherds and my sheep healthy, and give good health to me, my family and all who live in my house. For these reasons, for the purpose of purifying my farm, all my land, and of making an expiatory sacrifice, please accept these suckling animal victims, a pig, a sheep, and a calf. Father Mars, for these reasons accept this offering of a suckling *suovetaurilia*." Arrange the sacrificial cakes and the oblation cake, and then sacrifice the victims with a knife. When you sacrifice the pig, the lamb and the calf use these words: "For these reasons accept the sacrifice of this pig, lamb and calf." . . . If the victims do not yield favorable omens say this: "Father Mars, if for some reason you were not pleased with this sacrifice I offer you this new sacrifice as atonement for the first one." If there is some doubt about [the acceptability of] one or two of the animals, say these words: "Father Mars, since you were not pleased with that pig, I offer you this pig as atonement."

Divination: Livy, *History*, 8.9 and Suetonius, *Tiberius* 2

Much of Roman religion was based upon the belief that the gods revealed their will through various signs which could be read by those trained in the art of divination. Most Romans, and the government of Rome itself, made certain that the omens were favorable before beginning any serious undertaking.

Before the consuls led their soldiers into battle they offered up a sacrifice. The diviner who inspected the internal organs explained to Decius that the upper portion of the liver was lying in the correct position and that it was clear that the gods had found the sacrifice acceptable. He also said that Manlius, the other consul, had also received good omens. Decius replied, "Well then, if my colleague is satisfied then so am I." They then entered the battle . . . with Manlius commanding the right wing and Decius the left.

*

Claudius the Fair, when he was consul, took the auspices just before a naval battle off the coast of Sicily. When he discovered that the sacred chickens would not eat their feed he shouted, "If they won't eat then let them drink!" and fought the battle anyway. He lost.

Vestal Virgins: Aulus Gellius, *Attic Nights* 12

> The cult of Vesta, goddess of the hearth fire, was an important one in Rome, for the Romans recognized the importance of the hearth, home and family life. In fact, the temple of Vesta was a round stone building whose shape was clearly intended to recall the round huts in which the earliest Romans lived. Vesta was served by the Vestal Virgins, six priestesses who presided over her cult for terms of thirty years. During this period they were required to remain chaste, the punishment for unchastity being entombment while alive.
>
> The following excerpt from the second-century writer Aulus Gellius focuses on the criteria considered in the selection of a Vestal and offers an explanation of the old Roman saying that a new priestess was "taken" by the Pontifex Maximus. The references to the "emancipation" of the young girl refer to her passing from the state of being under the control of her father.

Those who have written about the "taking" of a Vestal Virgin, and of these the best is Antistius Labeo, have said that it is illegal for a girl younger than six or older than ten to be selected. In addition, both of the girl's parents must be living, she must not have any defects in her speech or hearing, nor should she have any physical impairments whatsoever. Moreover, such a girl should still be under the control of her father or, if she was born before her father had left his own father's house, she should still be under the control of her grandfather. Neither of her parents may have been slaves or engaged in any degrading form of work. . . .

When a Vestal Virgin has been chosen, taken to the House of Vesta and presented to the priests, she then and there leaves her father's control without the usual ceremony of emancipation or the loss of her civil rights and acquires the right to make her own will.

It is true that there are no good texts which describe the means and rituals involved in the selection of a Vestal, although it has been recorded that the first was chosen by King Numa. The Papian Law, however, provides that twenty maidens should be selected under the supervision of the Pontifex Maximus, that one of these should be selected by lot in the assembly, and that that girl should be "taken" by the Pontifex Maximus and be made a priestess of Vesta.

This practice of choosing a Vestal by lot is not often necessary these days, however, since if men of good birth go to the Pontifex Maximus and offer to give their daughters to the priesthood, then, as long as their candidacies do not violate any religious law or precedent, the Senate will suspend the Papian law.

It appears that a new Vestal is said to be "taken" because the Pontifex Maximus takes her by the hand and leads her away from the parent under whose control she has lived—just as if she had been captured in a war. The first book of Fabius Pictor's *History* contains the words which the Pontifex Maximus is supposed to say at this moment. They are: "I take you, Amata ["beloved"], as one who is legally qualified to be a priestess of Vesta and therefore entitled to undertake the sacred duties which it is lawful for a Vestal Virgin to perform on behalf of the Roman people."

Greek Gods Come to Rome: Livy, *History* 5.13

Beginning in the fourth century B.C. the influence of foreign religions in Rome increased steadily. At first the worship of new deities was restricted to the *Graecus ritus* (Greek ritual), but this paved the way for the later introduction of newer and stranger cults from Egypt, Syria, Asia Minor and other parts of the Empire. The earliest report of Greek ritual being performed in Rome concerns the introduction of the *lectisternium*, a public offering of a sacred meal to images of deities placed on special couches.

For some reason, possibly the sudden change from extreme cold to extreme heat, the severe winter [of 399 B.C.] was followed by a summer so hot that conditions were unhealthy. Disease was everywhere, and neither human beings nor animals were immune. No one was able to discover the origins of this plague or find a cure which would put an end to its awful effects, and so the Senate voted to consult the Sibylline Books. As a result, the two officials in charge of such matters celebrated the first *lectisternium* ever held in Rome. For eight days images of Apollo, Latona, Diana, Hercules, Mercury and Neptune received sacrifices as they lay on couches which were set up outside and draped and decorated as beautifully and luxuriously as the times allowed. Meanwhile, similar ceremonies were performed by people inside their homes. They say that throughout the city people left their doors wide open and allowed friends and strangers alike to come in and eat as much as they wished, friendly conversations were heard among men who were known enemies, and no one quarreled or brought another to court. Even the prisoners were set free, and by the time the ritual was over it didn't seem appropriate to send back to prison men who had been helped and befriended by the gods.

The Suppression of Foreign Religions in Rome: Suetonius, *Tiberius* 36.

The government of Rome was generally tolerant of the practice of a large number of religions. At the same time, however, it regarded the worship of Rome's traditional gods as a sign of patriotism and loyalty to the state. The monotheism of the Jews and their consequent refusal to worship any god other than their own often excited suspicion and resentment. Cults from Egypt and other parts of the East were also frequently regarded as subversive. The following excerpt from Suetonius' biography of Tiberius describes the action which that emperor took against them.

The emperor Tiberius suppressed foreign cults in Rome, especially the cults of the Jews and the Egyptians, and forced those who had embraced these superstitions to burn their religious vestments and other paraphernalia. He assigned Jewish youths of military age to provinces with the most unhealthy climates, and those who were too old or too young to serve (Jews and non-Jewish cultists alike) he banished from the city, threatening them with slavery if they defied his decree. He also expelled the astrologers, although he forgave those who asked his pardon and promised not to cast more horoscopes.

The Cult of Isis: Apuleius, *Metamorphoses*, 11.22–24

One of the most popular of the mystery religions was the cult of Isis, a goddess worshiped in Egypt long before the rise of Rome. Most of its rituals were mysteries known only to her devotees, who believed that immortality was one of the benefits conferred on them by their initiation. One of our best sources for the worship of Isis is the *Metamorphoses* or *The Golden Ass* of Lucius Apuleius, a second-century convert to the cult. In this romantic tale Apuleius describes how he was turned into an ass by a witch and eventually regained his human form through the grace of the goddess, whom he thanked by becoming an initiate and later a priest in her cult. The excerpt below illustrates the initiation rite and the concern for secrecy that surrounded it.

I obeyed the orders which the priest had given me and performed my daily duties in the temple as calmly and patiently as I could, for I wished to prove myself to the goddess. She did not subject me to a long and arduous trial, but soon after this demonstrated her grace by appearing to me in a vision in the dead of night and telling me in plain language that the day I had longed for had come at last. She gave me some details concerning the initiation rites and told me that she had chosen her High Priest Mithras, whose destiny was linked to my own by the alignment of the planets, to assist me at my initiation.

I was so thrilled by these and certain other words spoken by the goddess that I rose before dawn and went to tell the High Priest, whom I encountered just as he was leaving his room. I greeted him and was ready to beg him again, but now with the courage of one to whom a favor is due, to let me be initiated, when he spoke first. "Dear Lucius," he said, "how happy and blessed you are, you whom the goddess has chosen to honor in this way. Why are you just standing there? There is no time to waste! This is the day you prayed for. Today the many-named goddess has commanded me to induct you into her most holy mysteries."

With that the old man took me by the hand and politely led me to the doors of the great temple, which he opened with great solemnity. After performing the morning sacrifice he went into the sanctuary and brought out a number of books written in characters I had never seen before. Some were animal-shaped hieroglyphics, others were ordinary letters whose tops and tails were wreathed like vines' tendrils in circles around them in order to prevent profane people from reading them. From these books he read me the instructions concerning the clothes and other accessories I would need for my initiation. I went immediately to some of my friends and asked them to buy part of what I needed, and to spare no expense. The rest I bought myself.

In due time the High Priest and a crowd of cultic functionaries escorted me to the local public baths. There he prayed for the blessing of the gods, washed me, and purified me with a sprinkling of holy water. By then it was early afternoon. He led me back to the temple, where he presented me to the goddess by placing me at the feet of her statue. He whispered a few words to me—secrets too sacred to be spoken out loud—and then ordered me in a loud voice to abstain from meat and wine for the next ten days.

I obeyed his instructions to the letter. As the sun set on the day before my initiation a throng of priests came to me from every direction, each of them giving me presents and congratulations according to their ancient custom. When they had finished the High Priest commanded all those who had not been initiated into the mysteries to leave, presented me with a new linen robe and led me into the most secret and holy part of the temple.

Perhaps you would like to know, dear reader, the things that were said and done there. Believe me, I would quickly satisfy your curiosity if I were allowed to tell you and you were allowed to listen. But we are not allowed, and our indiscretion would mean suffering both for my tongue and your ears.

And yet I don't want to leave you in suspense, which would be torturous if you are religiously inclined, and so I will tell you what I can provided that you promise to believe me: I approached the very gates of Hades, even as far as the threshold of Proserpine, and then I returned here, transported through all the elements. I saw the sun shining brightly at midnight, I saw the gods of heaven and the gods of hell, I came near to them and worshiped them.

So, now you know. There's nothing more I can say to the uninitiated, and you must keep secret even the little I have told you.

The solemn rites ended at dawn and I came forth from the sanctuary sanctified by the twelve sacred stoles I wore (and which I may mention since a great many uninitiated people saw me wearing them). The High Priest then ordered me to stand upon a wooden pulpit which stood directly in front of the goddess' statue in the middle of the temple. I was wearing a gown of fine linen embroidered with flowers, and from my shoulders to my ankles hung a beautiful cloak on which were depicted in various colors beasts such as Indian serpents and Hyperborean griffins, winged lions which come from the far-off limits of the world. The priests call this cloak an Olympian stole. In my right hand I carried a lighted torch and on my head I wore a garland of flowers with white palm leaves sticking out all around it like rays of light.

And so I was dressed like the sun. I had been concealed by curtains, but now these were suddenly pulled aside, as at the unveiling of a statue, to reveal me to the crowd. I consider that day my spiritual birthday, and I celebrated it feasting with my friends. More ceremonies and a religious breakfast followed on the third day, when the proceedings were concluded. I remained there for several days, however, finding great pleasure and consolation in merely gazing upon the image of the goddess, for she had honored me with blessings I could never hope to repay.

Caligula and the Jews: Josephus, *Jewish War* 2.184–7, 192–203

In 39-40 A.D. the emperor Gaius (Caligula) nearly provoked a rebellion of the Jews of Judea by ordering that his statue should be placed in the Temple in Jerusalem. This amounted to a gross offense against the religious sensibilities of the Jews who, as strict monotheists, could not tolerate what the emperor intended. Josephus' account of the matter offers us portraits of a thoughtless emperor, a conscientious Roman governor (Petronius) and a people completely committed to its traditional religious beliefs and values.

The emperor Gaius [Caligula] defied fortune with an arrogance beyond measure. He wanted to be considered a god and to be hailed as such, he destroyed many of the promising young men of the aristocracy, and his impiety reached even as far as Judea. In fact, he sent Petronius to Jerusalem with orders to place statues of himself in the Temple there and, if any of the Jews tried to resist him, to put them to death and sell the entire nation into slavery. But God would have a hand in these matters, as future events would show. Petronius took three legions and a large force of Syrian auxiliaries and marched from Antioch toward Judea. . . .

The Jews gathered with their wives and children on the plain of Ptolemais and pleaded with Petronius to reconsider his intentions out of respect for the laws of their ancestors and, if that did not move him, for their own persons. Giving in for the moment to the pleas of this great multitude, Petronius left the statues and his troops at Ptolemais and went into Galilee where he called upon the people, and especially men of distinction, to meet with him at Tiberias. There he reminded them emphatically of the power of Rome, the emperor's threats and the danger of their request. He told them that there were statues of Caesar in the cities of all the other subject states, along with those of their other gods, and that their resistance amounted to insult and rebellion.

When the Jews claimed that their ancestral law and customs prohibited them from placing an image of God, not to mention the image of a man, not only in their Temple but even in any unconsecrated place in their entire country, Petronius replied, "But I must obey the law of my master; if I disobey him I will be executed, as I should be, and the one who sent me will make war on you. Both of us are under orders." Having heard this the multitude cried out that they were prepared to suffer anything for the sake of their law. Petronius asked for quiet and then asked, "Will you go to war against Caesar?" The Jews answered that they offered two sacrifices each day for Caesar and the Roman people, but that if Caesar truly intended to set up these statues he would first have to sacrifice the entire Jewish nation. They were ready, they said, to present themselves, their wives and their children to be slaughtered. The absolute devotion of these people to their faith and their sincere willingness to die for it filled Petronius with wonder and pity. And so, for the time being, he dismissed them with the issue left undecided.

In the days that followed he met privately with many of the aristocrats and also with the people in public. During these meetings he sometimes begged them, often advised them, but mostly threatened them, reminding them of the power of the Romans, the anger of Gaius, and the fact that he would be forced by circumstances to carry out his orders. The Jews, however, were unmoved, and when Petronius saw that the land was in danger of remaining unsown (for it was the sowing season, and the people had spent the last fifty days waiting for his decision and not working) he once again called them together and said, "I will be the one to take the risk. Either, with God's help, I will succeed with Caesar and have the joy of saving all our lives, or, if his fury is aroused, I will sacrifice my own life on behalf of yours." With these words he dismissed the crowd, who praised him profusely, collected his troops and left Ptolemais for Antioch. From there he immediately reported to Caesar about his expedition to Judea, described the pleas of the Jews, and advised the emperor that unless he wanted to destroy the entire country and its people he should respect their law and rescind his order concerning the statues. Gaius replied to this letter in terms which expressed his outrage and warned Petronius that he would be put to death for being so slow to execute his orders. But it just so happened that the bearers of his letter were kept at sea for three months by bad weather, while others, who brought the news that Gaius had died, had a much easier passage. Thus, Petronius learned of the emperor's death twenty-seven days before he received the letter which contained the order for his own execution.

Jesus on Ethics: *Gospel of Matthew* 13:44–46; 22:34–40; 5:17–48.

At the beginning of his account of the teaching of Jesus the author of the Gospel of Mark sums up his message in this way: "'The time has come,' he said 'and the kingdom of God is close at hand. Repent, and believe the Good News.'"

In the gospels Jesus speaks of the Kingdom of God (Kingdom of Heaven in Matthew) sometimes as the present reality of an intensely spiritual interior life enjoyed by those who are attuned to God and sometimes as a new world order to be established by God in the future. Whether present or future, Jesus understood the Kingdom of God to be worth the sacrifice of anything that stood in the way of its attainment (Matt. 13:44-46). His call for "repentance" (from the Greek *metanoia*, "a change of mind") was in effect a demand for the turning away from traditional values in favor of those consistent with the perfectly loving nature of God. That love is the most basic ethical principle is illustrated in Jesus' encounter with the Pharisees (Matt. 22:34-40). That God demands a commitment to the spirit, and not just the letter, of the Law of Moses—and even to perfection—is one of the major points made by Jesus in the Sermon on the Mount (Matt. 5:17-48).

Matthew 13:44-46

'The kingdom of heaven is like a treasure hidden in a field which someone has found; he hides it, goes off happy, sells everything he owns and buys the field.

'Again, the kingdom of heaven is like a merchant looking for fine pearls; when he finds one of great value he goes and sells everything he owns and buys it.'

Matthew 22:34-34-40

But when the Pharisees heard that he had silenced the Sadducees they got together and, to disconcert him, one of them put a question, 'Master which is the greatest commandment of the Law?' Jesus said, *'You must love the Lord your God with all your heart, with all your soul,* and with all your mind. This is the greatest and the first commandment. The second resembles it: *You must love your neighbor as yourself.* On these two commandments hang the whole Law, and the Prophets also.'

Matthew 5:17-48

The Fulfillment of the Law

'Do not imagine that I have come to abolish the law or the Prophets. I have come not to abolish but to complete them. I tell you solemnly, till heaven and earth disappear, not one jot, not one little stroke, shall disappear from the law until its purpose is achieved. Therefore, the man who infringes even one of the least of these commandments and teaches others to do the same will be considered the least in the kingdom of heaven; but the man who keeps them and teaches them will be considered great in the kingdom of heaven.

The New Standard Higher than the Old

'For I tell you, if your virtue goes no deeper than that of the scribes and Pharisees, you will never get into the kingdom of heaven.

'You have learnt how it was said to our ancestors: *You must not kill;* and if anyone does kill he must answer for it before the court. But I say this to you: anyone who is angry with his brother will answer for it before the court; if a man calls his brother "Fool" he will answer for it before the Sanhedrin; if a man calls him "Renegade" he will answer for it in hell fire. So then, if you are bringing your offering to the altar and there remember that your brother has something against you, leave your offering there before the altar, go and be reconciled with your brother first, and then come back and present your offering. Come to terms with your opponent in good time while you are still on the way to the court with him, or he may hand you over to the judge and the judge to the officer, and you will be thrown into prison. I tell you solemnly, you will not get out till you have paid the last penny.

'You have learnt how it was said: *You must not commit adultery.* But I say this to you: if a man looks at a woman lustfully, he has already committed adultery with her in his heart. If your right eye should cause you to sin, tear it out and throw it away; for it will do you less harm to lose one part of you than to have your whole body thrown into hell. And if your right hand should cause you to sin, cut it off and throw it away; for it will do you less harm to lose one part of you than to have your whole body go to hell.

'It has also been said: *Anyone who divorces his wife must give her a writ of dismissal.* But I say this to you: everyone who divorces his wife, except for the case of fornication, makes her an adulteress; and anyone who marries a divorced woman commits adultery.

'Again, you have learnt how it was said to our ancestors: *You must not break your oath, but must fulfil your oaths to the Lord.* But I say this to you: do not swear at all, either by *heaven,* since that is God's throne; or by *the earth,* since that is *his footstool*; or by Jerusalem, since that is *the city of the great king.* Do not swear by your own head either, since you cannot turn a single hair white or black. All you need say is "Yes" if you mean yes, "No" if you mean no; anything more than this comes from the evil one.

'You have learnt how it was said: *Eye for eye and tooth for tooth.* But I say this to you: offer the wicked man no resistance. On the contrary, if anyone hits you on the right cheek, offer him the other as well; if a man takes you to law and would have your tunic, let him have your cloak as well. And if anyone orders you to go one mile, go two miles with him. Give to anyone who asks, and if anyone wants to borrow, do not turn away.

'You have learnt how it was said: *You must love your neighbor* and hate your enemy. But I say this to you: love your enemies and pray for those who persecute you; in this way you will be sons of your Father in heaven, for he causes his sun to rise on bad men as well as good, and his rain to fall on honest and dishonest men alike. For if you love those who love you, what right have you to claim any credit? Even the tax collectors do as much, do they not? And if you save your greetings for your brothers, are you doing anything exceptional? Even the pagans do as much, do they not? You must therefore be perfect just as your heavenly Father is perfect.

Paul on Salvation: *Epistle to the Romans* 5:1–6:11

Working in the middle of the first century A.D., Paul of Tarsus was the most effective of the early Christian missionaries. Originally a persecutor of the Christians, after a dramatic conversion experience Paul came to believe that he had been called by God to be a Christian apostle to the gentile population of the eastern Mediterranean region. As a preacher of the gospel ("good news"), Paul focused on the soteriological significance of the death and resurrection of Jesus the Christ. For Paul, Jesus' obedience to God had been absolute, even to the point of his acceptance of an undeserved death by execution. But God had raised Jesus from the dead and thereby made it possible for those who identified with him through faith to share in his victory over death.

Faith Guarantees Salvation

So far then we have seen that, through our Lord Jesus Christ, by faith we are judged righteous and at peace with God, since it is by faith and through Jesus that we have entered this state of grace in which we can boast about looking forward to God's glory. But that is not all we can boast about; we can boast about our sufferings. These sufferings bring patience, as we know, and patience brings perseverance, and perseverance brings hope, and this hope is not deceptive, because the love of God has been poured into our hearts by the Holy Spirit which has been given us. We were still helpless when at his appointed moment Christ died for sinful men. It is not easy to die even for a good man—though of course for someone really worthy, a man might be prepared to die—but what proves that God loves us is that Christ died for us while we were still sinners. Having died to make us righteous, is it likely that he would now fail to save us from God's anger? When we were reconciled to God by the death of his Son, we were still enemies; now that we have been reconciled, surely we may count on being saved by the life of his Son? Not merely because we have been reconciled but because we are filled with joyful trust in God, through our Lord Jesus Christ, through whom we have already gained our reconciliation.

Adam and Jesus Christ

Well then, sin *entered the world* through one man, and through sin death, and thus death has spread through the whole human race because everyone has sinned. Sin existed in the world long before the Law [of Moses] was given. There was no law and so no one could be accused of the sin of 'law-breaking', yet death reigned over all from Adam to Moses, even though their sin, unlike that of Adam, was not a matter of breaking a law.

Adam prefigured the One to come, but the gift itself considerably outweighed the fall. If it is certain that through one man's fall so many died, it is even more certain that divine grace, coming through the one man, Jesus Christ, came to so many as an abundant free gift. The results of the gift also outweigh the results of one man's sin: for after one single fall came judgement with a verdict of condemnation, now after many falls come grace with its verdict of acquittal. If it is certain that death reigned over everyone as the consequence of one man's fall, it is even more certain that one man, Jesus Christ, will cause everyone to reign in life who receives the free gift that he does not deserve, of being made righteous. Again, as one man's fall brought condemnation on everyone, so the good act of one man brings everyone life and makes them justified. As by one man's disobedience many were made sinners, so by one man's obedience many will be made righteous. When law came, it was to multiply the opportunities of falling, but however great the number of sins committed, grace was even greater; and so, just as sin reigned wherever there was death, so grace will reign to bring eternal life thanks to the righteousness that comes through Jesus Christ our Lord.

Baptism

Does it follow that we should remain in sin so as to let grace have greater scope? Of course not. We are dead to sin, so how can we continue to live in it? You have been taught that when we were baptised in Christ Jesus we were baptised in his death; in other words, when we were baptised we went to the tomb with him and joined him in death, so that as Christ was raised from the dead by the Father's glory, we too might live a new life.

If in union with Christ we have imitated his death, we shall also imitate him in his resurrection. We must realise that our former selves have been crucified with him to destroy this sinful body and to free us from the slavery of sin. When a man dies, of course, he is finished with sin.

But we believe that having died with Christ we shall return to life with him: Christ, as we know, having been raised from the dead will never die again. Death has no power over him any more. When he died, he died, once and for all, to sin, so his life now is life with God; and in that way, you too must consider yourselves to be dead to sin but alive for God in Christ Jesus.

Nero's Persecution of the Christians: Tacitus, *Annals* 15.44

Under suspicion of setting the famous fire of 64 A.D. which destroyed a large part of the city of Rome, Nero managed to divert attention from himself by blaming the Christians for this crime. The result was the first official persecution of Christians in Rome. Nero's action against the Christians was limited to the faithful in the city and did not extend to other regions of the empire.

None of the emperor's efforts, neither the generous gifts he gave nor his attempts to appease the gods, would eliminate the ugly suspicion that he was to blame for the fire. In order to silence the rumors to this effect, Nero placed the blame on a group hated by the populace for their abominations and called Christians. These he punished with ingenious tortures. Christus, from whom their name derives, had been executed during the reign of Tiberius by our procurator Pontius Pilatus, but this deadly superstition, which had been controlled for a while, began to reemerge, not only in Judea, the cradle of this evil, but also at Rome where all sorts of hideous and disgusting things from all over the world became fashionable. At first those who confessed their guilt were arrested. Then, with the information they provided, a vast number of people were convicted—not so much of the crime of arson as of hatred of humanity. As they died they were subjected to insults. Some were dressed in the skins of beasts and torn apart by dogs. Some were crucified. Still others were sentenced to be burned so that the flames would light up the darkening sky at nightfall. Nero threw open his gardens for this spectacle and offered an entertainment at the Circus during which he moved about the crowd dressed like a charioteer or stood up high in his chariot. As a consequence, people sympathized with criminals who deserved extreme and exemplary punishment, for they were being killed in order to satisfy one man's appetite for cruelty instead of for the good of the public.

Trajan's Policy Regarding the Christians: Pliny the Younger, *Letters* 10.96–97

At some time between the years 100 and 113 Pliny the Younger, the Roman governor of Bithynia in Asia Minor, wrote to the emperor Trajan requesting specific instructions in the matter of dealing with the growing Christian movement in his province. Pliny was no friend of the Christians; he regarded their faith as a contagious superstition, regretted that it had penetrated both rural and urban areas, and believed that the temples of the old gods of Rome would soon be deserted unless steps were taken to combat the new religion. There may have been some rhetorical exaggeration in his correspondence with the emperor, but historians generally cite his letters as evidence for the existence of vigorous growth in the number of Christians in the areas along the shore of the Black Sea. In response to Pliny's inquiry as to how he should handle cases involving Christians, Trajan replied that while Christians brought to court should be required to demonstrate their loyalty by offering sacrifices to him, a truly enlightened state should not take the additional step of actually seeking out those suspected of being Christians.

Pliny to the Emperor Trajan

I have made it my practice, sir, to consult with you whenever I am in doubt about the proper course of action in public affairs. Who can better instruct me when I hesitate or enlighten me when I am ignorant? I have never been involved in the trials of the Christians and as a result I do not know what procedures to follow and what measures to take in investigating and punishing them. I have been particularly concerned about the following questions: Should young people accused of being Christians be treated leniently or tried in the same way as adults? Should Christians who renounce their faith still be punished? Should people be punished merely for being Christians, or are they to be punished for the crimes which are associated with the practice of Christianity?

Thus far I have employed the following procedures when dealing with those accused of being Christians. I have begun by asking them if they really were Christians. To those who replied that they were I repeated the question a second and then a third time, threatening them with capital punishment if they persisted. If they did persist I ordered their execution, for even though they did not confess to being Christians they deserved to be punished for their stubbornness and inflexibility. Other individuals similarly afflicted I had transferred to Rome because they were Roman citizens. But the problem has been made worse as more attention has been focused on it, and more and more cases are coming to light.

One case involved an accusation made by an anonymous informer against a large number of people who were individually named. Those who denied that they had ever been Christians I thought should be released, since they repeated a prayer I dictated to them and made a sacrifice complete with wine and incense to an image of you which I had ordered brought for this purpose along with statues of the gods. They also blasphemed Christ. All of these are things which it is said true Christians cannot be made to do. Other individuals named by the informer began by identifying themselves as Christians but then said that they were not, although they admitted to having been followers of Christ three, four or even twenty years earlier. These people were willing to worship your image and the images of the gods and also cursed Christ. They maintained that they had been guilty of nothing more than coming together on certain days before sunrise to sing a hymn to Christ, as if he were a god, and to take a solemn oath not to do anything criminal but to avoid fraud, theft, adultery, betraying a trust or denying one when asked to deliver it up. They said that after these rites were conducted they would disperse and then reassemble later in order to share a very ordinary and harmless meal, but they also claimed to have abandoned even these practices when I issued my edict which, in accordance with your wishes, forbade political associations. In order to get at the truth about this group I thought it necessary to examine two female slaves they call deaconesses, but under torture they revealed nothing but a perverse and excessive superstition.

I have suspended my proceedings against the Christians while I await your advice, and I believe that the large number of those involved justifies this decision. People of all ages, classes and both genders are now in danger and will be affected in the future, for this contagious superstition is not confined to the cities but is spreading to the villages and the countryside. Nevertheless, I believe that we can contain the problem and find some remedy for it.

Already the temples which not long ago had been almost completely abandoned are once again attracting worshippers, sacred rites are being restored after a long period of neglect and the flesh of sacrificial animals is being sold everywhere, although recently it was nearly impossible for vendors to find customers. All of these are evidence that there are many people who can be cured and reclaimed if given a chance to repent.

Trajan to Pliny

My dear Pliny, you have done well in your dealings with those who have been accused before you of being Christians, for you had no general rule which was applicable in all cases. We should not actively seek out these people. However, those who are accused before you and found guilty should be punished. If anyone denies that he is a Christian and proves that he is not by worshipping the gods, he should be pardoned as a reward for his denial even if he had been under suspicion in the past. Moreover, we should not pay attention to anonymous accusations, for this is a detestable practice which is unworthy of our times.

In Defense of Christianity: Tertullian, *Apology,* II.2–12

The second century African rhetorician Tertullian, who spent most of his life in Carthage, was a prolific writer who devoted his pen to the defense and promotion of Christianity. Of his more than thirty surviving works the most important may well be the *Apology,* which has been called "the noblest oration among all which antiquity has left us." In this work, which he addressed to "the rulers of the Roman Empire," Tertullian refutes point by point the charges which were made against the Christians. The selection below contains references to some of the more outrageous accusations against the adherents of the faith as well as Tertullian's argument that they suffered at the hands of a Roman judicial system whose policies were both unfair and illogical.

Now then, if it is really true that we are the most criminal of all people, why is it that you treat us differently from other offenders? Shouldn't all people guilty of the same offense receive the same treatment? When you charge others with the crimes you attribute to us they are allowed to defend themselves in court using their own powers of persuasion as well as the lawyers they hire. They are free to answer their accusers and to ask them questions in cross-examination, for the law forbids the condemnation of men who have not been given the chance to defend themselves and to present their own version of the story. But this is not the case with Christians. They alone are forbidden to answer their accusers, to defend the truth and to prevent their judges from committing injustices. The courts are interested only in giving the public what it most wants: confessions of the hated name of Christian. That is why the charges made against Christians are never thoroughly examined, even though in other criminal cases, when the accused confesses to being a murderer, temple-robber, adulterer or, to mention one of the labels pinned on us, enemy of the state, you are never willing to impose punishment until you have completed a lengthy review of all matters related to the case, such as the nature of the crime, the number of times it was committed, the time and place where it occurred and the accessories and accomplices who were involved. This procedure is not followed in cases involving Christians, though it ought to be. The courts should investigate the accusations made against Christians so that they will be able to determine just how many murdered babies we have eaten, how many acts of incest we have committed in the dark, and the precise number of cooks and dogs who witnessed these events. Imagine the fame that awaits the magistrate who proves that some Christian has eaten a hundred babies!

All of this in spite of the fact that it is illegal for the authorities even to seek us out! For when Pliny the Younger was administering his province and had convicted some Christians and forced others to renounce their faith, he became concerned about the large number of people who might be affected by his policies and asked the emperor Trajan for advice. Pliny explained that, apart from the Christians' stubborn refusal to sacrifice, he had not learned much about their practices. He had learned only that they held meetings before daybreak to sing hymns to Christ and to God and that they took oaths in which they bound themselves to avoid murder, adultery, dishonesty, treachery and other crimes. In his rescript, Trajan replied that such persons were not to be sought out, although they were to be punished if accusations were made against them before Pliny. What a decision! What confusion it was destined to cause! Trajan implies that the Christians are innocent when he says that they must not be sought out, and yet he suggests that they are somehow guilty when he orders Pliny to punish them. The emperor spares them on the one hand and attacks them on the other. He pretends not to be concerned about the Christians but, at the same time, he calls for them to be punished.

Why do you cheat yourselves with this game of deception? If you want to condemn Christians then why not seek them out? If you are not going to bother seeking them out then why do you persist in considering them guilty? The garrisons have been given the job of tracking down bandits in the provinces, and every man is a soldier in the war against traitors and public enemies—even their accomplices and accessories are hunted down. It is only the Christian who must not be sought out, although it *is* permissible to drag him before the authorities (as if it is possible for someone to be brought to trial without first having been sought out). Thus, even a man whom no one wanted to prosecute is condemned when dragged to court, a man whose punishment is not the consequence of his guilt but of the fact that, although he was not to be sought out, he was found!

And in such cases there is another way in which you deviate from the established procedures of criminal law. In the trials of other criminals you use torture to extract confessions of guilt from those who claim to be innocent, but when dealing with us you subject us to torture in order to get us to *deny* that we are guilty of the crime of being Christians. If we were guilty of a true crime, we would claim to be innocent and you would use torture to elicit confessions of guilt.

You refuse to proceed with judicial investigations of our crimes because you assume that a man's confession that he is a Christian provides proof of their commission. And yet, even though everyone knows what murder is, you ask confessed murderers for all the details and particulars of their crime. Your dealings with us are even more irregular when you assume our guilt from our confession of the name Christian and then proceed, through torture, to persuade us to recant our confession, so that by denying the name Christian we may also deny the crimes which you previously assumed we committed from our confession of the name.

Constantine's Vision: Eusebius, *Life of Constantine* 1.28–31

In 312, after his victories at Turin and Verona, Constantine marched on Rome and defeated his rival Maxentius at the Milvian Bridge. According to tradition, before the battle Constantine experienced a vision as a result of which he decided to fight under the auspices of Christ. Divine intervention, the Christians believed, had inspired the emperor to embrace Christianity and motivated him to push for the conversion of the empire to the faith which would be declared its only legal religion by the end of the fourth century.

As he prayed fervently in this manner a most marvelous sign appeared to Constantine in the heavens, an apparition which would hardly be credible had it been reported by any other person. But since the triumphant emperor himself described it to this writer a long time after it had occurred, at a time when I had the honor of knowing him and being his associate, and swore that his story was true, why should we not believe his account of his vision, especially since later events have argued for its authenticity? Constantine said that around noontime, when the day had just begun to decline, he saw in the sky above the sun a cross of light which bore the inscription "Conquer in This." The sight astounded him, and he was not alone in his astonishment, for the miraculous sight was also witnessed by the entire army that had accompanied him on this campaign.

Constantine said that at first he was not certain what the sign meant and that he continued to ponder and reflect on its significance as night came on. Then, as he lay sleeping, the Christ of God appeared to him with the same sign he had seen in the sky and ordered him to make a likeness of this heavenly symbol and use it as a means of protection in his engagements with the enemy.

The next morning Constantine informed his friends of this marvelous occurrence and summoned those artisans of his who were skilled in working with gold and precious gems. Sitting among them, he described his vision and ordered them to reproduce the symbol in gold and gems. The symbol was made in the following way. A kind of cross was fashioned by hanging a bar horizontally across a long spear covered with gold. A wreath of gold and precious stones was fixed on top of it, and within it was the symbol of the Savior's name—two Greek letters which stand at the very beginning of the name of Christ, the letter *rho* being intersected by a *chi* at the center [thus creating the symbol ⚥]. In later years the emperor was in the habit of wearing these letters as insignia on his helmet. . . . He wore this symbol of salvation as protection against every adversary and hostile power and ordered that replicas of it should be carried before all of his armies.

The Edict of Galerius: Eusebius, *Ecclesiastical History* 8.17

On April 30, 311 A.D., an edict of partial toleration of Christians was issued from Nicomedia in the names of Galerius, Constantine and Licinius. Sometimes called the "Edict of the Three Emperors," it has been preserved in Eusebius' *Ecclesiastical History* and Lactantius' *On the Deaths of the Persecutors.* The edict is most closely associated with Galerius, emperor of the East under the tetrarchy established by Diocletian and a former persecutor of Christianity. Its most striking features are its admission of the failure of the persecutions and its extension of freedom of worship to the Christians.

The Emperor Caesar Galerius Valerius Maximianus Invictus Augustus, Pontifex Maximus, Germanicus Maximus, Egyptiacus Maximus, Thebaicus Maximus, Sarmaticus Maximus five times, Persicus Maximus two times, Carpicus Maximus six times, Armeniacus Maximus, Medicus Maximus, Adiabenicus Maximus, Holder of Tribunician Authority for the twentieth time, Imperator for the nineteenth time, Consul for the eighth time, Pater Patriae, Proconsul; the Emperor Caesar Flavius Valerius Constantinus Pius Felix Invictus Augustus, Pontifex Maximus, Holder of Tribunician Authority, Imperator for the fifth time, Consul, Pater Patriae, Proconsul; and the Emperor Caesar Valerius Licinianus Licinius Pius Felix Invictus Augustus, Pontifex Maximus, Holder of Tribunician Authority for the fourth time, Imperator for the third time, Consul, Pater Patriae, Proconsul—to the people of their various provinces, greetings:

Among the other things we have done for the benefit and welfare of the state, we have attempted in the past to bring all things into harmony with the ancient laws and public order of the Romans and to provide also that the Christians, many of whom had abandoned the faith of their ancestors, should return to sound thinking. The Christians, for some reason, had been seized by such obstinacy and possessed by such foolishness that they would not honor the institutions of antiquity which happened to have been established by their ancestors. Instead, in accordance with their own judgment and pleasure, they desired to obey only those laws which suited their own way of thinking and their personal tastes. Moreover, they held meetings in various places.

When we finally ordered them to conform to the religious traditions of the ancients many of them obeyed us out of fear, but many others died for their faith. Now, in view of the fact that the majority of them have remained steadfast in their faith, and having observed that the Christians have since then neither worshiped our traditional gods nor given honor to the Christian god [because they have been forbidden to hold meetings for worship], we believe that in accordance with our clemency and consistent practice of granting pardons to all we ought to grant our pardon in this case as well, so that the Christians may be Christian again and hold their meetings, provided that they do nothing to threaten the public order. We shall give further instructions to the magistrates in a forthcoming letter concerning this matter. In gratitude for our clemency the Christians should pray to their god for our welfare, for the welfare of the state, and for their own, so that the state may be preserved on every side and that they may be able to live free from anxiety in their own homes.

The Edict of Milan: Lactantius, *On the Deaths of the Persecutors* 48

The Edict of Milan was published jointly in 313 by Constantine and Licinius, the emperors who controlled the western and eastern parts of the Empire respectively. Also known as the "Edict of Toleration," it went beyond the mere extension to Christians of freedom of worship granted by Galerius, Constantine and Licinius in 311. The Edict proclaimed freedom of conscience, accorded to Christianity full legal equality with other cults, called for the return of church property which had been confiscated during the persecutions and instructed the officials ("Your Devotedness," "Your Solicitude," etc.) to whom it was addressed as an imperial rescript to implement its provisions immediately. But the Edict did not mark the final victory of the church. In the decade that followed his meeting with Constantine, Licinius changed his policy and imposed severe restrictions on the public worship of Christians in his half of the Empire. Responding as a champion of the Christian faith, Constantine invaded his rival's territory in 324, eliminated him, and vigorously promoted the spread of Christianity throughout the Empire of which he was the sole master.

When I, Constantine Augustus, and I also, Licinius Augustus, had met together under happy circumstances at Milan and contemplated all the matters affecting the welfare and security of the Empire, we considered that, of all those things which seemed likely to benefit the people in general, it was our duty, first of all, to settle the matter of how the Deity should be revered by allowing the Christians and the members of all other religious groups to worship in any way they wished. We believed that this would incline whatever sort of divinity exists in the heavens to be benevolent and gracious to us and to all of our subjects. Therefore, we believed that we should establish this law, which provides that we shall by no means deny to anyone who has made a religious commitment the right to practice Christianity or any other faith that gives him personal satisfaction, so that the Supreme Divinity, who is worshiped freely, might continue to show to us in all affairs his customary good will and benevolence.

It is fitting that Your Devotedness should know that this is our desire and that all those conditions with reference to the Christians which were set forth in our earlier letters and sent to your office should now be removed, that all previous measures which are severe and contrary to our clemency shall be annulled, and that all who wish to observe the religion of the Christians may now do so without fear or injury. We believed that you should be made fully aware of this, Your Solicitude, so that you might know that we have given the Christians absolute liberty to practice their faith. Seeing that we have done this for the Christians, Your Devotedness should understand that we have also granted to others the same absolute liberty, in accordance with the peace of our times, to freely choose to worship as they see fit. We have done this to avoid the appearance of harming or dishonoring any person or religion. In addition, we have also decreed concerning the Christians that if those places in which they previously assembled and about which in previous letters to Your Devotedness we gave you different orders, if these have been purchased by someone, either from the treasury or from some other person, the purchasers shall return them to the Christians without requesting or accepting any money payment in return, all frustration and ambiguity being put aside. Persons who received such properties as gifts shall likewise return them to the Christians as soon as possible. In addition, if those who have bought these properties or received them as gifts wish to appeal to our benevolence, let them apply to the vicar so that some provision may be made for them by our clemency. You are directed to attend to all of these matters for the sake of the Christians and without delay.

Since these Christians, as is well-known, previously owned not only their customary places of assembly but other properties which belonged to them collectively, that is, to their churches rather than to individual Christians, all these possessions should now be returned to them in accordance with the aforementioned law, *i.e.,* to their churches and assemblies, without hesitation or litigation. The law also provides that those who freely return these properties should expect to be compensated by our benevolence, as we said before.

With respect to all these matters you must offer the Christians your most effective mediation so that our order may be implemented by our clemency for the public good. And may the divine favor which has already blessed us in so many ways continue to grant us prosperity and success, along with happiness for the Empire. So that everyone might know of this decree and of our benevolence we order you to publish this document upon its arrival, issuing it as your proclamation and bringing it to the attention of all so that this benevolent law may be concealed from no one.

V
Philosophy

A Roman Epicurean: Lucretius, *On the Nature of Things* 3.830–869; 5.820–877; 5.1193–1240

Very little is known of the life of the Roman poet and philosopher Titus Lucretius Carus. We can be certain only that he lived *ca.* 99–55 B.C., that he was an aristocrat, and that he was an associate of Gaius Memmius, the governor of Bithynia in 57 B.C., to whom his *De Rerum Natura (On the Nature of Things)* is addressed. According to St. Jerome, who mentions him in his Latin translation of Eusebius' *Chronica,* after Lucretius had composed his only known poem he became insane and, at the age of forty-four, committed suicide. However, there is no evidence to support this claim.

Lucretius' verse earned the praise of many of Rome's greatest literary figures, including Cicero, Virgil and Ovid. However, he considered himself more a philosopher than a poet. *De Rerum Natura* is, in fact, a faithful exposition in verse of the philosophy of Epicurus. Like that Greek thinker, Lucretius was a philosophical materialist who made the atomism of Democritus the foundation of his philosophical thought. Thus, he argued that there is no reality other than that which is constructed of atoms, that natural phenomena are not the work of the gods but the results of the chance movements of atoms, and that death should not be feared, since there is no possibility of an unhappy afterlife. Like Epicurus, Lucretius condemned religion for filling the heads of men and women with superstitions. These points are illustrated in the three excerpts which follow.

I

Therefore, death is nothing to us, it doesn't
matter a bit, for we know that the soul is mortal.
Just as long ago we felt no pain when the armies
of Carthage fell upon us from every direction,
when the whole world was rocked by the blows of war
and shuddered beneath high heaven,

when no one knew who was destined to govern those
who live on land and sea;
so, when we no longer exist, when
the body and soul of which we are made have separated,
then nothing will happen to us, nothing will
excite our senses,
not even if the earth crashes into the sea,
and the sea is mixed with the sky,
for we shall not be.
And what if the soul and the mind *did* have
sensory powers after their separation from the body?
It would make no difference, for we exist only
when our component parts are joined together.
Even if time should reassemble our atoms after we die,
so that we lived again, it would still not matter to us,
since any connection with that earlier self would
have been broken forever:
nothing about the we who we were before now affects us,
nor do we fear the we who we will become.
Think of the vast expanse of the immeasurable past
and, through it, the incalculable movements of matter,
and you may well conclude that the same atoms of
which we now consist were often ordered in just
the same way as they are now.
Yet we cannot remember this, for there has been a
break with the past, and the motions of our atoms have
lost their link with the motions of earlier sensations.
Similarly, if one is to be able to experience some
pain or trouble in the future, he must exist in the future.
Since death makes this impossible, and will not allow
the man who might otherwise experience such discomfort
the existence which this first requires,
we can be sure that there is nothing for us to fear
after death.
He who does not exist cannot be unhappy,
and it doesn't matter a bit if he lived before,
once immortal death has taken his life away.

II

And so time after time Earth has shown herself
worthy of the name mother, since she herself created

human beings, and at the proper time engendered every
animal that ranges at will across the great hills
and the birds of the air in every shape and color.
But since there must be an end to giving birth,
she ceased, like a woman tired and worn with years.
For all things in this world change with age, passing
from one state into another; nothing stays the same.
All things are in motion, for nature compels them
always to be turning into something else.
One thing rots, having grown weak and weary with time,
and from its remains another grows up.
In this way time alters the whole structure of the
universe as one state gives way to another,
and though Earth can no longer bear what she bore before,
she now bears what she could not bear before.
Then, too, Earth tried to create all sorts of amazing
monsters of weird construction and strange appearance:
some androgynous, two-sexed, lost between genders;
some footless; others without hands;
some mouthless, unable to speak;
some eyeless, unable to see;
others with their limbs held fast by flesh to their sides,
unable to move, to escape danger or take what they needed
to sustain life.
And so it was with all the other monsters and marvelous
beings that Earth made: she created them in vain,
for nature would not let them grow, reach maturity,
find food, or join together sexually.
We know that circumstances must be just so for living
beings to reproduce and forge the chain of generations:
food must be available, there must be some way for
life-bearing seeds to pass through the body when it
is relaxed, and couples must be able to join their
bodies and exchange delights.
Many species must have died out, being unable to
reproduce themselves.
Those which survived had either cleverness
or courage or quickness to guard and preserve them
from the very moment they came into existence.
Many were useful to us, and so they survived because
we took them into our care.
The lions, that fierce breed, were kept safe by

courage, the foxes by cunning, the deer by quickness.
But dogs (those light-sleeping and loyal creatures),
the beasts of burden, woolly sheep, and the horned
oxen—all these, Memmius, depend on man for
their protection.
They were eager to flee from the wild animals,
seeking the peace and sustenance that we give
them as the reward for their usefulness.
Others, to whom nature did not give the qualities
that would have enabled them to survive on their own
or make them useful to us and worth domesticating—
these creatures, trapped in the net of their own
fatal limitations, were at the mercy of others who
exploited and preyed upon them until at last
the workings of nature brought them to extinction.

III

O miserable humanity, thinking the gods responsible
for natural phenomena and attributing to them an angry
and malicious character as well!
What groaning they then brought on themselves, what
wounds for us now, what tears for generations to come!
Piety is not being often seen with one's head covered,
always turning toward some stone or altar;
nor is it falling prostrate on the ground with hands
outstretched before the shrines of the gods,
sprinkling their altars unceasingly with the blood of
beasts or taking vow after vow.
Rather, piety is the ability to observe all things with
a mind at peace.
For when we turn our gaze upwards to the vast expanse
of heaven, to the ether studded with sparkling stars,
and consider the movements of the sun and moon,
then in our hearts, already burdened by other cares,
yet another cause for worry is awakened:
the fear that there may be gods of immeasurable power
who have set the bright stars in motion, each in its
proper course.
The mind without knowledge is tormented by doubt:
Did the world have a beginning?
What of the walls of the universe?

Will they always be able to endure the stress and
strain of celestial motion, or have the gracious
gods granted that they should remain forever strong,
passing down through eternity untouched by the
wearing power of endless time?
Besides, whose mind is not paralyzed by fear of the gods,
whose body does not seek to creep away in terror when
the parched earth shakes under the horrifying pounding of
thunderbolts that echo through the heavenly halls?
Don't entire nations and peoples tremble, don't proud
kings curl up in terror of the gods, fearful that some
misdeed or proud word will bring the dread time of
retribution?
And when the violence of the unloosed gale casts the
fleet's admiral across the waves, together with his mighty
legions and elephants, doesn't he pray for the gods'
peace and in his panic beg for the stilling of every
wind, both fair and foul?
But to no avail, since often he is caught up by the
swirling wind and driven to his death in the shallows.
This is the extent to which some mysterious power
oppresses all humanity and even seems to trample on
and mock the symbols of the state's power.
And so, when the earth trembles beneath our feet,
when cities are shaken, totter, and fall,
is it any wonder that men feel contempt for themselves
and accept that the world is governed by wondrously
powerful gods?

On Law and Justice: Cicero, *Laws* 1.6–12

It is widely recognized that Cicero's philosophical treatises not only popularized the ideas of Plato and the Stoics but also gave a distinctly Latin flavor to classical humanism. In his *Laws* he described the laws of the ideal state which he envisioned in an earlier work, the *Republic*. The text takes the form of a dialogue involving Cicero (who is addressed as Marcus, his full name being Marcus Tullius Cicero), his brother Quintus and their friend Atticus. The excerpt below deals with the origin of justice and its relationship to law. Cicero's argument that both derive from that Reason which pervades and organizes the universe is a good example of his debt to Greek philosophy in general and Stoicism in particular.

MARCUS

Let us search for the origin of Justice. Now, the most learned of men have chosen to begin their own searches for its derivation by examining Law, and this would seem to be the right choice if, as they claim, Law is the highest form of reason which is implanted in Nature and which dictates what should be done and what should not be done. For them, Law is this very reason when it is is solidly established and fully developed in a human mind. Thus, they identify Law with intelligence and believe that its natural function is to command us to do what is right and to forbid that which is wrong. . . . Now, if they are correct, and I think that for the most part they are, then Justice is something which has its origin in Law, for Law is a natural force; it is the mind and reason of the intelligent human being and the standard for determining what is just and what is unjust. Since our discussion is about what the general population thinks, it will sometimes be necessary for us to speak as the people do and take the word "law" to mean the written decrees which require that some things be done and that others not be done. That is how the people define law. But we are trying to determine what Justice is, and so let us go back to that supreme Law which existed long before any decrees or states existed.

QUINTUS

Your suggestion is a good one. It will be useful for the purposes of our conversation.

MARCUS

Well then, shall we seek the origin of Justice at its very source? When we find it we will have a standard against which to test the things we are investigating.

QUINTUS

That is exactly what I think we must do.

ATTICUS

I agree with your brother.

MARCUS

I will make my argument brief. Your previous statements point to the conclusion that the animal which we call man, who is blessed with foresight and keen intelligence, is complex and sharp, possesses memory, reason and prudence—this creature has been given a special and distinctive status by the supreme God who created him, for he is unique among all the many and various species of living beings in that he reasons and thinks, just as the Creator does. This is an honor withheld from all other living things. And what is more divine, not just in man alone but in all of heaven and earth, than reason? Reason, which is justifiably called wisdom when it reaches a state of maturity and perfection! Since there is nothing better than reason, and since reason exists both in God and in man, reason is the first and greatest of the qualities shared by God and man. But those who have reason must have right reason, and since right reason is Law we must also conclude that men have law in common with the gods. Moreover, those who have Law in common must also have Justice in common, and those who share in both of these should be considered members of the same commmunity. This is especially true if they happen to obey the same powers and authorities, and in fact they do; for they are all obedient to the principles which govern this celestial system and acknowledge the authority of the divine mind and the God whose power sets him above all others. Thus, we should think of the universe as a single society whose citizens are gods and men. . . .

ATTICUS

By the immortal gods! Look how far back you have gone to discover the source of Justice! And you speak of it with such eloquence that I no longer have any wish to move on to our discussion of civil law, which I thought was going to be your subject. In fact, I wouldn't mind spending the entire day on your present theme since the points you have touched on in order to introduce another topic now seem more important than the topic they are meant to introduce.

MARCUS

Yes, the ideas we have been discussing are certainly important, but of all the ideas which provide material for philosophical discussion there is none more important than this: We are born for Justice, and that which is right is not determined by human opinion but by Nature. The truth of this becomes readily apparent once you clearly understand the way in which human beings relate to each other, for there are no two things so like each other, so completely identical, as two human beings. Indeed, if it weren't for the fact that some weaker minds have been damaged by bad habits and false beliefs and turned by these in different directions, no individual would be so like his own self as all individuals would be like all others. And so, no matter how we define man, a single definition will apply equally well to all men. This provides sufficient proof that no real differences distinguish one man from another; if the opposite were true a single definition of man would not apply to all men. In fact, reason, which is the single factor which raises us above the level of animals and enables us to draw inferences, to prove and refute, to discuss problems, devise solutions and reach conclusions, is indeed a characteristic common to all human beings, and although some individuals use it to greater effect than others, its capacity remains constant. . . . My next proposition is that human beings are designed by Nature in such a way that they share a sense of Justice and extend it to all of humanity. Now, I want you to understand that when I speak of Nature I mean any characteristic of ours which is implanted in us by Nature. I also want you to understand that the perversion which results from bad habits is so destructive that the sparks of light which Nature implants in us are extinguished by it, thus allowing the vices, which are the very opposites of those sparks, to establish themselves. If, on the other hand, the judgments of men were in harmony with Nature, so that, as the poet Terence proclaims, they considered "nothing alien to them which concerns humankind," then all people would practice Justice. For those creatures to whom Nature gave the gift of reason were also given right reason and, as a result, they received the gift of Law, which is right reason applied in relation to those things which must be done and those which must not be done. And if they were given Law they were given Justice as well. And, since all men have been given reason, all men have received Justice.

On Facing Difficulties: Seneca, *Moral Epistles* 96

The Roman philosopher Seneca (4 B.C.-65 A.D.), the son of Seneca the Rhetorician, does not conform to the ancient model of a philosopher without worldly concerns. Beginning his career as a lawyer, he quickly amassed a considerable fortune and then moved on to holding the office of quaestor and membership in the Senate. He was accused by Messalina, Claudius' wife, of adultery with Julia Livilla, the sister of Caligula, and sent into exile in Corsica. He was later recalled by Agrippina to assist her in restraining the violent and sadistic Nero, but apparently became involved in the emperor's plot to murder his mother. In 65 he was implicated in Piso's conspiracy to assassinate the young emperor and was asked by Nero to commit suicide. Although in his personal life he did not always exhibit the detachment one would expect to see in a Roman philosopher, his plays and philosophical writings are good examples of the influence exerted by Greek Stoicism on the Roman upper classes. His *Moral Epistles*, 124 letters written to his friend Lucilius, give us an excellent description of his views on a variety of philosophical issues. The letter which appears below presents his views on the proper way to deal with adversity.

Why, in spite of everything, are you still fretting and complaining? Why can't you understand that among all the terrible things you have been complaining about there is only one thing that truly is terrible—the fact that you *do* fret and complain? If you ask me, I think it's impossible for a man to be miserable unless he is convinced that there is something about the universe itself that is wrong and oppressive. I will not be able to endure myself on the day when I begin to believe that anything is unendurable. I am sick, but fate has decreed that I should be so. My slaves are ill, my income has fallen off and my house is in need of repair. I have been troubled by business losses, accidents, jobs to be done and anxieties, but all of these things are very common. No, that is an understatement; these things are inevitable. They do not occur by accident, but by design. Now, please believe me, for I am sharing my most heartfelt convictions with you. When everything seems to be going against me and life is an uphill struggle, I have taught myself not only to obey

God but also to fully accept his will. I follow him because that is my soul's deepest desire, not because I must follow him. And so there is nothing that the world can do to make me angry or cause me to grimace. I pay all my taxes willingly. You should realize that all of the things that make us moan and groan are part of the tax of life, and they are things, my Lucilius, which you shouldn't seek to avoid or escape.

Your troubles began with a bladder disease. You wrote depressing letters telling me that you were getting worse. In fact, it is closer to the truth to say that you were afraid you would die. But tell me, when you prayed for a long life, didn't you know that you were praying for exactly what you have gotten? A long life is full of troubles, just as a long journey is full of dust and mud and rain. But you say, "I wanted life *and* freedom from troubles." Such a womanish cry doesn't become a man. Think carefully about how you should react to my prayer for you, which I offer in the best possible spirit: "May all the gods and goddesses forbid that Fortune should give you nothing but leisure and luxury!" Ask yourself which you would choose if some god gave you the choice: life in a resort or life in a camp.

Life *is* like fighting in the army, Lucilius. That is why those who are buffeted about, who laboriously climb up and over the steepest obstacles, who take part in the most dangerous expeditions, are heroes and first-rank fighters. But those disgusting men who live the easy life while others toil, they are nothing but turtle-doves who are safe in their comfort only because other men despise them.

A Stoic's Views On Slavery:
Seneca, *Moral Epistles* 47

Like other Stoics, the Roman philosopher Seneca maintained that since all human beings are endowed with reason and are governed by the same universal laws they are essentially equal. His belief that slaves possess the same dignity and personal worth as free men and women is evident in the letter he wrote on the subject of slavery to his friend Lucilius.

I am pleased to hear from your associate, Lucilius, that you live on friendly terms with those who serve you. I would expect as much from a man as sensible and well-educated as you. "But they are slaves!" people will say. No, they are men. "Slaves!" No, they are comrades. "Slaves!" No, they are humble friends. "Slaves!" Then so are we, for all men are equally subject to the whims of Fortune.

That is why I laugh at those who think it is degrading for a man to dine with his slave. What is degrading about it? It is only because of our arrogance that the master of the house sits down alone to eat his supper while a throng of slaves stands around him. He stuffs and stretches his belly with such an enormous amount of food that he can barely digest and eliminate it. While he gorges himself the slaves may not so much as move their lips or even speak. The softest murmur brings a beating with the rod, and even an accidental cough, sneeze or hiccup does not go unpunished. There is a severe penalty in store for anyone who causes the slightest interruption of the silence, and so the slaves must stand there, sometimes for an entire night, hungry and wordless.

Slaves such as these speak disrespectfully of their masters behind their backs because they are not permitted to say anything at all in their presence. But in the old days slaves were allowed not only to speak when their masters were in the room, but even with them. In return for the freedom to speak they were willing to risk their own necks for their masters. The saying that a man has as many enemies as he has slaves is true only when slaves are treated with disrespect. They are not naturally our enemies, but we make them such. . . .

We Romans treat our slaves cruelly and arrogantly, but I do not wish to go into this matter more deeply at the moment. Let me just say that you should treat your inferiors as you would have your superiors treat you. And whenever you stop to think of how much power you have over a slave, remember the power that your master has over you. You say, "But I have no master." True. For now you are fortunate. But things change.

Epictetus on God and Life: Arrian, *Discourses*, selected excerpts

Epictetus (55-135 A.D.), a Greek from Hierapolis in Phrygia, grew up in Rome as a slave of Epaphroditus, one of Nero's freedmen, who allowed him to attend the lectures of the Stoic C. Musonius Rufus and later gave him his freedom. Epictetus became a teacher of philosophy in Rome and, after Domitian's expulsion of the philosophers from Italy in 89 A.D., continued his teaching in the Epirote city of Nicopolis. Although Epictetus left nothing in writing his lectures and conversations were preserved by his distinguished disciple, the Greek historian and philosopher Arnan.

Do you, my friend, who were given everything from the hands of another, complain and accuse the Giver when he takes something from you? Tell me, who are you and what is the purpose of your coming here? Was it not He who brought you into the world and made you see the Light and gave you co-workers and senses and the ability to reason? Tell me, how did He bring you into the world? Was it not as a mere mortal creature destined to die? As one who was to live out his life on earth in the confines of a small tabernacle of flesh? One who was to behold His rule and share with Him for a while the mighty parade of this great Festival? And now that you have beheld, while permission was granted to you, the solemn Festival and the Assembly, won't you depart gladly as He calls you forward with adoration and a gratitude for what you have seen and heard? "Yes," you say, "but I would have liked to have stayed longer at the Festival." The mystics would also have preferred to prolong their rites, and likewise the crowd at the Great Games would have liked to see more wrestling matches. But the solemn Festival is over, my friend. Come forward, then, and depart with gratitude and modesty. Give your place to others who must come into being just as you did.

Realize that the main source of all evils, the source of moral disgrace and cowardice, is not death itself but the fear of death. I beg you, therefore, to protect yourself against this fear by directing all of your reasonings, your exercises and your readings to the attainment of this goal. Then you will understand that only in this manner are men set free.

If you search for truth you will not be interested in winning by every possible means. And, when you have found truth, you will not fear defeat.

Keep in mind that you are an actor in a play which may be long or short, a play whose plot is decided by the Author. If He has the pleasure of assigning you the role of a beggar, a king, or a private citizen, it is your obligation to play your part well. Your duty is to act the assigned part. Choosing it is the prerogative of another.

When you feast, don't forget that you are entertaining two guests, body and soul. What you feed the body you lose. What you give to the soul is yours forever!

The Education of an Emperor:
Marcus Aurelius, *Meditations* 1

**Marcus Aurelius, the adoptive son of the Emperor
Antoninus Pius, succeeded to the imperial throne in 161 and
ruled until his death in 180 A.D. A student of the orator Fronto,
he ultimately turned to the study of the Stoic philosophy and
became one of its leading exponents. His *Meditations,* which he
wrote in Greek, rank among the most eloquent expositions of
this great philosophical system and reveal the mind and
character of the Emperor. In Book I, which appears below, he
described the contributions to his education of his family and
other associates.**

From my grandfather Verus I learned good morals and self-control.

From the reputation and memory of my father I learned modesty and a
manly character.

From my mother I learned piety, generosity and abstinence, not only from
evil deeds, but also from evil thoughts. She also taught me how to live simply,
avoiding the excesses of the wealthy.

From my great-grandfather I learned that a good private education at home
is better than a public education, and that a man should spend liberally on it.

From my governor I learned not to become involved in the factions at
the games in the Circus and at the gladiatorial contests. He also taught me how
to endure hard work, to have few wants, to work with my hands, to stay out
of the affairs of others and to avoid listening to slander.

Diognetus taught me not to waste my time in the pursuit of trifling things,
to ignore the things that miracle-workers and other charlatans say about
incantations, exorcising evil spirits and other things of a similar nature, and to
avoid the breeding of fighting birds and becoming passionately involved in such
things. He also taught me to respect freedom of speech, encouraged me to
become a student first of Bacchius and then of Tandasis and Marcianus, showed
me how to write dialogues when I was still a youth, and gave me a desire for
a plank bed and a pelt and all the other things that belong to the Greek regimen.

It was Rusticus who made me realize that my character needed
improvement and discipline. From him I also learned not to be led astray to
argumentative sophistry, not to write on speculative matters, not to deliver short
exhortatory speeches, not to show myself off as someone who practices much

discipline or does benevolent deeds, to abstain from rhetoric, poetry and fine writing, not to wear outdoor clothes inside the house and other such things, and to write my letters in a simple style, like that in which Rusticus wrote to my mother from Sinuessa. As for those who have offended me in word or deed, he taught me to be easily reconciled with them as soon as they express a desire to be reconciled with me. He taught me to read a book carefully and not to be satisfied with a merely superficial understanding of its contents. He also taught me not to agree too readily with people who talk too much. Finally, I am grateful to him for his knowledge of the discourses of Epictetus, which he made available to me in his own library.

From Apollonius I learned freedom of will, absolute constancy of purpose and always to rely on reason and reason alone. He taught me always to maintain the same disposition, whether in great pain, while suffering from a chronic illness, or even on the occasion of the loss of a child. He made me see clearly, by providing a living example in his own person, that a man can be both resolute and flexible, and not impatient in giving his instruction. He was for me the very model of the man who considers his experience and expertise in the exposition of philosophical principles as the least significant of his merits. Finally, I also learned from him how to accept from friends such things as are commonly considered favors without being either overwhelmed by them or appearing ungrateful.

Sextus taught me the value of a benevolent disposition, how to govern a family in a paternal manner and the concept of living in harmony with Nature. From him I also learned how to be dignified without affecting dignity, to watch out for the interests of one's friends, and to be tolerant of ignorant people and those who form opinions about things they don't understand. Sextus had the ability to accommodate himself to all sorts of people, so that conversing with him was more pleasant than being flattered by him; at the same time, he was very highly regarded by those who associated with him. He was able to discover and apply in an intelligent way those principles which are necessary for life. He never displayed anger or any other emotion, for he was entirely free from passion. He was also the most affectionate of men. Sextus could express approbation without much fanfare and, although he was a man of much knowledge, he was never ostentatious.

Alexander the grammarian taught me how to avoid the habit of finding fault with others and how not to reprove those who use barbaric, ungrammatical or odd-sounding expressions in their speech. I learned instead to introduce gently into the conversation, by means of a question or statement or some other appropriate means, the very expression which should have been used.

Fronto taught me to note the envy, duplicity and hypocrisy which are characteristic of tyrants, and that the people we call Patricians are, generally speaking, rather deficient in paternal affection.

From Alexander the Platonist I learned not to say frequently or without good reason, or to write in a letter, that I have no free time; also, not to constantly allege urgent occupations as an excuse for neglecting my responsibilities to those with whom I live.

From Catulus I learned not to be indifferent when a friend criticizes me, even if he has no good reason for doing so, but to restore him to his usual friendly disposition. In addition, he taught me to speak well of my teachers, as Domitius is said to have spoken of Ahenodotus, and to truly love my children.

My brother Severus taught me to love my family, truth and justice. Because of him I came to know Thrasea, Helvidius, Cato, Dion and Brutus. Severus gave me the idea of a state with one law for all and built on the principles of equal rights and freedom of speech as well as the concept of a monarchy which respects nothing more than the freedom of subjects. He taught me to be constant and uncompromising in my respect for philosophy, to be benevolent and generous to others, to be optimistic, and to be confident that I am loved by my friends. I observed him to be completely frank when expressing his opinions about those of whom he did not approve and noted that his friends never needed to guess what he wanted or did not want, for his desires were always quite plain.

From Maximus I learned self-mastery, how to commit to a cause, and to be cheerful in all circumstances, including sickness. He taught me the correct proportions in one's moral character of sweetness and dignity and how to do my duty without complaining. I noted that people believed him to be a thoughtful speaker and that in everything he did he had good intentions. He never seemed surprised or amazed. He never hurried, nor did he procrastinate. He was never perplexed or downcast. He never forced himself to laugh in order to hide his irritation, and he was never morose or suspicious. He taught me the meaning of beneficence, how to forgive, and how to be truthful. He impressed me as a man who walked the right path because it was his nature to do so rather than as one who had been improved by others. I noticed that no one ever felt that he was despised by Maximus or dared to think himself a better man. Finally, had an agreeable sense of humor.

I observed in my [adoptive] father a mildness of temper and an unwavering commitment to the philosophical positions he had taken after serious deliberation. He never found any particular glory in those things which are commonly regarded as honors, loved work and thoroughness, and was willing to listen to anyone who had a proposal for the improvement of society. He taught me how to be inflexibly firm in giving every man his due and, drawing on his own experience, how to know when to act or not to act. I observed that he had overcome all passion for boys, that he did not consider himself to be above the public, that he did not require his friends to take their meals with him or accompany him when he went abroad, and that those who did not, no matter what their reason, always found him to be a man of understanding. I also noted his habit of making careful inquiries into those matters which required his attention, his perseverance, and that he was never willing to conclude his investigations prematurely on the basis of first impressions. He had the habit of keeping his friends, rather than quickly becoming tired of them, and never displayed extremes of affection. It was his nature to be content and cheerful on all occasions and to exercise sufficient foresight to anticipate even the most unlikely eventualities.

In him I observed the habit of limiting popular acclamations and flattery, an ever watchful eye to the needs of the Empire, the wise management of its resources, and a patient endurance of the criticism he received from those who did not approve of his policies. He was not superstitious, nor did he attempt to make himself popular by giving gifts to the people or by flattering them; instead, he was always sober in all things, and firm, and never showed much interest in vulgar things or novelties. Those things which make life more comfortable or pleasant in some way, and which good fortune brings in abundance, he used without arrogance or excuse; when he had them he enjoyed them without calling attention to himself, and when he did not have them he did not want them. No one ever accused him of being either a sophist of a flippant slave or a pedant, but everyone agreed that he was a man perfect in his maturity, above flattery, and able to manage his own and other people's affairs. He honored true philosophers; as for those who merely pretended to be philosophers, he neither criticized them nor was he easily influenced by them. He was easy to talk to, and he made himself agreeable in conversation without offensive affectation. He took good care of his body's health, not because he was particularly attached to life or concerned about his personal appearance, but so that, by virtue of his own actions, he would rarely need physicians, medicines or other treatments. He was always willing to step aside without envy in favor of those who possessed some special talent or ability, such as eloquence or knowledge of the law of morals or anything else, and he offered them his assistance so that each might enjoy the reputation he deserved.

My father always acted in harmony with the institutions of his country, and in this his behavior was never forced, but natural. He was neither fond of change nor unsteady, but loved to remain in familiar places doing familiar things, and after suffering attacks of headache he would immediately return refreshed and full of energy to the pursuit of his usual routine. He had only a very few secrets, all of them concerning public matters and showed wisdom and restraint in what he spent on public spectacles, public buildings, distributions of money to the people and in other such things, for he was a man who was concerned with what ought to be done, and not with doing whatever would enhance his reputation. He did not go to the baths at odd hours, take pleasure in building houses for himself, or show much interest in the food he ate, the texture and color of his clothes, or the beauty of his slaves. His clothes came from Lorium, his villa on the coast, and from the region of Lanuvium generally. Everyone knows how he behaved to the toll-collector at Tusculum who asked his forgiveness; this was the way he always acted. There was nothing harsh, implacable or violent about him, nothing capable of bringing him, as they say, to the boiling point. He examined all things individually, as if he had plenty of time, and in an unconfused, orderly, vigorous and consistent manner. One might say of him what is said of Socrates, that he was able to abstain from those things which most people are too weak to resist and to enjoy in moderation those which most people enjoy to excess. Such strength and sobriety are the marks of the man who has a perfect and invincible soul, such as he showed when Maximus was ill.

I thank the gods that I have had good grandfathers, good parents, a good sister, good teachers, good friends and good relatives; nearly all of those around me have been good. I am also thankful that I never offended any of them, though I had the kind of disposition which would have led me to act offensively if an opportunity had arisen; by the grace of the gods, however, I was never put to the test. Moreover, I am grateful that I was not not brought up with my grandfather's concubine, that I preserved my virginity and waited to prove my virility until the proper time, that I lived under the authority of a ruler and father who was able to banish all conceit from me and make me understand that it is possible for a man to live in a palace without desiring guards, beautiful clothes, torches, statues and the like, and that it is within the power of such a ruler to live very much like a private citizen without being, as a consequence, either meaner in thought or more negligent in action with respect to those things which must be done, for the sake of the public, in kingly fashion.

I thank the gods for giving me a brother who was able, by his moral character, to teach me how to be vigilant over myself and, at the same time, to give me such delight by his respect and affection. I am grateful that my children have been mentally and physically sound; that I did not achieve greater proficiency in rhetoric, poetry and the other studies to which I might have given more attention had I noted I was making progress in them; that I quickly appointed to positions of honor, which they seemed to desire, those who reared me, and that I did so while they were still young instead of putting them off with nothing more than the hope that I would remember them later; that I came to know Apollonius, Rusticus and Maximus; and that I received clear and frequent impressions about what it means to live in harmony with Nature, so that, thanks to gods, because of their gifts and intentions, there was nothing to stop me from living in accordance with Nature, though I have fallen short of this goal because of my own faults and because I have not paid attention to the admonitions and, I might say, the instructions which the gods have given me.

I thank the gods that my body has lasted so long, considering the kind of life I have lived; that I never touched Benedicta or Theodotus; that after having fallen into erotic passions I was cured of them; that, although I often had difficulties with Rusticus, I never did anything which I lived to regret; that my mother, though it was her fate to die young, spent the last year of her life with me; that whenever I wanted to help someone in need, or do some other thing, I was never told that I did not have the necessary means; that I was never dependent on gifts from others; that I have a wife who is obedient, affectionate and unaffected; that I have had many good teachers for my children; that in dreams I have learned of remedies for bloodspitting and giddiness; and that, when I was attracted to philosophy, I did not fall into the hands of some sophist or waste time studying writers, analyzing syllogisms or looking for signs in the heavens, for these things can be done only with the help of the gods and fortune.

A Stoic Emperor: Marcus Aurelius, *Meditations*

While most philosophical writings are carefully composed works which undertake the sustained analysis of a given problem or theme, the *Meditations* of Marcus Aurelius take the form of a journal or diary in which the emperor often sets down only a few words on ideas which he presents in no logical order. Still, the work is perhaps the best extant exposition of the content of Roman Stoicism. The selections below are drawn from throughout the *Meditations* and express many of the basic features of Stoic ideology, such as the concept of the universe as a rational whole which works for the good, the doctrine of universal brotherhood, and the importance of indifference to the vicissitudes of fortune.

Begin each morning by saying to yourself, Today I will meet all sorts of people: busybodies, ingrates, arrogant people, and also those who are deceitful, envious and unsocial. They are what they are because they have no understanding of good and evil. But I have seen the essential beauty of good and the ugliness of evil, and I know that these wrongdoers and I are by nature the same—not that we are related by blood or seed, but that our minds are alike, and that we share equally in divinity—and so they can neither harm nor shame me. Neither can I feel anger against the wrongdoer or hate him, for we are brothers. We were born to work together, like hands, eyes, and the upper and lower rows of teeth. To work against another is to work against Nature, and to be angry with someone and turn away from him is to work against him.

*

Whether the universe is nothing more than atoms in motion or Nature is a system, one thing is certain: that I am a part of the Whole which is governed by Nature. I am related in some way to all its other parts and, remembering this, I will not be dissatisfied with any of the things which are assigned to me out of the Whole. Nothing is harmful to the part that works to the advantage of the Whole.

Whatever this is that I am, it is part flesh, part breath, and part intellect. Throw away your books and don't be anxious, for this is not your role in life. Instead, look on your existence as though you were dying. Despise your body, for it is nothing but blood, bones and networks of nerves, veins and arteries. Consider that your breath is air, and not even always the same air, that is continually exhaled and sucked in. Remember that the third part is the intellect, which directs the rest, and that you are an old man. Let this part be enslaved no longer, no longer manipulated like a puppet by selfish impulses, no longer either unhappy with your present lot or fearful of the future.

*

It is not often that a man is made unhappy by failing to take note of what is happening in someone else's soul; rather, it is those who do not pay attention to the disturbances within their own souls who are bound to be unhappy.

*

Keep in mind the nature of the Whole, your nature, and the way in which the two are related—that you are a part of the Whole. Remember that no one has the power to keep you from doing and saying the things which are according to the nature of the Whole of which you are a part.

*

No one can prevent you from living according to the reason which is a part of your own nature. Nothing can ever happen to you which is against the reason of the universal Nature.

*

The wise and modest man says to Nature, who gives and then takes away all things: "Give what you will and take what you will." He does not say this proudly, but obediently, and is satisfied.

*

Death reduced Alexander the Great and his groom to the same state; both were either returned to the seminal principles of the universe or dispersed among the atoms.

*

Accept wealth and prosperity without arrogance, and be ready to let them go.

*

Let your every word, thought and action be that of one who is ready at any moment to leave this life. There is nothing terrible in leaving the world of men since, if the gods exist, they would never allow you to fall into evil. If, on the other hand, they do not exist or do not care about us, then what point would there be in living in a world without the gods and Providence?

*

Even though you may be destined to live for three thousand years, and as many times ten thousand years, remember that a man cannot lose any life other than that which he is living now, nor can he live any life other than that which he is now losing. There is no real difference between the longest of lives and the shortest, for the present is the same for all, though we who perish are not the same, and so that which is lost is a mere moment. A man cannot lose either the past or the future, for how could anyone take from him what is not his?

*

Are you angry with someone because his body stinks? Are you displeased with another because she had bad breath? What good does it do to be angry? He does smell bad. She does have bad breath. . . . But they also have reason, and so they are capable of discovering, if they try, the way in which they are offending you. . . . And you, too, have reason. Use it to make them rational. Use it to show them their errors. If they listen you will have cured them, and without anger.

*

Men exist for the sake of one another. Instruct them, then, or put up with them.

*

Consider how much trouble is avoided by the man who, instead of concentrating on what his neighbor says or does or thinks, focuses instead on his own life in order to make it just and pure.

*

There is a kind of man who will charge another for a favor. A second kind will not go quite that far, but will always remember the favor he has done and think of the man he did it for as his debtor. But there is a third kind of man, the kind who really isn't aware that he has done a favor at all. Such a man is like a vine which has produced some grapes, but does not seek anything in return. Like a horse which has run, a dog which has tracked game, or a bee when it has made some honey, such a man, when he has done some good thing, does not call for the attention of others, but goes on to do some other good thing, just as a vine goes on to produce more grapes for the next vintage.

*

Get into the habit of paying careful attention to what the other person says. Try your best to be inside his mind.

*

The man who sins sins against himself. He who acts unjustly treats himself unfairly because he makes himself bad.

*

Look within yourself. Within is a fountain of goodness, and it will always bubble up if you will only search for it.

*

In the morning when you are not eager to rise, keep this thought in mind—I am rising to function as a human being. Why should I be dissatisfied if I am going to do the things I was made to do and for which I was brought into the world? Can it be that my purpose is to lie here under the covers keeping myself warm? It is more comfortable to lie here, but is it your purpose to be comfortable, and not to exert yourself or take action? Don't you see the little plants, the little birds, the ants, the spiders, the bees—how they work together to set in order their special places in the Whole? Are you, then, unwilling to do the work of a human being? Will you not hurry to do that which is according to your own nature?

*

Do not act as though you are going to live ten thousand years. Death hangs over your head. While you are alive, while you still have the power, be good.

*

Don't just talk about the kind of man that a good man ought to be. Be a good man.

VI
Ancient Lives

The Story of Cincinnatus: Livy, History, III. 26–29.

At the beginning of his history of Rome, Livy wrote that it was his purpose not merely to record events but also to trace the moral decline of the Roman people during the seven hundred years since the founding of their city. Among those he cites as exemplars of the noble character of the early Romans is Lucius Quinctius Cincinnatus. According to tradition, in 458 B.C., when the consul Minucius was trapped on Mt. Algidus by the hostile Aequi, Cincinnatus was appointed dictator and sent to his rescue. The dictatorship gave its holder six months of extraordinary military and political power for the purpose of dealing with some serious threat to the city. That Cincinnatus surrendered the office after a successful term of only fifteen days was, for Livy, evidence of his patriotism and lack of self-interest.

What follows will be of particular interest to those who think that great honor and virtue are in some way dependent upon money and can be found only among the wealthy.

At that time the one man in whom Rome placed all her hope, Cincinnatus, was working a little three-acre farm, now known as the Quinctian Meadows, across the Tiber and just opposite the place where the dockyards are today. It was there that the representatives of the state found him deeply involved in some farmer's task—digging a ditch, perhaps, or plowing. After an exchange of greetings, and expressing their wish that all would turn out well for him and the Roman people, they asked him to put on his toga and come with them to hear the orders of the Senate. Surprised, he asked, "Is something wrong?" He then asked his wife Racilia to get his toga from their cottage. After putting it on he wiped away the dirt and sweat and went out again to meet the representatives. As he approached they hailed him, with congratulations, as Dictator and asked him to come to Rome, all the while describing the frightening situation in which the city now found itself.

A boat owned by the state was waiting to take him, and when he had crossed to the other bank he was welcomed first by his three sons, then by other family members and friends, and finally by almost the entire Senate. Surrounded by all of these, and preceded by the lictors, he made his way to his lodgings. A huge crowd of plebeians had also gathered, but they were not at all pleased to see the Dictator since they believed that his authority was excessive and that he was likely to abuse it. No action was taken that night other then to maintain a watch in the city.

The next day Cincinnatus arrived before dawn at the Forum where he named as his Master of Horse Lucius Tarquitius, a patrician whose poverty had reduced him to service in the infantry but whose conduct in battle had earned him a reputation as Rome's finest soldier. Cincinnatus then appeared with his new Master of Horse before a meeting of the people to issue his orders: business in the courts was to be suspended, shops were to be closed, and private business of all kinds was prohibited. Next, he ordered all men of military age to bring their weapons, enough rations for five days and twelve stakes to the Campus Martius before sunset. Those who were too old to fight were told to prepare food for the soldiers while the latter were getting their equipment together.

And so the young soldiers ran about looking for their stakes [which they used for building palisades], and no one objected as they took them from wherever they could be found. They then reported to the Campus Martius as Cincinnatus had commanded. The men formed up into ranks suitable both for marching and fighting and then set out with Cincinnatus at the head of the foot-soldiers and Lucius Tarquitius leading the cavalry.

The two commanders exhorted and encouraged their men as the occasion demanded, shouting at them to quicken their pace and reminding them that they would have to move fast in order to reach the enemy during the night. The situation was grave: a consul and a Roman army had been under siege for three days; no one knew what might happen during the night or the next day; a single instant could determine the fate of the besieged. The men shouted too, pleasing their leaders with cries of "Faster, standard-bearer!" and "Follow him, soldiers!" At midnight they came to Mount Algidus and halted not far from the enemy camp.

After the Dictator had ridden around the camp and judged its size and shape as well as the darkness would allow, he instructed the military tribunes to have the men set down their packs in one spot and return to their ranks with only their weapons and their stakes. His orders were carried out. Then, leading the soldiers in the same long column in which they had marched from Rome, he had them surround the enemy camp. Their orders were to wait for a signal, whereupon each man was to raise a shout and then dig a trench and build a palisade in front of his own position. The signal came quite soon thereafter and the men did just as they had been commanded. Their shouting went up on all sides of the enemy camp and passed over it and into the camp of Minucius; in the one it caused terror, in the other it brought great joy. The beleaguered Romans congratulated each other that help had at last arrived, and their guards and sentinels now began to assume the offensive. Minucius himself determined that he should not delay his attack since the shouting meant not only that friends had come, but that they had already begun their own attack against the outside of the enemy camp. He ordered his men to take up their weapons and follow him. It was still night when the battle began, and the battle-cry of the encircled Romans told Cincinnatus and his men that their compatriots were in action at last.

The Aequi were already busy trying to keep Cincinnatus' troops from surrounding them when Minucius and his men, whom *they* had surrounded, began their attack. In order to prevent them from forcing their way through the middle of their camp, the Aequi turned to engage Minucius. This maneuver left Cincinnatus' troops unchallenged, and so they had time to work on their trenches and palisades while Minucius kept the Aequi occupied for the rest of the night. By dawn the Aequi were beginning to lose ground; moreover, they were now trapped inside the Dictator's fortifications. At this point Cincinnatus' men attacked them, forcing them to fight on two fronts. Before long they gave up and begged Cincinnatus and Minucius to allow them to drop their weapons and go home. Minucius referred them to the Dictator, who allowed them to surrender, but only with humiliation. He ordered that their commander Cloelius Gracchus and his lieutenants should be brought to him in chains and that the town of Corbio should be evacuated. Cincinnatus said that he would not demand the blood of the Aequi, but that he would require them to demonstrate the fact of their subjection to Rome by "passing under the yoke." And so a "yoke" was made from three spears—two of them stuck upright in the ground and a third laid across them—and the Aequi were forced to pass under it as they departed.

The Aequi had left behind all their military gear, and so the Romans found much that was valuable in their camp. Cincinnatus divided this only among his own troops; Minucius and his men got nothing. Shouting angrily, the Dictator told them: "You soldiers will get nothing from an enemy who nearly took *you*; and you, Lucius Minucius, will be my lieutenant until you learn to think and act like a consul." So Minucius resigned the consulship and took his place with the army as Cincinnatus' second-in-command. The men whom he had previously commanded were so impressed by their new leader and by the way in which he had rescued them from a humiliating defeat that they submitted to him completely and voted to honor him with a gold circlet one pound in weight and saluted him as their protector as he left them to return to Rome.

In the city the Senate was convened by Quintus Fabius, the City Prefect, and called upon Cincinnatus and his troops to pass through Rome's gates in a triumphal procession. Cincinnatus himself rode in a chariot. He was preceded by the standard-bearers and the enemy commanders. Behind him came the troops, who carried all the spoils of battle. They say that there were tables spread with food before all of Rome's houses, and that the soldiers feasted and sang and joked as they walked along, following Cincinnatus like men at some great party. That same day Lucius Mamilius of Tusculum was granted Roman citizenship by popular acclaim.

Cincinnatus would have resigned the dictatorship that very day had it not been for the upcoming perjury trial of Marcus Volscius [a former tribune whose testimony in the trial of Cincinnatus' son Caeso had ruined the family's fortune]. The tribunes were so in awe of the Dictator that they made no attempt to interfere; Volscius was found guilty and sent into exile at Lanuvium. Cincinnatus then surrendered his powers as Dictator after serving only fifteen days in a office he had been given to hold for six months.

During the same period Nautius defeated the Sabines at Eretum, adding this disaster to the previous devastation of their fields. Quintus Fabius was sent to replace Minucius at Mount Algidus. Toward the end of the year the tribunes called again for passage of the law [proposed by Gaius Terentillus Arsa, which would limit the power of the consuls], but the Senate insisted that no proposal should be put before the people when two armies were away from the city. The plebeians did gain a victory, however, in electing the same tribunes for a fifth term. They say that at that time wolves were seen being chased by dogs on the Capitol—a sign that the Capitol had been purified. Such were the events of this year [458 B.C.].

A Roman of the Old School:
Plutarch, *Marcus Cato* 4, 22, 23

Marcus Cato (234-149 B.C.), also known as Cato the Elder and Cato the Censor, fought in the Second Punic War and went on to hold many public offices in Rome. A conservative, he used his political power and remarkable oratorical skill to attack the immorality of the Roman upper class and to reestablish traditional Roman values and institutions. The latter, be believed, had fallen into decay because of the wealth and foreign ideas and practices which flowed into Rome as the consequences of a growing empire. Cato found Greek civilization in all its aspects especially pernicious and sought to limit its influence in Rome by delivering impassioned speeches against it and philhellenes such as Scipio Africanus and his family.

Catos' eloquence brought him considerable power, and many went so far as to call him a Roman Demosthenes. But his lifestyle was even more famous and talked about. This was so because the pursuit of oratorical skill was something quite common in those days, while a man such as Cato was very rare: a man who worked with his own hands as his father had done, who was content with a cold breakfast, a light dinner, plain clothes and a simple house, who was more interested in doing without luxuries than in possessing them. Now, by this time Rome had grown too large to preserve the purity of its original values and habits. So many peoples and places had come under its control that the city had become a kind of cultural mixing bowl from which many Romans eagerly sampled and adopted all sorts of foreign ideas and customs. It was with good reason, then, that Cato was so admired, for while such men could be seen weakening under the burden of their work and made soft by their pursuit of pleasure, he was victorious over both. And this was true not only when he was young and ambitious for honor, but also when his hair was white with age, after a consulship and triumph. Like a victorious athlete he continued to train, keeping his strength of character and clarity of mind until the very end.

Cato himself says that he never wore clothing worth more than a hundred drachmas and that even when he was praetor or consul he drank the same wine as his slaves. He tells us that the fish and meat he bought in the market never cost more than thirty *asses,* and that the only reason he ate meat at all was for the city's sake, so that his body would be strong for war; that he once inherited an embroidered Babylonian robe, but sold it immediately; that not one of his farmhouses had plastered walls. He never paid more than fifteen hundred drachmas for a slave since he did not want soft and beautiful ones but hardworking types who could care for the horses and cattle; and he believed that these should be sold again when they became old, so that he would not have to feed them when they were useless. In general, Cato believed that no unnecessary thing could be had for a good price, no matter how small, and that money spent on land for growing or grazing was well-spent while that invested in acreage covered by sprinkled lawns and swept paths was wasted. . . .

When he had grown quite old two philosophers came to Rome from Athens: Carneades the Academic and Diogenes the Stoic. They came as ambassadors to request the reversal of a judgment in which a fine of five hundred talents had been imposed on Athens. The suit had been brought by the people of Oropus and judged by the Sicyonians; the Athenians themselves had not offered a defense. As soon as the philosophers arrived all of the studious young men of Rome hurried to meet them and sat entranced as they spoke. Carneades was the better speaker, his words having elegance and power and a reputation to match. Large and approving audiences came to hear him, and before long news of him spread throughout the entire city like a mighty wind. It was said that an amazing Greek whose eloquence enchanted and won over all who heard him had filled the young men of the city with such an enthusiasm for philosophy that they had abandoned all their other pleasures and pastimes. Most of the Romans were pleased to see their young men taking an interest in Greek culture and associating with these admirable men, but Cato was disturbed by this passion for rhetoric and discussion as soon as it began to fill the city, for he was afraid that the young men would lose sight of their true goal and come to love words more than work and war. When the fame of the philosophers continued to grow and a man of such distinction as Gaius Acilius asked to be their interpreter at their first appearance before the Senate, Cato resolved to have all philosophers expelled from the city. He strode into the Senate and scolded the senators for keeping such persuasive ambassadors in suspense for so long. "We ought to make up our minds," he said, "and vote on the ambassadors' petition, so that they may return to their own schools in Greece and lecture to Greek children; then the youth of Rome will turn their attention back to the laws and rulers of their own country."

He did not do this out of anger toward Carneades, as some think, but because he had nothing but scorn for philosophy in general, and because his patriotic pride prompted him to scoff at anything Greek. He used to say, for example, that Socrates was just a big talker who tried to tyrannize the Athenians by destroying their ancient customs and enticing them into opinions contrary to their laws. He ridiculed the students of Isocrates, saying that they continued to study with their master until they were old men, as if they intended never to exercise their legal and oratorical skills until they had died and gone to the court of Minos in Hades. In order to set his son against all things Greek, he did something unbecoming a man his age: speaking in a loud and angry voice, as if he were a prophet, he "predicted" that Rome would fall when it became infected with Greek literature. Time, of course, has shown how wrong he was, for it was precisely when the city was at the peak of its power that Greek learning had its greatest influence there.

It was not only Greek philosophers he despised, but also the Greek physicians who practiced their art in Rome. It seems he had heard how Hippocrates, when the king of Persia had offered him a fortune just to examine him, had sworn that he would never use his skill to help barbarians who were the enemies of the Greeks. Cato argued that all Greek physicians had taken the same oath and warned his son to beware of them. He himself had written a little book full of medical notes to which he turned whenever a member of his household was sick.

Hannibal: Cornelius Nepos, "Hannibal" 1-2 (in *On Illustrious Men*)

The story of the great Carthaginian general Hannibal's oath of eternal hatred of Rome was recorded by Cornelius Nepos (*ca.* 99-24 B.C.), a native of Gaul who lived in Rome and was a friend of Cicero. His *On Illustrious Men* does not match the high standard in biography set by Suetonius, Plutarch and others. Nevertheless, in ancient times his historical and biographical works (most of which are lost) were highly regarded by such luminaries as the poet Catullus, and modern historians consider his brief accounts of the lives of illustrious men to be a valuable source for the history of antiquity.

If it is true, and no one denies it, that the Romans were superior to all other peoples in military virtue, then it must also be said that Hannibal was superior to all other generals in strategy. Indeed, he won every battle he fought against the Romans in Italy and might well have gone on to conquer Rome had he not been undermined by envious and spiteful politicians in Carthage.

Hannibal inherited from his father a legacy of such hatred of Rome that he cared more for his hostility than for his own life. Even when he had been exiled from Carthage and forced to depend on foreign peoples for protection he worked relentlessly against the interests of the Romans. Far away [in Macedon] he turned Philip V against the Romans, and there was also King Antiochus of Syria, a man considered to be the most powerful potentate of his time. Hannibal filled him with such anger toward the Romans that he made preparations for moving his army from the Red Sea toward Italy. Roman envoys came to Antiochus to examine his plan of action and to make him suspicious of Hannibal. In fact, they succeeded in making him believe that they had succeeded in bribing Hannibal to switch allegiances. When Hannibal learned of this development, and that he was no longer invited to participate in the King's councils, he managed to arrange an audience with Antiochus during which he explained his enmity toward Rome: "When I was a boy of nine," he said, "my father Hamilcar asked if I would like to go with him to Spain. At that time he was offering sacrifices to Jupiter Optimus Maximus in preparation for his departure from Carthage. I said yes, of course, and begged him not to change his mind. He assured me that he would take me along, but only if I did what he asked. He then led me to the sacrificial altar, placed my hand on

247

it and ordered me to swear that I would never befriend the Romans. I have kept that sacred pledge to my father so faithfully that there is no reason why anyone should doubt my intention to hold to it for the rest of my life. Therefore, if you have plans to make an alliance with Rome it would be best to keep them hidden from me, but if your intention is to fight the Romans you would be wise to make me commander of your army."

A Roman Billionaire: Plutarch
Crassus, 1-2

Marcus Licinius Crassus was one of the more colorful figures in the history of the late Republic. An aristocrat, he gained immense wealth through real estate speculation and used it and his talent for easily making friends to gain political influence and offices. While he generally promoted the interests of the equestrians instead of those of his own class, it is difficult to determine whether he had any other political goals beyond the mere acquisition of power. He served as consul in 70 B.C. and then again, in 60 B.C., as a member of the First Triumvirate, which also included Pompey and Julius Caesar.

Marcus Crassus was the son of a man who had been a censor and honored with a triumph, yet he was reared in a small house with his two brothers. The brothers married while their parents were still alive, and all of them continued to share the same table. This may very well explain why Crassus' style of life was one of temperance and moderation. When one of his brothers died, Crassus married his widow and had children with her, and in his relations with his family he was as proper and well-disciplined as any Roman. And yet when he was older he was accused of having sexual relations with one of the Vestal Virgins, Licinia, who was prosecuted by a certain Plotius. Now, Licinia owned some nice property in the suburbs that Crassus was hoping to get for very little money, and this was why he was always following and flattering her until at last he fell under suspicion of being her lover. And, in a way, it was his well-known greed which led the jurors to clear him of the charge of corrupting one of the Vestals. But he never let her go until he had managed to get possession of her property.

The Romans say that Crassus' many virtues were obscured by the vice of avarice, which became stronger than his other faults and actually weakened them. The chief proofs of his avarice are the means by which he got his wealth and the actual amount of it. In the beginning he had no more than 300 talents. Then, during his [first] consulship, he gave a tenth of what he owned to the god Hercules, provided a feast for the people, and even gave every Roman out of his own pocket enough money to live on for three months. And yet, when he made a private inventory of his property before his campaign against the Parthians, he found that he had 7100 talents. The truth, however scandalous, is that he acquired most of this through fire and war. Public disasters were his greatest source of income.

For example, when Sulla seized Rome and sold the property of the men whose deaths he had ordered, identifying it as "spoils of war," he wanted to involve as many influential men as he could in his crime. Crassus never wasted an opportunity to buy or receive such property. In addition, since he knew how often buildings in Rome burned down or collapsed because they were too heavy and close together, he bought slaves who were architects and builders. When he had more than five hundred of these he began buying houses that were on fire and houses next to those that were on fire, for he knew that their frantic owners would sell them for almost nothing. In this way he became the owner of most of Rome. Curiously, although he owned so many workmen he never built for himself any house other than the one in which he lived. In fact, he used to say that men who loved building too much would bring about their own undoing without help from anyone else. And even though he owned many silver mines and much valuable land complete with laborers, all of this was nothing next to the value of his many and valuable slaves.

Cornelia, Mother of the Gracchi:
Plutarch, *Tiberius Gracchus* 1 and
Gaius Gracchus 19

Roman tradition glorified few women more than Cornelia, the mother of the reformers Tiberius and Gaius Gracchus. The daughter of the great Scipio Africanus and wife of Tiberius Sempronius Gracchus, she was gifted with great intelligence and a political acumen which she used to help shape the careers of her famous sons. Cornelia was highly regarded for her wisdom and nobility of character, and there were many who came to her for advice and conversation even long after the deaths of her husband and sons. Later writers portrayed her as the ideal Roman mother, among them the Greek biographer Plutarch. In the following excerpts he describes Cornelia's management of her household as a young widow and how she later dealt with the deaths of Tiberius and Gaius.

There is a story according to which Tiberius once found a pair of snakes in his bed and was told by the augurs that he should neither kill both of them nor allow both to escape. Their interpretation was that he would have to kill one of them; if he killed the male he would bring about his own death, and if he killed the female Cornelia would die. Gracchus loved his wife and was well aware that, while he was rather old, she was still quite young. Reasoning that it would be better for him to die, he killed the male snake and let the female slither away. He died soon thereafter, leaving Cornelia with their twelve children.

Cornelia took charge both of the family and the estate and showed herself to be so sensible, loving and noble that it was thought Tiberius had done well in choosing to die and allowing his wife to live. In fact, when Ptolemy, the king of Egypt, asked her to marry him and be his queen she refused. It was as a widow, then, that she lost all but three of her children. One, a daughter, married Scipio the Younger, and her two surviving sons, Tiberius and Gaius, are the subjects of this biography. Cornelia reared her boys with such great care that although everyone agrees no other Romans were given more in the way of natural gifts, they were thought to owe their virtues even more to their education than to nature.

They say that Cornelia bore her misfortunes with nobility and grace, and that she said of the holy places where her sons had been killed that they were tombs worthy of those who occupied them. She went to live on the promontory called Misenum, but otherwise kept to her usual way of life. She had many friends and kept a good and generous table, she was always surrounded by Greeks and other learned men, and all the reigning kings exchanged gifts with her. Her visitors and close friends loved to hear her tell stories about the life and habits of her father, Scipio Africanus, but they admired her most of all for being able to describe the achievements and deaths of her sons without sorrow or tears, as if she were speaking of men from the early days of Rome. This led some to conclude that old age or the great burden of her grief had dulled her mind, so that she was insensitive to her misfortunes. But the truth of the matter is that such people themselves are insensitive, for they do not understand that a noble nature, an honorable ancestry and a good upbringing can give us immense strength in the face of grief, and that even though fate may thwart the efforts of the virtuous to avoid evil, it can never take from us our power to endure it with peace of mind.

The Character of Caesar: Suetonius, *Julius Caesar*, 45–54

Gaius Julius Caesar's multi-faceted genius was a unique phenomenon in Roman history. Lavishly endowed with energy, intellect and versatility, he made his mark as a soldier, politician, statesman, orator and historian. However, his biography by Suetonius, an administrator who served as secretary to Hadrian, is not entirely laudatory. Making use of hostile as well as complimentary sources, Suetonius produced a fascinating portrait of this complex and important figure in the history of Rome.

According to tradition Gaius Julius Caesar was a tall man endowed with a light complexion, well-formed limbs, a relatively broad face and intense dark-brown eyes. He enjoyed good health, although in his later years he was afflicted by sudden fainting spells and nightmares; moreover, the fainting sickness [epilepsy?] attacked him on two occasions during his campaigns. Caesar was somewhat overly concerned with his personal appearance: his facial hair was always trimmed and shaved and, as some of his detractors say, he even had certain other hairy parts of his body shaved as well. His baldness was a weakness that annoyed him greatly because it was often used by his enemies as a subject of jokes. To conceal it, he would comb his hair forward from the top of his head, and of all the great honors given to him by the people and the Senate of Rome none pleased him more than the right to wear a laurel wreath at all times. It is also said that Caesar was a peculiar dresser. He used to wear a senatorial tunic whose fringed sleeves extended to his wrists, and over it he always placed a fairly loose belt. This mode of dressing, they say, inspired Sulla's witty warning to the nobles of Rome to watch out for the boy with the loose clothes.

Originally, Caesar lived in a modest house in the Subura, but he occupied the official residence on the Sacred Way when he became Pontifex Maximus. Much has been written about his love of elegance and luxury. They say that after conceiving the idea of building a country villa on his estate at Nemi and completing the project at great expense, he proceeded to demolish the entire structure because he was not totally satisfied with every detail of the work, and this happened while he was still a poor man and heavily indebted to his creditors. They say, moreover, that while campaigning he carried with him tessellated and mosaic floors and pavements.

It is said that Caesar was induced to invade Britain by the hope of procuring pearls and that he would occasionally weigh them with his own hands in order to estimate their worth. They also say that he would collect with great zeal gems, carvings, statues and ancient paintings. He was also an avid collector of slaves of exceptional beauty and accomplishments, paying exorbitant amounts of money to acquire them; in fact, he was so ashamed of the enormity of these payments that he did not enter them in his accounts.

It is also said that during the years he served abroad he would always use two separate rooms for dining, one for his own staff of officers and Greek friends and another for Roman citizens and the most prominent provincials of the region. Caesar was so concerned with the proper running of his household, paying attention to its minutest details, that on one occasion he actually put his baker in irons for serving him one kind of bread and his guests another. He also ordered the execution of one of his favorite freedmen for seducing the wife of a knight in spite of the fact that the injured husband had not made any complaint.

Caesar has been accused of only one specific case of perverted behavior, namely that he had been the lover of Nicomedes, king of Bithynia. This charge, which stained his reputation for life, was often brought against him by his adversaries. One of them, Licinius Calvus, went so far as to compose the infamous line: "the riches of the Bithynian king abused in bed by Caesar." Another detractor, Dolabella, referred to him as the rival of the queen and "intimate sharer of the royal bed," while Curio the Elder called him the "Bithynian brothel of Nicomedes."

The man who shared the consulship with him, Bibulus, once referred to Caesar in an official public proclamation as "the Queen of Bithynia . . . who once merely aspired to sleep with a king, but now aspired to be a king." Marcus Brutus wrote that during those years a man named Octavius who was mentally ill and would say anything he wanted once came to a crowded assembly and proceeded to salute Pompey as "king" and Caesar as "queen." Insults of this nature should not be taken seriously save for the fact that Gaius Memmius clearly implicates Caesar as a participant, along with some other corrupt young friends of Nicomedes, in a banquet where he served as the king's cup-bearer. Memmius states, moreover, that a number of Roman merchants were also guests at the party, and gives their names. In addition, Cicero writes about this affair in several of his letters.

According to our sources, Caesar's intrigues and affairs with women were many and extravagant. Among the numerous women of noble families whom he seduced were Postumia, wife of Servius Sulpicius; Lollia, wife of Aulus Gabinius; Tertulla, wife of Marcus Crassus; and even Mucia, wife of Gnaeus

Pompey. In any case, Pompey was rebuked by both Curio the Elder and Curio the Younger, as well as others, for marrying Caesar's daughter Julia, since it was Caesar, whom Pompey had often despairingly called an Aegisthus, who had caused his divorce from Mucia, the mother of his three children. But Caesar loved the mother of Marcus Brutus, Servilia, more than any other women and gave her, in his first consulship, a pearl worth six million sesterces. Besides this, Caesar gave her many additional gifts during the civil wars and knocked down some valuable estates to her, at a public auction, for a ridiculously low price. When people expressed their surprise, Cicero made a witty comment: "The price is even lower than you think, since a third of it is discounted." This was said because Servilia was also rumored to have prostituted her daughter Tertia ["third"] to Caesar.

The fact that Caesar was also involved in affairs with provincial women while serving abroad is demonstrated in a couplet which was sung by his soldiers in his Gallic triumph: "Romans, guard closely your wives, for here we bring a bold libertine who spent the gold you lent him in his Gallic escapades." Caesar was involved with several queens as well. Among them were Eunoe, wife of Bogudes the Moor, who received, along with her husband, many valuable gifts from Caesar, as Naso tells us. But the most notable of his royal mistresses was Cleopatra, with whom he often partied all night long and with whom he would have sailed in an official barge down the Nile to the borders of Ethiopia if his soldiers had not refused to follow them. In the end, he invited Cleopatra to Rome and would not allow her to leave the city before he had bestowed high honors on her and given her costly gifts. Caesar went so far as to allow Cleopatra to name the son she had borne him Caesarion, a son who, according to some Greek writers, had inherited both the looks and bearing of his father. Mark Antony revealed to the Senate that Caesar had, in fact, recognized the boy as his own son, and this was also known to Gaius Matius, Gaius Oppius and other friends of Caesar. But Gaius Oppius, who seems to have felt the need to clear his friend's reputation, later published a book to prove that the son of Cleopatra, Caesarion, was not fathered by Caesar.

Helvidius Cinna, a tribune of the people, confessed to several individuals that on instructions from Caesar he had prepared a bill which was to be submitted to the people for their approval when Caesar was absent from Rome. The bill would have made it legal for Caesar to marry any one woman or as many women as he wished "for the purpose of procreating children." However, in order to prove beyond doubt that Caesar had a bad reputation for both unnatural vice and womanizing, I need only record here that Curio the Elder referred to him in one of his speeches as "every woman's man and every man's woman." Yet even his enemies denied that he drank much. In fact, a saying of Marcus Cato has come down to us which states that "Caesar was the only man who, while sober, undertook to overthrow the state." Moreover, Gaius Oppius informs us that Caesar did not care much for gourmet foods and relates how once, at a dinner when his host served rancid oil instead of fresh and all the other guests refused to touch it, Caesar consumed more than his usual portion because he did not want to embarrass his host for his carelessness or bad manners.

Caesar's lack of integrity in fiscal matters was manifested both during his service overseas and when he held office in Rome. Several authors indicate in their memoirs that when he served as proconsul in Spain he not only begged his allies to give him money for the repayment of his debts but also attacked and sacked without provocation several towns of the Lusitanians in spite of the fact that these people had readily accepted his terms and opened their gates to him as soon as he arrived. In Gaul he robbed sacred shrines and temples of their votive offerings and usually sacked towns for the purpose of plunder rather than as a response to hostile actions. By these means he came to possess more gold than he could manage. He then began to sell it in all parts of Italy and the provinces at 3,000 sesterces per pound. In the year of his first consulship he stole 3,000 pounds of gold from the Capitol and replaced the stolen gold with an equal weight of gilded bronze. Alliances and thrones were sold for money; he had King Ptolemy alone give him and Pompey nearly six thousand talents and later managed to finance the enormous costs of the civil wars and the expenses of his triumphs and entertainments by means of unconcealed extortion and sacrilegious behavior.

Augustus: Suetonius, *Augustus* 79–80

**Although it has been said that no one had greater influence
in determining the course of Roman history than Augustus, it
is also clear that in many respects the emperor was quite
ordinary. The following excerpt from Suetonius' biography of
Augustus gives us a glimpse of his personal characteristics and
habits as well as a catalog of his physical ailments.**

Augustus was a very handsome man who was graced throughout his life
with a noble bearing, although he was not much concerned with his physical
appearance. In fact, he was so indifferent to his grooming needs that he would
employ two or three barbers to work on him at the same time, cutting his hair
or shaving him while he kept busy writing or reading one thing or another,
thus saving time. Augustus always gave the impression of being a tranquil man
no matter whether he was talking or resting, a fact which prompted the chief
of a Gallic tribe to confess to his people "When Augustus was crossing the
Alps I made an appointment to see him so that I would have an opportunity
to throw him over the cliffs, but when I saw his serene face my heart grew
soft with compassion and I could not bring myself to kill him"

Augustus was endowed with clear and luminous eyes which shone with
a kind of divine brilliance, or so he liked to think, and he was always very
pleased when people who looked him in the eye lowered their gaze as if they
had been overpowered by the splendor of the sun. In the last years of his life,
however, his left eye was partially blind. He had a few small teeth which were
in a state of decay and his hair was light and slightly curly. His eyebrows were
so close together that they met above his nose. He had ears of normal size, a
typical Roman nose and a complexion which was neither very dark nor very
fair. According to Julius Marathus, a freedman and statistician in Augustus'
employ, the emperor was five feet seven inches tall. This figure is probably an
exaggeration, but his body and limbs were so nicely proportioned that his small
stature was not really noticeable unless a tall person stood beside him.

They say that Augustus' chest and stomach were marked by a combination
of seven birthmarks which corresponded exactly to the constellation of the Great
Bear and that his body was blemished with many hard, dry patches resembling
ringworm that had resulted from a skin irritation and too much scraping at the
baths. Augustus had a weak left hip, thigh and leg which sometimes gave the
impression that the emperor was limping, but this condition was successfully
treated with the sand-and-reed therapeutic method. In addition, the forefinger

of his right hand was occasionally paralyzed by cold to the point that it became useless for writing, even with the aid of a long horn finger-stall. Augustus was also afflicted for a time with bladder problems but was cured after passing sand in his urine. He survived a number of serious illnesses in his lifetime. The worst of these occurred when, after his Catabrian conquest, he developed abscesses on his liver which caused him so much discomfort that he was willing to try a most unorthodox remedy, namely cold fomentations, which his physician Antonius Musa administered to him with success after the usual therapy of hot fomentations had failed to relieve him. He also suffered from certain other maladies associated with the change of the seasons. In early spring he experienced a tightness of the diaphragm, and when the warm southern wind blew he experienced difficulties arising from the inflammation of his mucous membranes. These conditions had such an impact on his health that he suffered greatly both in hot and cold weather.

The Germans: Tacitus, *Germania* 1-4, 7-8, 14-15

The Roman historian Tacitus (*ca.* 55-120) is best known for his excellent accounts of the early Empire, the *Histories* and the *Annals,* but he is also the author of several other important works, among which is the *Germania,* a description of the German tribes which inhabited the lands beyond the Rhine and Danube. This brief but important work deals with the geography, political and social life, and customs of the Germanic peoples. While it is clear that Tacitus' first purpose was to provide his readers with useful information about the Germanic peoples, he also wished to offer whatever moral instruction might be gained from a comparison of the Germans and the Romans. Thus, while the *Germania* contains frequent references to the Germans' laziness, gluttony, drunkenness and love of warfare, the great historian contrasted the simplicity, energy and other virtues of the Germans with the degeneracy and corruption of his fellow Romans who would one day be conquered by them.

The land of Germany is separated from the lands of the Gauls, Rhaetians and Pannonians by the Rhine and Danube rivers, while mountain ranges and the fear which each feels for the other keep its people apart from the Sarmatians and Dacians. Germany is elsewhere bordered by the sea, which embraces wide peninsulas and unexplored islands where the existence of various tribes and kingdoms has only recently been revealed to us by war. The Rhine has its source in the steep and inaccessible heights of the Rhaetian Alps, after leaving which it bends a little westward and finally empties into the Northern Ocean. The Danube pours down from the gentle slope of Mount Abnoba and crosses the lands of many peoples before making its way to the Black Sea through six separate channels; a seventh channel disappears in the marshes.

In my opinion the Germans are an indigenous people who have not mixed their blood with that of others as a result of the immigration of foreigners or social intercourse with them. This is supported by the facts that in ancient times it was not by land, but by sea, that immigrants traveled and that even today the vast and forbidding ocean which stretches beyond us is rarely entered by ships from our part of the world. Besides, even if we were to discount the dangers of that rough and unknown sea, what inhabitant of Asia, Africa or Italy would want to leave his homeland for Germany with its wild country, harsh climate, sullen manners and general gloominess, unless he had first been a native of that land?

The Germans celebrate in their ancient songs the only tradition and historical recollections they have. These relate how the Earth-born god Tuisco and his son Mannus were the fathers and founders of their race. Mannus is said to have fathered three sons from whose names are derived those of the Ingaevones, who occupy the coastal regions, the Herminones, who live inland, and all the rest, who are called Istaevones. Some authorities assert, with the license permitted in the recollection of ancient events, that the god left many descendants and that the German tribes once had very many names, such as Marsi, Gambrivii, Suevi and Vandilii, and that these were their most ancient and authentic names. They say that the name Germany, on the other hand, is new and only recently introduced, and that it derives from the fact that the tribes which are now called Tungrians, who were the first to cross the Rhine and drive out the Gauls, were called Germans back then. Thus, the use of what was originally a tribal and not a national name gradually spread until all the tribes adopted this newly invented name of Germans, which was first employed by Germanic conquerors to frighten their enemies.

They say that Hercules once came to their land, and when going into battle they sing about him before any of their other heroes. They have special songs by the recitation of which (baritus is their word for it) they seek to encourage each other and whose sound is supposed to augur the successful outcome of the contest. It is not a clear, intelligible sound, but rather a more primal expression of courage which they make by shouting into their shields a confusion of coarse notes which echo and combine into a full, deep sound. Some believe that Ulysses, too, visited the land of the Germans in the course of his long legendary wanderings. They say he found his way into the Northern Ocean and then, having made landfall, he founded and named the town of Asciburgium on the bank of the Rhine, which is still inhabited today. They also claim that an altar dedicated to Ulysses and bearing the name of his father Laertes as well was once discovered there, and that some monuments and tombs marked with inscriptions in Greek can be found on the border of Germany and Rhaetia. I have no intention of arguing either for or against the truth of these claims. Let the reader come to his own conclusions.

I accept the view of those who hold that the tribes of Germany are entirely free of contamination by intermarriage with foreign peoples and that they have remained a distinct and pure race, unlike any other. Hence, the physical characteristics of the Germans are quite uniform among the population despite the fact that it is so large. They have fierce blue eyes, reddish hair and huge bodies which are more suitable for the release of short bursts of energy than long, tedious work. They cannot stand either heat or thirst, though they are used to the cold and hunger because of their harsh climate and poor soil.

The Germans follow the hereditary principle in choosing their kings, but their generals are chosen for their valor. The kings do not enjoy unlimited or arbitrary powers, and the generals lead more by example than by the exercise of authority; they command because they win the admiration of the people when, full of vigor, they fight with conspicuous bravery in the front lines. The generals do not punish soldiers but leave this to the priests who are the only ones authorized to execute, imprison or flog miscreants, and do so not at the command of any general, but rather that of the god who inspires them in battle. They bring into battle figures and images taken from their sacred groves, but the real explanation for their great courage is the fact that their divisions of horsemen and footsoldiers are not comprised of men selected at random, but of members of the same families and clans. Moreover, those who are most beloved by them are placed nearby, so that the shrieks of their wives and the crying of their children can be heard above the din of battle. These are to every warrior the most sacred witnesses to his bravery, these are his most enthusiastic applauders. The warriors bring their wounds to their mothers and wives, who are not averse to counting them, or even to demanding them, and who provide their men with food and words of encouragement.

Tradition relates how in some instances armies on the verge of retreating have been rallied by women who with bared breasts encouraged the warriors by shouting frightening descriptions of the horrors of captivity, which the Germans fear more for their women than for themselves. Indeed, this fear is so intense that tribes which exchange maidens of noble birth as hostages form the strongest bonds in their treaties. The Germans even believe that women have a special spirituality and the gift of prophecy, and so they take their advice and counsel quite seriously. We saw during the reign of Vespasian how the lady Valaeda was thought by many to be a goddess. And in earlier years they venerated Aurinia and many others as true divinities and not with servile flatteries or as if they really believed that the women were mortals who had been deified.

When the Germans go to war it is considered shameful for the chief to be outdone in courage and a disgrace for the warriors not to match the valor of the chief. Moreover, eternal infamy and everlasting condemnation accrue to the warrior who survives the chief and escapes injury in battle. This is because, for them, true loyalty means defending the chief and ascribing one's own heroic deeds to his glory. The chief fights for victory, the warriors fight for their chief. If the tribe sinks into a state of laziness and inaction as a result of prolonged peace and tranquility many noble youths will voluntarily join other tribes which are still fighting wars, for a life of inaction is repulsive to them and they stand to gain fame and glory more readily when in the midst of danger. Also, it is impossible for a leader to maintain a large following of warriors except through war and violence, for the warriors depend on the generosity of their chief for their war-horses and their bloody and victorious spears. Simple feasts and entertainments, which are liberally provided to them, are their only pay. All of these things come from war and rapine.

The Germans are not as easily persuaded to cultivate the soil and wait for the harvest as they are induced to fight the enemy and win the honor of war wounds. As a matter of fact, they consider it tame and stupid to earn by their sweat and labor what they can acquire with their blood. In times of peace they spend some of their leisure time hunting, but for the most part they remain idle, sleeping and feasting, the bravest and most warlike among them doing nothing, while the women, old men and weaker members of the tribe assume the responsibility of managing their households and lands. The men lie in a slothful state, demonstrating a strange combination in their nature of a fondness for idleness and an aversion to peace.

It is the practice of the members of the tribes to offer the chiefs gifts of cattle or grain which, though they are accepted as compliments, are actually necessary for their sustenance. The chiefs are greatly pleased when they receive gifts from their neighbors, both individuals and states, such as fine horses, heavy weapons and various trappings and ornaments. These days we have even taught them to accept money.

The Gauls: Ammianus Marcellinus, *Res Gestae* 15.12

In 390 B.C. the Gauls defeated the Romans on the banks of the Allia river and then went on to sack Rome, an event that was long remembered as one of the most catastrophic in the early history of the city. They were later conquered by Caesar in the middle of the first century B.C. and remained under Roman rule until the fifth century A.D., when Rome withdrew its garrisons from France. In the following excerpt Ammianus Marcellinus (fl. 360 A.D.), the last of the great historians of Rome, offers an interesting description of these remarkable people.

Nearly all Gauls are tall in stature and endowed with a fair complexion, red hair and fierce eyes which give them a forbidding aspect. They are an exceedingly ferocious and warlike people. If a Gaul fighting in the midst of a battle asks his wife for help the wild-eyed woman will show herself to be quite capable of handling several of the enemy at once, for she is even more formidable than her husband. The women are especially impressive when, with their muscles tightened and their teeth gnashed, they swing their long white arms and deliver volleys of kicks and punches resembling the missles shot by a catapult. They make frightening and menacing sounds with their voices, no matter what their mood, and yet they are without exception clean and tidy in appearance; in fact, in the region of Aquitania and throughout the entire country you will rarely encounter the filthy women dressed in rags who are such a common sight in other lands.

The Gauls are always prepared for war, regardless of their age. Older men exhibit as much spirit in battle as the younger ones, and because their bodies are toughened by exposure to the elements and by constant labor there is no chance they would ever be unfit for fighting. No Gaul would ever mutilate himself by cutting off his thumb in order to avoid military service, though this is common in Italy, where such people are called *murci*.

The Gauls are accustomed to drinking. They enjoy numerous alcoholic beverages which taste like wine, and there are many disreputable individuals who spend their time wandering aimlessly from place to place in a condition of perpetual drunkenness, a state described by Cato as self-inflicted insanity. Thus, Cicero was not far from the truth when, in defending Fonteius, he said,

"From now on the Gauls will mix their drinks with water, a practice which they have hitherto considered the equivalent of drinking poison."

Rome conquered Gaul, and particularly those regions closer to Italy, gradually and without great difficulty. Fulvius was the first to move against the Gauls, and Sextus further reduced their strength in a series of minor military operations. Fabius Maximus managed to defeat the warlike tribe of the Allobroges, thus completing the conquest of these people and winning for himself the title Allobrogicus. Then, as Sallust relates, Caesar conquered the entire land of Gaul (with the exception of its remote marshlands) in a difficult ten-year campaign and made it subject to Rome by means of a treaty of perpetual alliance.

The Huns: Ammianus Marcellinus, *Res Gestae* 31.2

By 370 A.D. the Huns, a Mongolian tribe from northwestern Asia, had advanced into Europe and forced the Ostrogoths to abandon their kingdom between the Dnieper and the Don in order to find safety within the Empire. In 376 they crossed the Danube into Roman territory, following the Visigoths who had earlier forced their way across the frontier in order to escape their savagery. In 451 the Roman general Aeitus defeated the Huns and their chieftain Attila in central France. The following excerpt from the *Res Gestae* of Ammianus Marcellinus describes the Romans' fear of the various tribes which invaded Europe in the last years of the Empire and illustrates their tendency to view their enemies as brutish and uncivilized.

The people known as the Huns, a name scarcely mentioned in the records of the past, occupy a region beyond the sea of Azov on the periphery of the frozen ocean and are a race surpassing all others in savagery. When an infant is born among them they burn his cheeks with a hot iron so that the scars which form will prevent hair from growing on his face when he reaches adulthood. As a result, the Huns grow up beardless and devoid of beauty.

The Huns have firm, powerful limbs and thick necks. They are very large, but their legs are short, so that one can almost think of them as similar to two-legged animals or to the sturdy, roughly hewn figures which one finds on the posts that support the ends of bridges.

The Huns are definitely human in form, no matter how uncouth they may be, and are so vigorous and durable that they need neither fire nor fancy food but subsist on whatever roots they find in the fields or on the animal flesh that they heat quickly by placing it between their thighs and the backs of their horses as they ride.

The Huns never take shelter in roof-covered structures. Instead, they avoid these as places unfit for human use just as other people avoid taking shelter in places such as tombs. Even reed-thatched huts do not exist in their world, for they are wanderers who roam over mountains and through forests and are accustomed from birth to a life of cold, hunger and thirst.